ROCKFORD

American Historical Press
Tarzana, California

ROCKFORD

An Illustrated History

Jon W. Lundin

*Above: The circus is in town! Courtesy, Rockford
Museum Center*

© American Historical Press, 1996
All rights reserved
Published 1996
Printed in the United States of America
Library of Congress Catalogue Card Number: 96-78830

Includes bibliographical references.

ISBN 0-9654754-1-7

Contents

Acknowledgments

Many people helped me during the preparation of this book. Dr. John Molyneux of the Rockford Public Library (Local History and Genealogy) directed me to many valuable primary sources, clarified details, and offered suggestions; his review of the completed manuscript also saved me from making several errors of fact. I have benefitted from discussions with Milton Mahlburg, Armour VanBriesen, Carl Linde, Dick Rundquist, Tom Boyer, Don Lunquist, Webbs Norman, and Karl Jacobs, especially in the development of a perspective on Rockford and its past. Many people have assisted me in locating and identifying old photographs, but I would like to recognize the following people for efforts above and beyond the call of duty: Ruth Lunde, Scott Prine, Sandy Bryden, Beverly Whitehead, Lucille Wilson, Frances Porter, Joe Lamb, Shirley Fideli, Jane and Norman LaGrande, Chris Sjostrom, and Captain Gene Coots of the Rockford Detective Bureau. My thanks also go to Dave Connolly and Margaret Anderson for information relating to Fay Lewis; to Guy Fiorenza for background on the W.B. Reynolds Circus; to Tony Mandell for information about his relative Sammy Mandell; and to Bob Lindvall for several helpful suggestions relating to Rockford politics. I have benefitted, in a general way, from reading portions of the Swedish Historical Society's history of the Rockford furniture industry (still in preparation). Finally, I want to remember my father, Leonard Lundin, who many years ago gave me his collection of Rockford memorabilia and went out of his way to hunt down and acquire for me a copy of Charles Church's 1916 *History of Winnebago County.*

N.C. Thompson's Reaper Works in the Water Power District was the principal manufacturer of the John P. Manny combination reaper-mower. Painting by George Robertson. Courtesy, Collection of the Illinois State Museum, Springfield

Prologue: "Jonesville"

Rockford is one of the places in the Midwest that sophisticated easterners like to visit to confirm their notions of Middle American culture. "It is as nearly typical of the U.S. as any city can be," *Life* magazine said in 1949, taking a cue from the fact that the well-known sociologist W. Lloyd Warner had used Rockford as a model for a hypothetical middle-class community named "Jonesville" in an earlier study of social class. The Joneses of the world were average, hard-working folks who believed in the value of home and family, and they tended to live in cities such as Rockford, where—according to *Life*—people still got together in lodges and clubs, went to church on Sundays, and shopped at neighborhood stores. Margaret Bourke-White's photo essay for *Life* captured the steady optimism of a Rockford factory worker at the bottom of the economic ladder and compared this favorably to that of his management counterpart at the top, both men alike in their tastes and social habits. The American Dream was alive and well in Rockford if the only things that kept a person from climbing the ladder were "the tools, the education, the will to do and a little luck."

The *Life* article helped to establish Rockford's democratic credentials, but it also marked it out as one of this country's basic four-square communities. There was something endearingly honest about a place in the heartland that took its name from an actual limestone river ford instead of the classics or romantic literature, and that tried to promote itself for many years as a distant cousin of one of the most congested manufacturing areas in the Merrimack Valley—Lowell, Massachusetts. This seems odd to us today, perhaps, because so many of our notions of the Good Life in America have been shaped by images of suburban culture. Yet a hundred years ago, before the national media made factory work (and factory communities) unfashionable, the situation was different, and Rockford could refer to itself as the "Lowell of the West" with the same kind of unrestrained enthusiasm that most Midwestern chambers of commerce now reserve for comparison to Silicon Valley.

The comparison to Lowell was actually not farfetched at all. By the 1860s, Rockford was a mill town with a waterpower district just like its eastern counterpart and a booming farm implement industry that rivaled Chicago's in the production of self-raking reapers and mowers. By the turn of the century, Rockford made hosiery and furniture in large quantities as well, the latter at such a rate that only one other city in the entire country, Grand Rapids, Michigan, surpassed its production. For a time, it seemed, every homemaker in the U.S. wanted a Rockford-made desk-and-bookcase combination known as the "side-by-side," a durable, workmanlike piece that epitomized the virtues of plainness and practicality. Rockford also built what may have been "the largest gas range plant and the largest piano action plant in the world"; it made similar claims for a group of cavernous wooden buildings known as the Hess and Hopkins Company, a manufacturer of leather harnesses.

Was the comparison to Lowell really fair? People here admittedly began to have serious second thoughts about the wisdom of appropriating the name and reputation of an old New England textile center for their city of various business enterprises. "Two decades ago the vastness of her

The Edwin Bulkey Homestead on East State Street survives today as a part of the First of America Bank. Courtesy, Rockford Museum Center

manufactures gave to her the sobriquet of the 'Lowell of the West'," a local writer explained, "and this clings to her still, although it is not worn with as much pride as in other days, for Rockford, mind you, is passing this namesake of hers, and it may soon be that Lowell will feel a dignified desire to be known as the Rockford of the East."

Try as it might, however, Rockford never seemed to be able to earn the respect of the people that counted most in this country, especially those east of the Alleghenies.

New York journalists, who offered themselves as authorities on just about everything having to do with culture and social status, were unimpressed by manufacturing statistics. Lowell, to them, was one of the nondescript little towns in the East that did the necessary dirty work of an industrial society, and if some place in Illinois wanted to pattern itself after Lowell, then so much the worse for it. Rockford failed most of the tests that were used to determine high-status communities. It had what social scientists would call a neg-

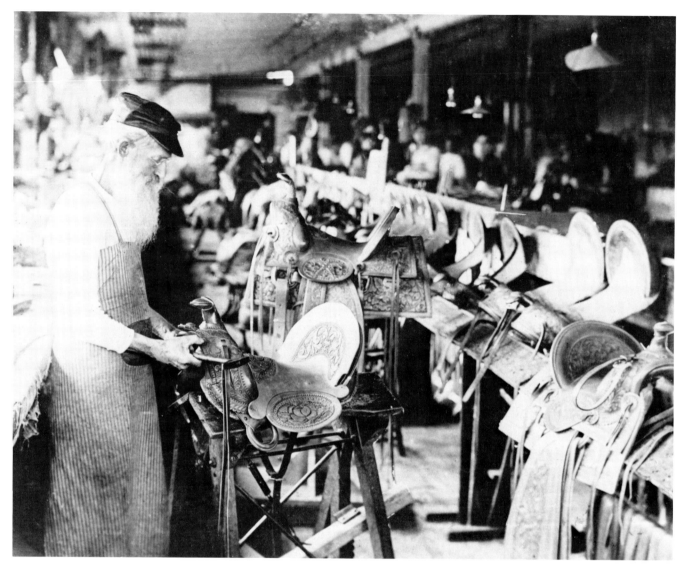

Saddlemaking survived the longest of Rockford's handicraft industries. This view of the Hess and Hopkins Company was taken in the late nineteenth century. Courtesy, Rockford Museum Center

ative blue-collar index, and its average income level was low enough to scare away all but the most adventurous fashion-and-money people.

"Rockford is not a show place of magnificent residences," the *Morning Star* conceded in a 1912 promotional booklet, taking pains to emphasize that the beauty of its homes was of a "far more subtle" variety. Instead of mansions and elaborate fretwork, one saw plain carpentered houses and workaday facades. The less pretentious revival styles, like the Romanesque and Neo-Classical,

were favored over the wedding-cake fantasies of Eastlake architecture that so often endeared themselves to the Chicago suburbs. In fact, the best, most expensive Rockford houses were primarily utilitarian—"good, substantial, convenient" buildings (as the *Morning Star* would say). This was a working-class town that preferred solid comfort to the charm of picturesque effects.

Almost in spite of itself, Rockford has kept a low profile. Not even the fact that it is now the second-largest city in Illinois and a national leader in certain fields of metalworking has overcome its lack of recognition, since, as Calvin Trillin discovered in researching an article for the *New Yorker* in November 1976, "a Rockford resident on an out-of-town visit [still] runs the risk of meeting people from Chicago who have never heard of Rockford, Illinois."

If they have heard of it, they are unsure of where it is. Many Chicagoans to this day picture Rockford among the Kewanees and Danvilles of "downstate" Illinois, a prairie crossroads with gigantic grain elevators

perhaps. These impressions merge easily with ideas of corn-pone Americana. Urbane easterners like Trillin have tended to view Rockford as a time warp of older, conservative Midwestern values—distrust of government, opposition to taxes, etc.— much as though its anonymity over the years has resulted in a kind of attitude isolation. It has become for them the prairie equivalent of the proverbial backwoods Appalachian community where sociologists sometimes go to study American folkways. As a result, their observations on Rock-

A circus parade passes the Winnebago County Jail on Elm Street in the early 1900s. Courtesy, Rockford Museum Center

ford have usually been presented as important discoveries.

The reasons for Rockford's low profile are no doubt many and complex, but simple geography explains a lot about its feelings of isolation. Separated from Springfield by 200 miles of Route 51, for years no more than a glorified country road, and (now) from Chicago by 90 miles of tollway, it has long felt itself to be cut off from the main centers of Illinois government and commerce. Its sense of identification with other parts of the state, particularly the southern half from Decatur to the Ohio River, has been tenuous at best; Rockford residents are probably right in thinking that, socially and economically, they belong to another culture. This feeling of separateness goes back to the very beginning of Rockford's history, to the years before the Civil War when the area was dominated by settlers from New York and New England, and southern Illinois was dominated by settlers from Kentucky and Tennessee, many of them former slave owners.

"Between the people of the southern and northern portions of the state was a great gulf fixed," Charles Church wrote in 1900 in his *History of Rockford.* "Each misunderstood the other. The Illinois and Michigan Canal was opposed by the people of southern Illinois for fear it would flood the state with Yankees." In the 1840s Rockford residents were equally alarmed by a huge state debt that had been incurred for "improvements" in the southern counties. Because of it, a referendum was held in Winnebago County in June 1842 to secede from the state of Illinois and annex itself to the Wisconsin Territory. This proposal passed 971-6. For years afterward, until Wisconsin was admitted

to the Union and its boundary with Illinois defined by Congress in 1848, Rockford continued this campaign. Even today, it feels as much akin to Wisconsin as it does to most areas of Illinois.

If Rockford has been more or less isolated from downstate Illinois, it has also been overshadowed at different times by two of its northern neighbors, Galena and Chicago. In the 1840s and 1850s when Rockford was still a frontier town, Galena was one of the state's leading commercial centers, a river port with a thriving lead mining business and some of the finest brick and limestone residences in the Midwest. Chicago emerged from the obscurity of a tiny garrison settlement (Fort Dearborn) in the 1830s to become the manufacturing hub of the Upper Great Lakes region by the time of the Civil War. Its rapid growth during this period made it a dominant force in Illinois politics. It was Rockford's misfortune in some ways to end up in the same state as Chicago—a proximity that may well have inhibited the growth of Rockford's own "cultural and mercantile institutions," as Trillin has suggested.

One of the ironies of Rockford's "Jonesville" reputation, its typical-hometown-in-the-heartland image, is that Rockford has been anything but typical in the way it earns its money. Economists point out that more than half of the earnings in Winnebago County over the last 30-40 years have come from manufacturing, and that this level is far above the national average. As anyone who has had even a nodding acquaintance with Rockford history will tell you, this has almost always been the case in this community. In fact, Rockford has actually reduced its dependence on manufac-

turing in the last few decades, so that now only two out of every five people you pass on the street are likely to have some connection with industry.

Since John H. Manny started making reapers in the old Water Power District in 1853 and a number of people got into the business by doing job work for him, Rockford has had a rich culture of mechanical invention. John Barnes was so good at building reaper models for the factory of Emerson & Company, for instance, that he packed his homemade tools up and went to work for himself—making more of the tools that he used to construct his models. To develop a foot-powered scroll saw, he invented a foot-powered circular saw; to produce them both, he perfected a foot-powered lathe. John Clark, who ran a hardware store here at the turn of the century, designed a folding flue stop to save room on his shelves because he was annoyed by the bulkiness of his existing supplies and because his own strong sense of order prevented him from wasting anything—even space—if he could help it. The popularity of his invention eventually led to the full-scale production of the "Gem Flue Stopper." To salvage the scraps from the flue's tin pieces, in turn, he decided to manufacture a small metal container known as the "Gem Ointment Box," a product that was later the basis of a multi-million-dollar corporation.

The trouble with these stories—and they seem to be endless in Rockford—is that they are often too esoteric for people to appreciate. Ask anyone to explain the function of a universal joint, the specialty of Rockford's Mechanics Machine Company for many years, or the purpose of a hollow chisel mortiser, the "signature piece" of the early Greenlee Tool Company portfolio, and unless the person you ask is already quite mechanical or a student of Rockford history, the odds are better than five-to-one that he can't answer the questions and at least ten-to-one that he doesn't care. Since World War II, Rockford has devoted itself to the production of things that are virtually invisible to the average consumer. Consider all the machines Rockford builds to make other machines, like the big Ingersoll mills or the specialized tools for the auto industry, and the mechanical components manufactured here for the *inside* of some-

Passengers on the Chicago and Northwestern Railroad had this view of the east side while crossing the river in the late nineteenth century. The W.F. & John Barnes Company appears at upper left; the Ward Pump Company is in the center; and the Rockford Watch Company is at upper right. At the crest of the hill (partially obscured by the Ward Pump building) is the roof of Rockford High School. Photo by F.C. Pierce/Rockford Public Library

thing else, like prime mover controls, heavy-duty clutches, and drive generators. Think of Rockford's development of the horseshoe calk, knotting bill, and automatic quiller, and then ask yourself if a place that routinely manufactures such strange-sounding items could ever honestly hope for much social cachet.

Rockford has probably been recognized more often for being unrecognized than any other city in the country. "I am greatly pleased to be able to meet the people of Rockford," General Ulysses Grant said in a speech during the 1880 presidential campaign. "It is strange that I should have lived so near you as long as I have [in Galena] and never paid you a visit." And strange, too, to find a well-developed economy. "You have manufacturing interests enough," he went on, "to warrant an increase in population to three times its present size." Rockford's strength as a manufacturer has usually exceeded its ability to promote itself to outsiders—and

to interpret itself to its own people. When it was known as the "Reaper City" in the 1860s, its farm implement industry had already started to decline. When it was the "Furniture City" in the 1920s, the woodworking industry was beginning to turn its attention to the associated fields of machine tools, fasteners, ornamental hardware, paints and varnishes, glues, and glass. Long after a New York journalist had given Rockford the nickname of the "Forest City" and the nickname itself had been widely adopted by business and civic groups here, Rockford decided to go to the trouble of actually counting all the trees inside the city limits because it questioned its exclusive right to such a common title. (The survey showed that there were 142,044 trees in Rockford in 1915, or about 122 trees for every city block.)

Obviously it was important to be the best at something. Rockford in the past has pioneered an oil-hardening process for reaper blades, opened the first malleable iron foundry west of Pittsburgh, and designed the largest palletized automatic transfer machine (then) in existence. Moreover, the winner of the 1937 Indianapolis "500" drove a car with Rockford piston rings in the engine, and the 1952 U.S. Mens' Olympic Basketball Team wore "Rockford Socks" when it captured the gold medal. These were things to be proud of (more or less), even if they were not exactly the kind of things that you could take very far in the status competition among American cities.

Rockford's biggest claim to fame in recent years has been its hardware industry. Most of the screw factories here go back in one way or another to a single furniture-affiliated business at the turn of the century, the National Lock Company, which had originally developed a mortise lock for cabinets and then branched off into hinges, trim, and screws. The "Lock," as the company was widely known, became Rockford's largest employer. During its years of expansion, a number of Lock employees

Visitors to this Rockford circus, probably held in the County Fair Grounds (present Fairgrounds Park), could meet "Pharoah's Daughter." Courtesy, Rockford Museum Center

left the company and got into the business themselves. Thus, while furniture declined here after the Great Depression, the fastener trade increased proportionately, a change of focus that somehow seems all the more inevitable now in light of Rockford's fascination with low-profile commodities. One of the best ways to visualize the evolution of Rockford manufacturing in the twentieth century, in fact, would be to put together a kind of chronological exhibit of its major furniture products, beginning with the famous desk-and-bookcase combination, proceeding through a variety of dressers, chests, mantels, sewing machines, pianos, and radio cabinets, and finishing with a little pile of nuts, bolts, and screws. After years of defining itself according to someone else's standards—"playing second city to the Second City [Chicago]," in Trillin's words—it became the self-declared "Metal Fastener Capital of the World" in the 1960s, enjoying a celebrity of its own devising for a few years at least, before the Japanese industrial invasion of this country in the 1970s challenged the claims of American fastener superiority.

Rockford's image problems obviously have a lot to do with its difficulties in deciding exactly what it is today—a small town in its final stages of development? A big town in embryonic form? This is where the "Jonesville" thing keeps coming in, for every time that Rockford has tried to promote itself as a serious candidate for big-town status, someone has appeared on the scene to burst its bubble. *Newsweek* ran a major article on the arts in Rockford on December 24, 1973. The article celebrated the achievements of its symphony and theater, but also recalled enough of its immediate past,

its reputation especially as Jack Benny's "stiffest audience" on the old vaudeville circuit, to make any news of a renaissance in Rockford entirely a matter of local importance. Regardless of how it has tried to make itself over, those small-town habits have come to the surface. When the Rockford Symphony performed at the CherryVale Mall in 1973, *Newsweek* said, "Rockford husbands and wives rose from their tables and waltzed. It was a cornball-wonderful, very American moment."

The more you know about Rockford, the more you come to recognize an element of independence in the place—call it localism, provincialism, or what you will. Germanicus Kent was the first person to give expression to it, in 1834, when he bucked the whole trend of American westward migration in the nineteenth century and founded Rockford by traveling *east* (he set out from Galena in the general direction of Chicago). Rockford settlers nominated the first Republican candidate for Congress in Illinois (E.B. Washburne in 1854) and voted for John Fremont, who was running on the Free Soil ticket, over Democrat James Buchanan in the 1856 Presidential election. (Republicans and Free-Soilers were the radicals of their day and the Democrats the party of the status quo.) Unsuccessful in their efforts to secede from Illinois, Rockford voters repudiated the 1862 state constitution by a vote of 3,367-602. Two decades later, in 1883, they rejected the General Free School Law of Illinois by more than 1,200 votes rather than surrender their authority under the existing city charter.

Rockford has always produced its share of mavericks. Before the Civil War, there was the well-known judge and political activist, Selden Church, who worked in the secessionist campaign of 1840, introduced a controversial antislavery resolution at the 1848 state constitutional convention, and helped to nominate the Republican E.B. Washburne for Congress. Church's friend and sometime colleague, William Lathrop, was likewise distinguished by his early advocacy of women's rights in Illinois. As a legislator, Lathrop drew up the bill that allowed women to practice law, and he championed the cause of Alta Hulett, the first female admitted to the state bar (he encouraged her to prepare for the bar by reading under his supervision). His daughter Julia worked with Jane Addams at Hull-House in the 1890s and established this country's original juvenile court; in 1912 she was the first woman ever appointed to head a governmental agency at the federal level, the U.S. Children's Bureau. Rockford has had a long tradition of conservative politics—Trillin says it was a "resolutely Republican blue-collar town" until the 1970s—but this town has obviously had a lesser radical tradition as well, and sometimes it's hard to tell where one begins and the other leaves off.

Think of John B. Anderson, the Rockford native who in 1980 became the most successful third-party candidate for President in the history of the United States. During his early years in the House of Representatives, his conservative credentials were impeccable, but the longer he served this Congressional District, the more he seemed to gravitate to the other side of the political spectrum (beguiled, say his detractors; enlightened, say his friends), so that eventually he left the Republican party altogether to form his own new Party of National Unity. This in many ways was a *Rockford* solution, entirely in line with a self-reliant attitude that has characterized the business community here.

Generalizing about Rockford politics is a tricky business, especially if you throw in a certain amount of ethnic stereotyping and think you can summarize the place with sweeping references to "Main Street, Illinois," as *Newsweek* did during Anderson's presidential campaign (June 9, 1980). "Rockford is a Corn Belt city of 150,000," Peter Goldman ex-

Theodore Roosevelt campaigned in Rockford before the 1912 Presidential election. Courtesy, Rockford Museum Center

For much of the late nineteenth and early twentieth centuries, Rockford was a temperance town, with the sale of liquor either severely restricted or abolished entirely. In this photograph, what appears to be a large temperance parade moves along East State Street. Courtesy, Rockford Museum Center

plained, "settled heavily by Swedish immigrants who came, like Anderson's parents, seeking freedom to practice their own threshing-floor, fundamentalist Protestantism." This may be good enough for *Newsweek*, but threshing floors disappeared around Rockford long before the main wave of Swedish immigration began (they were replaced by machine shops that *made* threshing machines), and there was a whole group of Swedes who came to Rockford after the turn of the century to get away from precisely that brand of fundamental Protestantism that *Newsweek* says was characteristic of the place. It was, and it wasn't; and here we run into one of those Rock-

ford paradoxes again, the lesser radical tradition feeding off the dominant conservative one, at times merging with it, recombining, and throwing out new forms like the National Unity Party.

Take, for example, the period of the First World War, when Rockford factories were booming (the payroll of industry tripled between 1914 and 1918). The Chamber of Commerce had successfully persuaded the U.S. War Department to locate a new army training camp on farmland south of town (Camp Grant), and every saloon in the vicinity had been closed by temperance forces under the leadership of the Reverend F.M. Sheldon of the First Congregational Church. Then, no doubt, Rockford really deserved its reputation as a sewed-up company town. Right up to the Great Depression, Wayne Whitaker wrote, "New buildings and additions went up one after another . . . Money flowed freely and everybody's credit was good. An economist of the day wrote that Rockford was the most prosperous city in the United States."

Here, certainly, is a good case of consensus politics, of resolute Republicanism! Yet you only need to look at a few of the flaws in the otherwise smooth surface of Rockford's war-time prosperity—at the demonstrations, for example, and police arrests—to realize that there was also a strong counterforce at work.

During the general period of the First World War, say 1912-1920, Rockford conservatives like the temperance candidate W.W. Bennett occupied the mayor's office (the Drys regularly defeated the Wets when local option elections were held), but before and after the war the city's highest office was almost the exclusive property of trade unionists, a situation unprecedented in Rockford's 75-year history. Mark Jardine of the Leather Workers' Union was elected in 1907 and again in 1909. Herman Hallstrom of the Bricklayers' and Stone Masons' Union was elected in 1921, 1923, 1925, 1929, and 1931. Hallstrom, one should add, was both a trade unionist and a Socialist (though he ran for office on the Labor League ticket) and was well-known, especially in the immigrant community, as one of the main organizers and driving forces in the old Swedish Socialist Workers' Club (Svenska Arbetara Socialist Klubben), a group that sometimes agitated against American involvement in the war. In 1915 the Socialists nominated Oscar Ogren, another Swede, to oppose Bennett for mayor (Ogren lost, but only by a fraction of the men's vote, 4,702-4,048), and two years later the Socialists captured five of the seats on the Rockford City Council, a full third of those available. These were times of great patriotism and One-Hundred-Percent Americanism; but in 1917 a group of 118 Rockford Socialists, mostly Swedes, marched to the courthouse to refuse induction into the military. And in 1919, a much larger group, estimated variously at between 1,000 and 3,000 people, paraded with red flags through the downtown to the National Guard Armory, where Ogren and Charles Johnson, a Rockford alderman, addressed the crowd on the evils of capitalism, all this at a time of unparalleled peace-time prosperity.

During the Palmer raids of 1920, when the federal government cracked down on subversives and suspected Bolshevists across the country, Rockford's arrest totals were higher than those of any other city of its size. Among the people arrested and later acquitted here was Alice Beal Parsons, the granddaughter of a former Rockford mayor (Henry Nevin Starr), who later described her ordeal in an autobiographical novel entitled *The Trial of Helen McLeod*. Shunned by many people in Rockford after her arrest and divorced by her husband, Parsons moved to New York in the summer of 1920 to begin a new career as a writer. In the 1930s she helped found that state's Liberal Party and was installed as its honorary vice-chairman. It was this party, oddly enough, that made one of the earliest endorsements of the candidacy of John B. Anderson in the 1980 Presidential campaign.

The Palmer Raids broke the

The Swedish Socialist Workers' Club, which was active at the time of the First World War, produced one of Rockford's most popular twentieth-century mayors, Herman Hallstrom (1921-1927 and 1929-1932), a journeyman bricklayer and stone mason who is shown at the end of the second row at left. Courtesy, Rockford Museum Center

back of the Swedish Socialist Worker's Club, but not the Swedish Socialists. Hallstrom was born again as a Labor League activist to become the dominant political figure of his time; by 1929 he had drifted far enough to the right of the political spectrum locally—a John Anderson in reverse, as it were—that his own party decided to drop him in favor of another candidate (Hallstrom won the election anyway). In 1933, when Hallstrom finally went down to defeat, it was at the hands of an upstart alderman named C. Henry Bloom, who had picked up the pieces of the old Labor League Party and made them into the new and formidable Progressive Party. And who was Bloom? One of the five Rockford Socialists elected to

the City Council at the time of the First World War.

Between the two of them, the Labor League and Progressive Party influenced the course of local elections until the 1950s; Bloom won a fifth term for mayor as late as 1949. This did not mean that voters here abandoned the Republican party at the state and national levels, however, since many of the same people who backed the Labor League ticket also supported the candidacies of Harding and Coolidge. "While the ancestors [sic] of the old Socialist Party were holding effective control of the April elections for mayor," Jack Winning wrote in *Sinnissippi Saga*, "November continued to belong to the Republicans . . ." Rockford was really Republican, in other words, but not resolutely.

If there is one thing that has characterized Rockford politics down through the years, it is a resistance to outside controls. This was a motivating factor in the secessionist movement, the nomination of Washburne, the beginnings of the Rockford Socialist Party, and one of the reasons that Anderson left the Republican Party in 1980 and launched his Campaign of National Unity. If we are to believe the anonymous author of *Manufacturing Rockford,* published in 1892, it even played a part in this area's early industrialization, a strategy the city fathers pursued to make them "independent of the tributes of agriculture." Remember that the last and most dramatic holdout in the international scheme to refinance the loans to Chrysler Corporation in 1980 was the American National Bank and Trust Company of Rockford, Illinois. Despite the enormous pressures brought to bear on the bank at every level of business and government—and in part, no doubt, because of them—its president, David Knapp, was "determined to hold out to the bitter end." His position was, "I'm sorry, but if you take a loan you've got to pay it back" (*Iacocca. An Autobiography*).

Rockford has always resisted efforts to smooth out its rough spots. Despite the Chrysler lesson, debt accumulation and compound interest levels continue to be regarded with great suspicion. Rockford would still rather make things than exchange paper commodities, and in America's gradual evolution toward a national service economy, it has pursued a deliberate policy of manufacturing reinvestment. All the old Jonesville values—self-reliance, living within one's means, distrust of government bureaucracies—seem pretty well entrenched here, and it

may be years, even decades, before Rockford shakes off the dust of its small-town inheritance.

● ● ●

This book is a summary of the people and events that have contributed to this inheritance. The story is illustrated with photographs from local archives and picture collections. The book is in all respects a highly personal history whose approach is both qualitative and selective. I have left out some stories and included others for the simple reason that I liked some stories better than others, and I have depended on anecdotes to make my points because I think they are more apt to be remembered than simple facts. I have also omitted a good deal about the arts, religion, and education in Rockford, not because they were unimportant in the past, but because they are covered in extensive detail elsewhere. There are whole sections on these subjects in the previous histories of Charles Church, William Kett, and Hal Nelson that have relieved me of the need to be comprehensive here.

This book is not intended to be a piece of booster literature, and no one is responsible for its contents except myself. Local history is always a mixed bag of fact and fantasy, including a number of things of questionable authenticity that we are reluctant to ignore. I have made every effort to corroborate the accuracy of the details in the following pages and have tried to be objective in recounting them; but I still believe the only real reason for writing a book such as this is that it's interesting, and whether entirely true or not, that it makes a good story.

Jon Lundin
Rockford, Illinois

Founding and Early Settlement

N orthern Illinois in the early nineteenth century was a sea of tall prairie grasses whose occasional groves and timbered uplands served as reference points for travelers. "From Galena go directly east until you come to and cross Apple river," Germanicus Kent wrote an acquaintance in the fall of 1834, "thence turn in a southeasterly course to Plum river, and from there to Cherry Grove. There leave some timber on your left, and a small grove on your right and then keep on until you strike Rock River from which a blind path will lead you to Midway." This little community was the first permanent white settlement within the existing city limits of Rockford. Kent had established it a few months earlier at a shallow crossing in the river that was more or less "midway" between Galena and the village of Chicago, but the difficulties that the first visitors had

George Robertson, a Rockford College professor of art, painted this view of the Kent Creek limestone bluffs in about 1860, before the railroad's arrival. Courtesy, Collection of the Illinois State Museum, Springfield

experienced in finding it had tended to outweigh the potential advantages of its location. There were no roads, and the few trails that existed generally followed meandering waterways like the Rock River rather than lines across the prairie. Travelers from Galena to Midway had to make their way overland as best they could by heading for "points of timber" and high ground, standing in the stirrups to get their readings over the tops of bluestem grasses sometimes eight feet tall, and trusting to Providence and their own instincts to get them through.

The first roads to Midway began as solitary paths, one rider following the tracks of another, and each in succession wearing the trail down a little further, often widening it in places where rain had turned the existing tracks to mud. Trees were blazed and girdled to make the trail easier to find; and on the open prairie there were other signposts that travelers left behind—rock piles and so-called "mile stakes." It was said that a trail in Illinois became a road as soon as the second wagon passed over it, since these things were normally calculated by the width of the track and not by the condition of its bed. Road improvements consisted of dragging a tree trunk behind a team of oxen and felling trees on riverbanks where the crossings seemed to be the safest. Yet no one worth his salt would have thought of crossing a waterway in warm weather without checking the condition of the bottom first. Wagons and their entire contents were known to have disappeared in the shallow waters of a muddy-bottomed stream. A shallow-water crossing with a rock bottom was attractive to travelers, and Kent's choice of a claim at the western end of the best natural limestone ford in the entire northern portion of the state was not entirely by accident.

Most accounts of early Rockford suggest that Kent had come here with the intention of finding a good place to start a sawmill. Kent was in fact a land speculator, what was known at the time as a "locater," a familiar figure in many Illinois frontier communities who made his money by selling homesteads to settlers. He no doubt started the mill in part as a way of increasing the attractiveness of his various properties at Midway, since sawmills, blacksmith shops, and saloons were the three seeds of most new settlements in the region. He wanted to provide for all these services to some extent (he was later to add both a forge and tavern to his claim), though a sawmill would undoubtedly have been the primary attraction of such a community in its earliest stages of development.

Little is known about Kent except in the broadest outline. A native of Connecticut, he had gone south to seek his fortune as a young man and had worked for a period in both Virginia and Alabama, where he is said to have owned several slaves. At one time he had been a partner in a cotton factory on the Flint River near Huntsville. By the early 1830s he evidently had liquidated his business interests in the South and moved to Galena to be closer to his brother Aratus, who

was stationed there as a Presbyterian home missionary. (Aratus Kent, with youthful zeal, had asked the missionary board to send him to "a place so hard that no one else would take it.") Germanicus Kent may have intended all along to settle on the Rock River, but in looking for land he had at least investigated a few possibilities in the Lead Region first, riding north into the Wisconsin Territory as far as the Pecatonica River, and then descending the Pecatonica in a canoe that he acquired from a settler named Ransom and eventually entering the Rock not far from the cabin of the Indian trader Stephen Mack. Kent had been accompanied on his trip by Thatcher Blake, another native of New England who had been drawn to the Galena area by the prospect of unclaimed land in the wilderness tracts of the Upper Mississippi Valley.

After locating a mill seat on the lower Rock in the vicinity of Kent Creek, and after surveying the surrounding countryside for its other natural advantages, Kent and Blake took temporary squatters' possession of the site at Midway and went back to Galena for provisions. This was most likely in June 1834. Two months later, in late August or September, they returned to the Rock River in a lumber wagon with two other men to begin the actual task of improving the claim. For most of the next year Kent made regular trips to both Galena and Chicago for additional men and supplies while work at the site continued. The Rockford historian Charles Church has identified at least 10 people who were employed by Kent at Midway in 1834-1835; Blake himself was hired, according to Kent's journal, "at eighteen dollars per month . . . to take charge of my business,

Germanicus Kent established his sawmill in 1834 in this area of Kent Creek. Some early Rockford accounts identify Robert Tinker's little dam (foreground) as a remnant of the retaining wall of Kent's original millpond. Courtesy, Rockford Museum Center

and to do all kinds of work."

One of the laborers that Kent brought to Midway was a black slave named Lewis, who had followed him north from Huntsville the previous year. Lewis apparently had been given the choice of remaining in Alabama with another master or of traveling to Illinois as a kind of indentured servant. Kent was an eminently practical man. He had originally paid $450 for the slave in 1829; and in order to recover his investment, he proposed that Lewis buy his freedom by working for him at Midway over a period of six years and seven months. A deed of manumission, which is on file in the Winnebago County Clerk's office, shows that Lewis actually became a free man after only four years and four months of servitude, since Kent was willing to certify on September 6, 1839, that Lewis had by then been fully emancipated, or, as the Rock River *Democrat* later put it, "sold to himself."

There was an old Indian saying that white settlers were like spots of raccoon grease on a blanket. No one could tell from the first little stains that they would spread as rapidly and widely as they did. Long before Kent finished erecting his buildings at Midway he was joined by other speculators who were intent on establishing claims of their own in the area.

Daniel Shaw Haight, described by Church as a "rugged, roistering pioneer and a shrewd man of affairs," moved into the woods on the east side of the Rock River near the present intersection of State and Madison streets sometime in the spring of 1835. He is said to have lived in a tent under a large burr oak tree while he constructed his cabin. His plot was at the crest of a steep hill that ran down to the river

(this hill has since been graded and greatly reduced in elevation) and his cabin would probably have been visible to Kent's people on the river's west side, then living less than a mile away. Haight, who was from Warren County, New York, brought his wife and child with him, as well as his wife's sister and a hired man.

A year later a man from Virginia named Charley Reed located a claim on the west side about a mile and a half above Midway. This was near the river in the present Auburn Street area. Though he resided at Joliet, Reed had been in the habit of exploring the prairies of northern Illinois as far west as the Apple River, marking out the best homesteads. His contemporaries remembered him as "Friend Charley," a genial character, always well-dressed, with a small hatchet for blazing trees as a regular part of his outfit. Reed had become associated with a former Indian agent from the Wisconsin Territory, Nicholas Boilvin, who himself had acquired some property in the vicinity of Midway through the sale of Indian lands that had been granted to half-breeds under the 1829 Treaty of Prairie du Chien. Together they laid out a number of streets and plots, erected a two-story hotel, a blacksmith shop, and a lime kiln, and went into business as land agents, with Reed assuming the duties of general manager. Their settlement was given the name of Winnebago.

Both "Haightville" and "Kentville," as the east and west sides of the river at Midway eventually came to be known, acquired their share of new buildings during this time. Most of them were crude log structures built in the so-called "pioneer style" without nails, the logs notched at the corners and carried up horizontally to a gable roof of oak shakes. These structures were usually situated at the edges of groves, which offered protection from the elements, and were distributed somewhat randomly through the settlement. There was little sense of an organized community here, more a patchwork of small cabins and gardens; though both Haight and Kent hired the surveyor Don Alonzo Spaulding to plat their lands for future development and both envisioned mature settlements with streets, public squares, and commercial riverfronts that were reminiscent of the best New England towns. Between 1836 and 1838 Midway gained several new hotels, saloons, and general stores, and if the east side built two hotels to the west side's one during this period, the west side had the distinction of putting up the first brick building, the Winnebago House, a short distance from the river. Midway was not exactly like the phantom villages of some land agents in the state who advertised in the East for settlers without doing much more than platting barren lands. But the earliest surviving map of the west side, which was published by Millers' Lithographing Company of New York in 1839, does show a fairly complicated grid of 47 city blocks, a broad levee known as Front Street, and a public cemetery—and most of these features were bogus.

The liberties that Kent took in promoting his settlement were typical of speculators on the Illinois frontier. In a lowland area known as the "Big Bottom" a few miles north of Haightville, a homesteader named Wattles staked off streets and residential lots on his farm and christened the area "Scipio" after a leading citizen of ancient Rome. Below Midway, at the mouth of the

Kishwaukee, another phantom village came into being when speculators erected the wooden frames of some 40 buildings as an inducement to immigrants to settle there; the village was known as "Kishwaukee" to its promoters and "Rib Town" to its detractors, who took a certain malicious delight in observing that the ribs of these houses were never fleshed out. East of Haightville, ten miles or so from the Rock ford on the edges of what was then known as the "Big Woods," Colonel James Sayre founded the village of Newburg, building a sawmill to rival Kent's, as well as the first grist mill in the region. "The immigration to this locality in the years 1837 and 1838 was simply immense," Rockford's John Thurston later wrote, "a regular 'boom.' The roads were thronged with immigrants, many of them driving cattle, horses, and hogs, and as each had a little money, trade was excellent." Every homesteader along the way hawked his wares, trading animal skins for whiskey and grain for salt, and always extolling the virtues of land that was capable of growing the tallest corn and fattest hogs in the country.

KENT AND HAIGHT

The history of Rockford's early development is really the story of two men, Haight and Kent, who worked hard to promote the ford and its surroundings, but who later found themselves at odds with each other after Midway emerged as the dominant trading center in the region. They were the most determined and resourceful of all the early speculators, and they took the greatest pains to cultivate their political connections.

When the Illinois Legislature established Winnebago County and authorized the first elections in 1836, Kent offered his house as a polling place and made sure that his candidate, William Dunbar, was nominated to the court of county commissioners. Dunbar eventually played an important role in determining the location of the county seat, for it was his decision that helped to disqualify the preliminary bid of Nicholas Boilvin & Company (Boilvin and Charley Reed) and to ensure that the courthouse was built instead in either Kentville or Haightville. Charles Church tells us that Dunbar disassociated himself from Kent and moved to the east side (Haightville), evidently in the late 1830s. He also points out that William Hulin, who became a county commissioner while living on the east side, crossed the river in the other direction and allied himself with Kent.

Kent and Haight hired the same surveyor to plat their settlements, but they were unwilling to modify their plans when it was discovered that several of the main streets running east and west would not line up, thus insuring that the area's first bridges would be built diagonally across the Rock River. Each felt that it was the others' responsibility to change, even though it would involve moving only a handful of wooden stakes. Both men established their own commercial districts and "Main streets" (Haight's was later renamed "Madison Street"), while at the same time becoming grudgingly aware of the ways that their fortunes had already been linked by geography and circumstance.

Haight and Kent both stood for public office. In 1836, Haight became sheriff of Winnebago County. A year later, in August 1837, he was appointed the county's first postmaster.

Kent, who served as an election judge in 1836, had the honor of being the area's first representative in the Illinois General Assembly in 1838.

Local elections were great social occasions in those days, with each voter being required to vote out loud in front of the candidates, who usually sat on a bench. Judges were present to record the votes in special "poll books." Crowds alternately cheered and groaned as the votes were cast, and influential people such as Kent and Haight took the measure of everyone who came forward. It is evident that few people in Winnebago County in 1836 had ever voted before. No one owned a copy of the Illinois statutes or admitted to knowing what such a book looked like. Kent was given the job of election judge because he claimed to be familiar with the laws of Alabama and Virginia, and he usually got his way, unless he was opposed by Daniel Shaw Haight. After the first election, the winning candidates administered the oaths of office to each other and drew lots for the lengths of their respective terms.

Haight was able to get himself appointed to a special commission that was responsible for surveying and locating a permanent state road between the Fox River and Midway. In 1836 the Illinois Legislature directed that the road be fixed on what the commission found to be the "most advantageous ground." Almost inevitably, Haight located the road in front of his own house.

Not to be outdone, Kent established a ferry service at that point on the riverbank where the state road came to an end. He wanted to ensure that travelers would have access to the businesses in his settlement as well, but in opening the ferry he made the passage easier both ways, and he considerably reduced the difficulties of those people on the west side who wanted to cross the river to Haightville.

In the early years of Midway, public religious services alternated between the east and west sides. The very first service was held in Kent's cabin in the summer of 1835 on the occasion of Aratus Kent's visit from Galena; every white resident in the area was said to have been in attendance that day, including Haight and his family. Beginning in 1837, Congregational Church services were held on the east side near the present intersection of State and Third streets, in a stage barn belonging to Haight. The church, which had been organized in May with nine members, made arrangements to construct a permanent frame building a half mile or so to the north, and work on this had progressed to the point of actually enclosing the walls when it was learned that Kent and George Brinckerhoff, another land agent, had started to erect a Congregational church of their own on the west side with money obtained from some of their friends in New York. Kent's action effectively put an end to work on the east-side building, which almost certainly was his intention, and the west side added a new Greek Revival edifice with a cupola and fluted columns to its list of public attractions.

Midway eventually eclipsed in size and reputation all other settlements in the region. With the loss of the county seat, both "Scipio" and Charley Reed's "Winnebago" passed into oblivion. The surveyors' stakes were pulled up and the buildings dismantled. Farmers went to "Rib Town" to ransack the house frames for lumber. Whole structures were moved across the prairies on wagons to become parts of new homesteads miles from their

Shepherd Leach, an English immigrant, erected this little shanty on his claim near Montague Road, in 1837. From Rockford: Yesterday—Today & Forever, *1904*

original locations.

"Midway" was Kent's name for his claim, and one must suppose that Haight objected to it as a name for the east side. As settlers moved into the vicinity of the ford, and as the terms "Haightville" and "Kentville" gained in currency, it became expedient for the settlers to adopt a new name for the entire area that was free of sectional prejudice. According to John Thurston, a meeting was held in Chicago for precisely this purpose between Haight, Kent, Dr. Josiah Goodhue, and several other people with business interests in the settlement. "Rock Ford," Thurston says, was Goodhue's suggestion and unanimously adopted by the men to replace "Midway." Historians have been unable to agree on the exact date of the name change and even on whether the change occurred in the way that Thurston remembers it, but a terminus of sorts is provided by one of Kent's own letters in 1837, where "Rockford" appears as part of the inside address.

Frontier Life

I

n its early years, from the time of Kent's arrival in 1834 until the coming of the railroad at mid-century, Rockford was virtually indistinguishable from hundreds of other small frontier towns, a collection of frame buildings with false wooden fronts, log houses, dirt streets, and milling livestock. Living conditions were primitive to a degree that most people today would have difficulty imagining. There is little in the standard histories of Rockford that gives us much more than a passing notion of life in Rockford in the nineteenth century.

The one exception is Thurston's 1891 *Reminiscences, Sporting and Otherwise, of Early Days in Rockford*, which is full of the sensations and small details of the frontier.

"In the early forties," Thurston writes,

the people of this county were so poor they 'couldn't cast a shadow' . . . I venture to say that in 1841-1842 there were not twenty farmers in the county who possessed a suit of clothes suitable to wear to church or to court, which they had purchased with the avails of

labor on their farms. Alas for those among the settlers who had passed their prime physically. Too old to withstand the hardships of pioneer life, they sickened, and in some instances they straggled back to the old homes at the east to die.

The hard, grinding reality of life on the prairies was that the settlers were bound to the soil. They lived outdoors to a far greater extent than most farmers do today, and they had little relief from its storms and summer heat. They truly lived off the land, raising crops and livestock for barter and keeping their own tables supplied with whatever they could kill or grub out of the ground.

At times game was so plentiful that this was not a problem. They could shoot deer almost from their doorsteps. Quail and grouse appeared in such numbers that a single shot occasionally brought down several birds; rabbits and muskrats were easy to trap. At other times, particularly in the winter, settlers had to exist on roots and a coarse corn bread baked in grease. Even tree bark, pulverized and boiled to a grainy consistency, helped them to control their hunger.

Yet the problem that they faced was not so much in staying fed as it was in staying dry. They were always damp. They developed painful sores on their legs and feet because they could never find a way to dry their boots entirely or to change their clothing often enough to keep it from irritating their skin. Some regularly went down with the chills, like "Uncle Stone," a well-known Rockford character whose grumblings in the throes of a malarial fever ("ague") were mimicked in Worcester Dickerman's contemporary account: "I had an awful time yesterday; thought I would shake my teeth out; folks all sick; but I'm goin' ter wear the ager out this year or quit. It comes only once a week now."

Life on the prairies was simple in its fundamentals. Settlers got their water from the river, kept time by the sun, and tested the fertility of soil with drops of vinegar. They believed that the phases of the moon determined the best times to harvest crops and slaughter livestock, and they worried that when they accidentally stepped on a toad their cows would give bloody milk. They found springs with a hazel dowsing rod and underground mineral deposits with the leaves of a prairie plant. They were practical inventors, as most farmers are to this day, rubbing raw onion on bee stings, and a mixture of fresh butter, chimney soot, and hog's lard on burns.

When Rockford settlers were plagued by a rash known as the "prairie itch" in 1837-1838, they experimented with a variety of home-made ointments and salves until someone in desperation spit tobacco on his arm—and found relief. They distrusted most forms of "book learning" as well as most books. They were just as likely to break the binding on a new volume and paper the walls of their cabins with it as they were to examine the pages. Even more than books, they

distrusted paper currency and the men who issued it. Whenever they received bank notes, they got rid of them as fast as they could.

The first settlers tended to avoid the prairies. They thought that treeless land was unsuited to farming and looked instead for oak and hickory groves. White oaks were supposed to have been among the best indicators of fertile soil. Haight himself selected a field or "barrens" in an oak forest south of today's State Street to put into cultivation and enclosed it with a stake-and-rider worm fence. Oak Street in this area today has taken its name from this early feature of the landscape.

Settlers farmed the forest edges and hillsides first, then the flats along the Rock River, and finally the prairies, though few were prepared for the difficulties they encountered in working the grasslands. "The prairie grass grew in small bunches or tufts," Thurston remembered, "the blades of the grass having sharp edges which cut out the leather on the toes of a pair of boots rapidly, unless protected with a strip of tin tacked to the sole of the boot, a practice almost universal."

Breaking the sod required several yoke of oxen, as well as someone to ride on the plow beam so that the point would stay in the ground. Young boys walked alongside the breaking team with sticks in order to scrape the wooden blade when it became clotted with soil, and the driver watched for snakes as the sod turned over and killed them with his whip. Thurston said that the prairie's tough root system sometimes brought the team to a halt. The driver would then have to break the roots with an axe, as he did in planting sod

Some of the early log houses in Rockford survived as farm outbuildings well into the twentieth century. This structure, which was built by Alfred Mather in 1839, was apparently moved from its original west side location to a farm in the vicinity of Loves Park. From Rockford: Yesterday—Today & Forever, 1904

corn, and realign the plow blade in the trench before continuing.

Generally speaking, the size of the trees on a claim determined the size of a settler's cabin—the taller the trees, the larger the dwelling. Since oak was a desirable building material, the selection of a mature stand of oak trees close to a steady supply of running water would have been considered advantageous. In the case of Haight, the choice of a wooded hilltop overlooking the river with a commanding view of the countryside to the west would have been doubly attractive. According to Church, his original cabin was erected at the very "brow" of this "tableland." He built it approximately 18 feet square, with two windows and a plank door that was attached to the walls with wooden hinges, everything "gotten out by hand" from oak. Haight decided to leave the bark on the log walls, though he furnished his cabin with

a puncheon floor and an iron cooking stove.

Most of Haight's contemporaries were far less enterprising home builders, living at first in crude huts and half-faced shelters of animal skins. Thomas Lake's original cabin, while slightly larger than Haight's, had a dirt floor beneath a carpet of basswood bark. Settlers' tables were improvised by wedging puncheons into door openings and by straddling the notched corners of the rooms. Sleeping quarters were arranged by heaping up prairie grass on the floor under a hogskin blanket. This kind of bed, which was as hard as a rock, was called a "prairie feather" mattress, and it was widely adopted on the Illinois frontier.

A few settlers did their cooking outdoors, even in the winter, but the majority tried to fashion a hearth of some sort on the inside of their dwellings because of the greater warmth and convenience it offered. Hearths varied from a simple fire in a circle of stones—hence the advantage of an earthen floor—to a relatively sophisticated stick-and-mud fireplace. The more lackadaisical homesteaders got by without ever constructing a chimney or cutting a hole in the roof. For them, the existing cracks between the logs of the cabin sufficed for ventilation, while the smoke that built up inside the structure was tolerated and even welcomed because it drove out the "mosche-toes" and the green-headed prairie flies that made life miserable in the summer.

It is debatable whether a twen-tieth-century visitor to one of these hovels would have been more of-fended by the cramped quarters or by the lack of sanitation. There was little chance for privacy, little separa-tion of the sexes. People shared the same beds (as many as three to a blanket), the same clothes, the same eating utensils. The same iron kettle might be used to bring water from the river or fire from a neighbor's hearth prior to cooking a meal—such an implement, according to Thurston, "being well adapted to bake, stew, fry, boil, washing dishes, and also available for toilet pur-poses in the early morning."

When Rockford celebrated its first Independence Day in 1837, guests were served food on wooden shingles, a common practice among frontier families at the time, most of whom could scarcely have afforded real crockery even if they could have figured out a way to bring here without breaking it. People ate with their fingers and afterward rubbed their plates clean on the grass. Travelers at country inns ate off each others' plates and even shared the same cutlery. As a rule,

people were not bothered by these things because popular science had not yet established a connection in their minds between personal hy-giene and the prevention of disease. If they bathed in the river, it was seldom. The only soap that they had was an alkaline concoction made by leaching ashes, and from time to time they rubbed this on their hands and faces. Most of the time, however, they went around unwashed.

The taverns and hostelries on the frontier—commonly referred to as "doggeries" and "dog holes"—were little better than the settlers' cabins, and in many cases they were worse. People of all types slept together in a room on beds of rope and cleft oak planks, their modesty protected by blankets that hung be-tween the beds from the ceiling raft-ers. In the Rockford House, which Thurston's father operated for many years on the east side, the dormi-tory room was located on the third floor and was accessible by a crude ladder that had been built into the wall studs. (Thurston's job as a boy was to light the way up the ladder at night with a tallow dip.)

When frontier inns were crowded, strangers of the same sex were expected to share beds, though anyone could sleep alone in a wooden chair or spread a blanket on the floor on top of prairie feath-ers if he wanted to. Most people slept in their clothes because of the presence of the opposite sex. Plank beds were generally too hard, and rope beds, like hammocks, too soft in the middle, the latter throwing sleeping companions on top of one another when either moved a mus-cle. Fleas and bed bugs tormented everyone, and travelers cursed and flailed about in the darkness under their attack.

CLAIM JUMPERS AND "TOMAHAWK RIGHTS"

Hard times produced hard people. In a frontier community where families were used to killing and dressing their own meat, where ague and horse cholera were common and infant mortality considerably higher than it is today, people developed a familiarity with death that now seems callous. It was not unusual in the early days of Rockford for wagons loaded with hundreds of dead quail and grouse to be brought in from the prairies. The carcasses of deer, beaver, and rabbit hung in the open on the walls of sheds and on fences in the settlement. When it pleased them, farmers would, as they used to say, "send death through an animal" on the very streets of the town.

The frontier developed its own curious code of ethics. You could kill a man in a duel or in another so-called affair of honor if you killed him fair and square. You could also kill a horse thief or a claim jumper in good conscience if that person threatened you with bodily harm. The point, of course, was that horse stealing and claim jumping were assumed to be life threatening in almost every instance. "The loss of his team was often bitter ruin to the settler," Thurston recalled, "and he was ready to protect his property regardless of preliminary legal proceedings."

The early laws of Illinois provided a rude framework within which most people were left to do more or less as they pleased. Rockford was 240 miles away from the state capitol of Vandalia, and in between were a series of stump roads that few people willingly traveled. Daniel Shaw Haight, the sheriff of Winnebago County, was given little actual power to enforce the law. He was only one man in a society of back-country settlers, a figurehead sheriff who got his way when it suited the rest. Many homesteaders declared themselves simply too busy or ornery to bother with such things and went about their business indifferent to legalities. Germanicus Kent, who walked the streets of Rockford an honored man, brought the slave Lewis with him from Alabama in spite of the fact that slavery had been prohibited by both the ordinances of the Northwest Territory and the Illinois Constitution of 1818. People praised his generosity in freeing Lewis, overlooking the fact that Kent had already recovered his investment in the slave two-fold by the time that he set him free. (Kent also realized that the growing number of abolitionists in the county had limited the days of Lewis's "indentured servitude.")

Lawmakers talked about right and wrong as abstract concepts, but the ordinary homesteader knew in his bones that these were only fancy words for a kind of survival-of-the-fittest ethic that recognized a person's strength and potential for violence as the final arbiters of disputes on the frontier. People called them "tomahawk rights"—when there was little government and even less law enforcement, the strong man always won.

The first settlers in northern Illinois had only temporary squatters' possession of their lands, an authority that was based on an old notion that possession was nine-tenths of the law. Claim holders proved their worth by building houses and tilling the soil. Residents of west Rockford were unable to obtain their actual legal titles until 1839, and because of certain

This stone building, identified only as "Winnebago County House," is typical of the plain, unadorned style of the earliest dwellings in the Rockford area. Courtesy, Rockford Museum Center

the neighbor a new pasture for his 40 head of cattle. Lake eventually got well enough to pull the fence down; and when his neighbor put it up again, Lake resorted to a more elemental approach. "At last," he wrote in his memoir, "lightning struck a pair of oxen, and in burying them, marks of Galena were found, and I suppose a mineral abounded in the claim. Cattle did not trouble me much after that."

Homesteaders banded together in impromptu judiciaries known as claims committees to deal with suspected lawbreakers. In the winter of 1838-1839, more than 100 residents of Rockford assembled on the prairie to pry the house of a claim jumper off its foundation and move it by ox sled into the center of town. There they unloaded it on the front yard of George Brinckerhoff, Kent's business associate, who was believed to be the mastermind behind the illegal claim. Brinckerhoff was informed that the house had been lost on the prairie, and that they had felt obliged as good neighbors to bring it home again.

Occasionally these vigilante groups meted out much rougher punishment. When a homesteader named Brown put up a cabin on land that was thought to belong to Don Alonzo Spaulding, the government surveyor, a claims committee decided to storm the cabin and evict him, only to be met by Brown's musket poking through a window. Unwilling to test him, the committee resorted to trickery, promising a new house and a better claim in another section of the county if Brown agreed to vacate the premises. Once a deal had been struck and the door opened, the crowd rushed forward to tear the cabin down and set it on fire, leaving Brown and his

technicalities, most settlers on the east side had to wait until Congress finally authorized a land sale in 1843. For almost a decade, people were left to themselves to resolve boundary disputes and other questions of ownership. And because so much of the land in the vicinity of Rockford was inadequately surveyed, disputes were fairly common.

People sometimes tried to enlarge their homesteads at a neighbor's expense by moving their fence lines at night or by depositing ready-made cabins in remote areas where boundaries were in doubt. When John Lake was bedridden with a fractured skull, his wife awakened one morning to see a strange fence "running near the house," with a neighbor who had earlier called to inquire about her husband's health providing most of the locomotion. The new fence enclosed some 90 acres of the Lake homestead, most of it already planted, while offering

The dignified stone edifice of the First Baptist Church on North Church Street was the finest in the city at the time of its construction in 1850. Courtesy, Rockford Museum Center

family of seven children in the woods to brave the winter cold and an eight-inch snowfall as best they could. (Spaulding later said that the crowd had made a mistake; the claim wasn't really his.)

Fairness required that suspects be given the right of due process, and claims committees and other vigilante groups went through the motions to ensure that their juries had the appearance of legitimacy. A citizens' group known as the Regulators, which was made up of residents of both Winnebago and Ogle counties, took the trouble to adopt by-laws and rules of conduct, elect officers, and even got the blessing of a circuit-riding judge. For much of the spring of 1841 the Regulators, thus "legalized," dealt with suspected lawbreakers in the territory by flogging them with blacksnakes. According to Jacob Miller, a Rockford lawyer, "Everyone who happened to fall under the suspicion of one or more of their gang was at once brought before their self-constituted tribunal, where there was no difficulty in procuring the ready testimony for convicting him of any crime which should be named . . ."

The judge himself had recommended 36 lashes as a first warning for offenses and 60 lashes as a second, but one account of these incidents placed the penalties as high as 300 lashes for first-time offenders, who were usually advised to leave the territory before they received a second dose. Regulators who wanted to adhere to the strict letter of the judge's recommendations could apply 36 lashes in unison to the back, buttocks, and legs of a prisoner. Unwilling to trample on the rights of the minority, the Regulators did nothing to punish or otherwise censure a small group of its own members who expressed their outrage at a jury's acquittal of a man named Daggett by dragging him into the woods at night and flogging him nearly to death.

INCORPORATION AS A CITY

By the 1850s Rockford had changed. Livestock still ran loose in the streets and manure piles abounded, but the town had its own courthouse and jail and a rickety lattice bridge that spanned the Rock River where the ferry had previously operated. Frink, Walker & Company, the Chicago stagecoach line, carried passengers to Galena several times a week across the bridge, which trembled under the weight of wagons and livestock and looked from a distance like a crooked cow path, or, as one person put it, "the longest horse barn in the world."

Rockford residents had also constructed a brush and gravel dam upstream near the present Beattie Park as a means of harnessing the river's power. There was a headgate for steamboats (which was never used) and long sluiceways running parallel to the river on both the east and west sides to receive the water diverted by the dam. Three sawmills, a gristmill, a carding and fulling mill, and a foundry had been built on these waterways in 1845-1846. When the dam broke in 1851, the water rushed downstream with such force that it tore out the bridge's west embankment and twisted the first two trestles. Yet the bridge, whose old oak planks were said to have been "as tough as whalebone," held together, and people used a block-and-tackle mechanism to haul the trestles back into place.

Deratus Harper, who later became Chicago's city engineer, was responsible for the construction of Rockford's bridge and courthouse in the mid-1840s. Harper was a kind of rural mechanic who made his living as a smith and house joiner

while tinkering in his workshop with axles, cylinders, and wooden joints. Thurston said that he "possessed mechanical skill and ingenuity of a high order." Harper's skill as a finisher was displayed in the courthouse, which stood behind a symmetrical wooden fence on the west side public square facing State Street. Working with the carpenter John Beattie, he designed a single-story frame structure that was 17 feet high and 56 feet long. Its classical facade was among the most graceful in the area—certainly the finest of any Rockford building used for public meetings. There were two wings and a central auditorium (courtroom), each with a

This is the earliest surviving photograph of Rockford. It was taken from the east side in 1853 and shows the irregular outline of Deratus Harper's 1844 bridge. From Rockford: Yesterday—Today & Forever, *1904*

colonnade in front. A triangular pediment rose above the main entrance, like the gable end of a Grecian temple. Its style appealed to Rockford, which was always ready to imagine itself as more civilized than it actually was.

Of all the municipal improvements, however, none was more eagerly anticipated than the railroad. As early as 1836, a charter had been issued to the Galena & Chicago Union Railroad to build a track across northern Illinois, but the company had lacked the means to finance the project, and work had not begun in earnest until 1848. In the meantime, Rockford residents had explored a number of other possibilities for transportation, including the construction of a plank road to Chicago and the navigation of the Rock River. These had stalled for the same reason: a lack of capital. The Panic of 1837, which had been intensified in Illinois by a huge state debt and a banking system that lacked adequate gold and silver reserves, had made investors wary of risking their money.

Germanicus Kent himself had lost most of his money in the Panic and had given up his business interests in south Rockford. By 1844 he had moved back to Virginia for good. His long-time rival Daniel Shaw Haight had little better luck despite his many investments. Three years later he too had left the area and taken up residence in eastern Texas.

After the departure of Kent and Haight, the leadership of Rockford civic affairs was assumed by men like John Holland and Thomas D. Robertson, who were bankers and business partners and somewhat more sophisticated in their understanding of finance. As the Galena & Chicago Union track moved steadily westward from Cook County in the late 1840s, interest in the railroad remained high, especially among farmers hoping to sell their produce on the eastern grain markets. Stock in the company was sold in Galena, Chicago, and Rockford, in addition to the various rural locations along the proposed line. Robertson, who was elected a company director in 1849, was one of its most active promoters. By August 1852 an engine (the Pioneer) and six freight cars were greeted by

One of the finest Greek Revival structures in Rockford was the 1844 courthouse, which was designed by Deratus Harper and John Beattie. It was built on the west side public square (present courthouse site) entirely through public subscription. "The main building was a court room," Worcester Dickerman remembered, "with two rooms in rear for jury, and a wing on each side, occupied respectively by the county clerk, recorder, sheriff, circuit clerk, and probate justice of the peace." Courtesy, Rockford Public Library

ringing church bells and cannon blasts as they entered Rockford for the first time.

In many ways the year 1852 was a watershed in the early history of the area. Rockford was officially incorporated as a city in April, and the first mayor and aldermen were elected. Willard Wheeler, a tinner from Canada whom Thurston remembered as a "bad man" in a quarrel, had the honor of being chosen the city's chief executive. In June the Illinois Legislature authorized the city council to borrow money for the construction of a new bridge across the Rock River to replace Deratus Harper's wobbling structure.

Work also proceeded south of State Street on a more permanent masonry dam to replace the one constructed in 1845-1846. The site chosen was the old ford, the shallowest point in the river rapids, which Kent had envisioned as one of the keys to the development of his little community. Under the name of the Rockford Water Power Company, a massive 800-foot wall was built across the river, a long sluiceway excavated in the adjacent bedrock of the west side, and a six-foot headway created upstream to drive the water wheels of the city's future mills and shops. This, as Charles Church has pointed out, was the first step in the transformation of Rockford from a regional trading center into a manufacturing city of national importance.

Anson Miller was a state senator from Rockford in the 1840s. A presidential elector at the time of the Civil War, he was given the honor of reporting the Illinois vote to the Electoral College in Washington in 1864. Courtesy, Rockford Public Library

Rockford's second State Street Bridge, constructed in 1854, offered two lanes of traffic, pedestrian walks, and reasonable protection from the elements. From Rockford: Yesterday—Today & Forever, *1904*

Industrial Development

W ith the coming of the railroad in 1852, Rockford entered one of the decisive periods of its development. In less than a decade, the population of Winnebago and Boone counties increased by more than 1,600 people and Rockford itself tripled in size. Land values doubled practically overnight after the Galena & Chicago Union completed its line to Freeport in 1853. Chicago grain markets, hitherto accessible to farmers only by arduous wagon trips across the prairies, could now be reached in half a day. Grain production rose sharply. Eastern merchandise, particularly high-grade pine lumber for new buildings, followed the rails west, chasing the money that the farmers were earning on the region's agricultural surpluses.

Whatever its advantages as a distribution center and way station on the railroad, Rockford owed most of its development in the 1850s to the use of hydraulic power. The Rock River was easily

dammed, and the limestone ford proved to be a secure base for the new masonry wall. It was from all accounts an ambitious enterprise, particularly the financing. "I was astonished at the magnitude of the undertaking," Ralph Emerson wrote of his first visit to Rockford. "I knew that to build the Lawrence dam required the heaviest New England capitalists, and I took it for granted that it must be Eastern capital that was building this stupendous work. How great then was my astonishment to learn that it was being built by citizens of the town." Under an 1849 general act of the Illinois Legislature concerned with the "improvement of the Rock River" and "the production of hydraulic power," Rockford's business leaders had pooled their resources to create the Water Power Company in 1851. Robertson and Holland, the chief promoters of the Galena & Chicago Union Railroad, were once again in the forefront.

Orlando Clarke, who had opened a foundry on the original west-side race just north of the city bridge in 1845, was one of the first people to move his business to the Water Power District. During the spring, in partnership with Isaac Utter, Clarke began to manufacture a new reaper for a young inventor living in Stephenson County.

The inventor was John H. Manny, a farm hand of 27, then

ABOVE: John Chick, a native of Devonshire, England, operated both the Forest City and Reaper City flour mills on South Water Street in the late nineteenth century. This view of the Chick milling complex also shows the diagonal line of the Rockford dam. Photo by F.C. Pierce/ Rockford Public Library

BELOW: Joseph Emerson, who was the rector of the Second Congregational Church, built this Italianate residence on North Church Street in 1855. Three years later he sold it to his cousin, Ralph Emerson, who enlarged it into a 30-room mansion during the next half century. Courtesy, Rockford Public Library

practically penniless from his inventions (he owned several patents for a reaper-mower) but widely recognized in the area as a gifted mechanic. Manny and his father, it was said, had started experimenting with farm implements at their home in Waddam's Grove after seeing a popular grain cutter, the Esterly Header, exhibited at the Chicago Mechanics Institute. They had purchased two Esterly machines, torn them apart, and rebuilt them according to their own designs. Manny's own reaper-mower had been manufactured in limited quantities in 1852, and was gaining a reputation throughout the Midwest as a lighter, more compact version of the celebrated McCormick Virginia Reaper.

According to Charles Church, Clarke persuaded Manny to come to Rockford in 1853 to take advantage of its developing hydraulic power. Aware of Manny's "financial embarrassment" and genuinely impressed by the commercial potential of the North-

ern Illinois Reaper, Clarke proposed making machines for him as a licensee. Wait and Sylvester Talcott, prosperous Rockton farmers who owned a Manny harvester, were taken into the company in 1854 as investors. Later in the same year, Ralph Emerson and Jesse Blinn also joined the company by extending credit to Manny for metals and other materials from their hardware store in Rockford in exchange for a percentage of his future sales.

Manny's move to the Water Power District was the most important event in the early history of Rockford manufacturing. Because of him, the new hydraulic company became a credible enterprise, and a number of jobbers were attracted to the city to produce parts for his reaper. John Pells Manny, a cousin from Stephenson County and an inventor in his own right, arrived in 1854 to make knife sections. Liberal assignments were made under the Manny patent for the manufacture of patterns and castings.

Production rose from 150 machines in 1853 to 1,030 in 1854. By the end of the following year, when the Northern Illinois Reaper was exhibited at the International Exposition in Paris (one machine was purchased there by Napoleon III), production had risen to 2,893. So rapid was the growth of the farm implement trade during this time that a labor shortage became one of the chief obstacles to its further expansion. Production outstripped the existing facilities.

Almost inevitably, Cyrus McCormick came to regard Manny & Company as a serious threat to his business. He was convinced that the Rockford firm had simply altered the design of his own machine in order to evade patent restrictions. Though the original patent had expired in 1848, McCormick sued, contending that the subsequent patented "improvements" in the Virginia Reaper construction entitled him to a virtual monopoly of the existing trade. He hired two nationally prominent lawyers, E.N. Dickerson and Reverdy Johnson, and his strategy seems to have been, at least in part, to encumber the fledgling Rockford operation with legal expenses while making a public example of it. McCormick claimed $400,000 in damages, warning farmers in his advertisements that they would be guilty of patent infringement themselves if they purchased a Manny machine. Manny chose a one-time Rockford farmer and iron founder named Peter Watson to organize his defense. Watson had helped him obtain the patents on the Northern Illinois Reaper and possessed an exceptional understanding of mechanics. It was his decision to retain Edwin Stanton of Pittsburgh and Abraham Lincoln of Springfield, Illinois, as associate counsels.

Stanton and Lincoln had never met, and they would not actually come together until the eve of the trial in 1855. Lincoln was chosen because of

his reputed skill as a debater and because Watson considered it politically expedient to have an Illinois lawyer arguing the case in an Illinois courtroom. Lincoln visited Rockford during the summer of 1855 to study the construction of the Northern Illinois Reaper. He was not, however, allowed to argue the case, as he had hoped. When the trial was moved to Cincinnati in the fall (it was then part of the same judicial district), Lincoln's Illinois residency became a disadvantage. Stanton, moreover, considered him oafish, a long-limbed "baboon," and let others make the arguments.

Manny & Company nevertheless won the case, and Lincoln received $1,000 for his trouble—the largest legal fee that he had ever collected. Along with the initial retainer of $500, the payment enabled him to begin the construction of his Springfield home, and, eventually, to launch his candidacy for the U.S. Senate. Lincoln, as President, appointed Stanton as his secretary of war and Watson as his assistant secretary, overlooking the former's treatment of him at Cincinnati. Justice McLean, who heard the case on January 16, 1856, granted John Manny "full possession of his invention" and dismissed McCormick's suit "at the cost of the complainant."

The John P. Manny Mower Company manufactured knife sections for several Rockford reaper businesses. This was one of the Manny buildings located in the Water Power District. Photo by F.C. Pierce/Rockford Public Library

Manny's legal expenses amounted to $60,000, a huge burden for a company of its size. Given a period of less dynamic growth, McCormick might well have succeeded in driving Manny out of business in spite of losing the suit. As it was, Manny won the trial and lost his health. The strain of the lawsuit made him ill. On the last day of January, barely two weeks after the trial had ended, Manny died of tuberculosis at his home on South Main Street in Rockford.

Manny's widow made assignments under her husband's patents to Emerson and Talcott, as well as to F.H. Manny, another relative, who arrived in Rockford to manufacture the combined reaper-mower. Emerson solidified his relationship with his partner by marrying Adaline Talcott; the business was renamed Emerson & Company in 1860. The firm acquired the rights to two popular farm implements,

Emerson & Company promoted the New Manny Reaper and Mower as "the best Combined Self-Rake Reaper and Mower ever offered to the public."

the Marsh Harvester and the Jones Hand Corn Planter, and began to produce these in great quantity. When the owners of the Rockford Water Power Company offered Emerson a controlling interest at 66 cents on a dollar of stock, he accepted, and in a short time he had "harvested" 225 cents from his investment.

Others began to diversify their businesses. F.H. Manny added seeders and cultivators to his product line. The firm of Bertrand and Sames, which was established outside the Water Power, manufactured colters (vertical plow blades), plows, and sulky cultivators. The blacksmith shop of James Skinner expanded its capacity to eleven forges, turning out a wide variety of plows. Clarke and Utter, who had lost the license for the Northern Illinois Reaper, now manufactured a mechanized seeding machine that had been invented by Marquis L. Gorham; they also began to make sugar mills, evaporators, and steam engines. John Pells Manny left his job with Emerson and Talcott to spend time on his inventions. In the early 1860s he brought out a combined reaper-mower of his own design in competition with that of his former business associates. This was a commercial success and made him a wealthy man. Unlike his late cousin who never realized the benefits of his inventions, Manny earned royalties of $15 for every one of his machines sold. The N.C. Thompson Company, given exclusive rights to the John P. Manny Reaper, produced 4,000 of the machines a year.

THE CIVIL WAR

By the late 1850s, Rockford industry included not only farm implement manufacturers, but flour and planing mills, carriage makers, pump

Emerson & Company acquired the rights to the popular Marsh Harvester in the 1860s.

factories, "wind engine" (windmill) builders, foundries, tanneries, and blacksmith shops. It was no longer a country trading center. The steady stream of immigrants from New England had been joined by increasing numbers of foreign-born, initially the Irish after the Great Potato Famine of the late 1840s, and then the Swedes after the crop failures in Scandanavia at mid-century. Agricultural prices in Europe were depressed by the arrival of cheap American grains from states like Illinois, which led the rest of the nation in the production of wheat and corn. The bounty of northern Illinois farms, delivered by rail to the port of Chicago and other places farther east, thus indirectly helped to stimulate emigration.

Irish immigrants built the Galena & Chicago Union track to Rockford, the new State Street covered bridge in 1854, and many of the factories that sprang up in the Water Power

N.C. Thompson's Reaper Works in the Water Power District (1857) was the principal manufacturer of the John P. Manny combination reaper-mower. In this photograph, the millrace is visible in the foreground.

District. They settled on the southwest side of the city in an area later known as the "Potato Patch," and on the northeast side near the public square; the Swedes lived on the southeast side in the general vicinity of the Galena & Chicago Union station.

Rockford was a Whig stronghold and hotbed of abolitionist feeling in the 1850s. Anti-slavery and temperance resolutions were introduced into the charters of various churches and social organizations, and in 1856 Rockford voters approved a prohibitory liquor law by a margin of more than 10 to 1. The City Council refused to license the sale of intoxicants within its corporate boundaries. It passed an ordinance to "prohibit and suppress" gaming houses, tipling houses, and dram shops, as well as "ball alleys" (bowling alleys) and billiard tables. Whigs routinely swept the local elections, playing upon a certain well-established reverse class prejudice—a suspicion of the gentleman stranger. In promoting its candi-

dates at election time, the party paraded them through the streets in coonskin caps in celebration of the old-fashioned virtues of free labor, self-reliance, simple meals, and homespun garments.

After the passage of the controversial Kansas-Nebraska Bill in 1854, a mass meeting was held in Rockford to denounce the "treachery" of the "trading politicians" in Congress—Democrats, Free Soilers, and Whigs alike—and to "protest the rapidly increasing influence of the Slave-Power." According to the official minutes of the meeting, ". . . E.B. Washburne was nominated by acclamation as the candidate of the Republican party of the First Congressional district of Illinois, for Congress, to be supported at the coming election." This had nominally been a Whig gathering, given the fact that it was actively promoted by local Whig leaders. Washburne himself had already been elected to Congress as a member of that party. Yet Whigs at the national level had been in eclipse since the 1852 Presidential election, and the loyalties of many of its old-line adherents in Illinois were weakening. What began as a more or less spontaneous protest against the Nebraska Bill had ended, after some strange political maneuverings, in the birth of the Republican Party in Rockford and the nomination of the first Republican candidate for Congress in the state.

Church has recorded the comments of a local newspaper at the time: "After settling a few other matters, the convention adjourned, and the Republican Party was supposed to be born." How did a Whig convention turn into a Republican one? It appears that Stephen Hurlbut, a Belvidere lawyer and unannounced candidate for Washburne's Congressional seat, had seen an opportunity in the uproar over the Nebraska Bill to embarrass Washburne and to force him either to endorse a radical anti-slavery resolution or to disavow it publicly. Rockford, he knew, would support a radical measure, and Hurlbut had bet that Washburne would be unwilling to endorse it. This was not the case. Washburne, with a far keener sense of the political realities in his own district than the policies of distant Washington,

had announced at the meeting that he gave Hurlbut's resolution his "most hearty approval." Whereupon, it appears, the crowd had roared its own approval back and renominated Washburne by acclamation as a Republican—the only party with an unequivocal position on slavery. James Loop, a Rockford lawyer and one-time business associate of Hurlbut's, is said to have commented sarcastically afterward that Washburne would "swallow anything." The new Republican had only proved to be a superior kind of political chameleon, however, since he solicited and received the official endorsement of the regular Whig convention as well six days later. In 1856 Rockford gave the Republican candidate for President, John C. Fremont, a 3,000 vote majority, his "Old Pathfinder" reputation evidently appealing to the Whig loyalists here.

In 1857 a volunteer militia known as the Rockford City Greys was organized. Like good soldiers, its members agreed to avoid drinking and gambling and to conduct themselves at all times in public with proper military deportment. They wore uniforms consisting of

This view of the intersection of South Main and Elm streets in the late nineteenth century includes the Winnebago National Bank (foreground), which was organized as a private banking company in 1848. The four-story Hotel Holland, also shown, was the city's largest hostelry with more than 150 rooms. It was erected in 1855. Photo by F.C. Pierce/Rockford Public Library

The Rockford Silver Plate Company, which formerly stood on South Wyman Street, manufactured a variety of silver and tableware. Photo by F.C. Pierce/Rockford Public Library

crossbelts, epaulets, swords, plumes, and bearskin hats. Each man pledged to devote himself to the business of the company, which not only meant adopting an ascetic lifestyle but learning the complicated drills that the Greys performed in public.

The United States was moving gradually towards civil war, and the sectional strife in places like "Bleeding Kansas" between slavery and anti-slavery settlers, reported regularly in the press, made Rockford conscious of the value of a militia. A new drillmaster from Chicago, Elmer Ellsworth, arrived in 1858 to instruct the company in the rapid, athletic movements of the French Zouaves, the first time that such a system had been used to train an American cadet corps; and the Greys' early proficiency in these drills made it one of the best performing regiments in the state.

During the summer Ellsworth made arrangements for a "Grand Military Encampment" at the annual Winnebago County Agricultural Society Fair, inviting two other state militias, the Chicago National Guard Cadets and the Washington Continental Artillery of Elgin, to compete against the Greys in skirmish and

bayonet exhibitions. Drummers kept up a steady cadence through the performances, which culminated in the Greys' own "Grand Review," the "Drill of the Chasseurs de Vincennes and the Zouaves of the French Army." The companies demonstrated difficult tumbling maneuvers in full regalia.

The "Zouaves" open-order drills were conducted against a background of working windmills and corn planters, while a cornet band led a parade of farm implements, the "agricultural procession," around the trotting track. The new reapers of John P. Manny, Ralph Emerson, and Fountain & Company were driven up and down in front of the grandstand cutting imaginary wheat. Yokes of oxen pulled a steel breaking plow of the John Deere Company of Moline. Close behind it, teams of horses drew threshers, grain drills, and hay wagons.

During the Presidential Campaign of 1860, Cassius Clay, a muscular Kentuckian with a reputation for both oratory and bowie knives, addressed a Republican "Rally Day" crowd of 12,000 on the courthouse square, and uniformed "Wide-Awakes" marched through the streets in support of Lincoln's candidacy. The marchers, who were commanded by a one-time Rockford City Grey named Garrett L. Nevius, organized themselves into a new military company, complete with fifer and drummers, at the conclusion of the November election. When Fort Sumter was attacked in April 1861, Nevius' group, composed mainly of former Wide-Awakes and Greys, responded to the President's appeal for volunteers. Their name, the "Rockford Zouaves," assumed a special significance after word reached Illinois that Elmer Ellsworth, the Grey mentor and the main popularizer of the Zouave system nationally, had been murdered by a Confederate symphatizer in Alexandria, Virginia on May 24. Ellsworth, whose body was taken to the White House, became the first official casualty of the American Civil War and a martyr to the Union cause.

Rockford raised a total of six companies of volunteers within three weeks of the surrender of Fort Sumter, including an all-Irish group, the "Mulligan Guards." The Winnebago County Board of Supervisors met in emergency session to appropriate $10,000 for equipment and monthly payments to the families of the volunteers. Sewing machines were set up in Concert Hall on South Main Street and women were recruited to make uniforms out of bolts of blue flannel, the work continuing even on Sundays to meet the volunteers' departure dates.

Camp Fuller, a temporary rendezvous point for Illinois volunteers from the northern counties, was established on the west side of the Rock River in July 1862. Initially a tent encampment, the site was transformed in August by the construction of buildings for the quartermaster and

sutlers, and four large wooden barracks, giving the area the vaguely familiar look, one person said, of a "young Dublin." Between August and November, four regiments of men from eight different Illinois counties (including Stephenson, Winnebago, and Boone) were organized and trained at the camp in response to the President's renewed appeal for volunteers. When the last regiment, the Ninety-fifth Illinois Volunteers, left Rockford on November 4, Camp Fuller was closed for good. The wooden buildings were eventually sold for salvage at public auction in January 1863.

At the end of the Civil War, Rockford became a force in the development of the national Grand Army of the Republic, a fraternal organization of Union veterans that was founded in Illinois to keep the reforming spirit of the North alive. Members "waved the bloody shirt" at political rallies and lobbied for Republican candidates who demonstrated the proper patriotism. Stephen Hurlbut, E.B. Washburne's old antagonist and a popular major-general in the army, became its first Commander-in-Chief in 1866.

The plain classical revival styles of Rockford's earliest commercial buildings gave way to more elaborate Italianate facades that featured fancy iron work and rounded window hoods. The southeast corner of West State and Wyman streets, with the offices of the Rockford Gazette *and its neighbors to the east (left) adjoining the earlier Prouty Shoe Store building, illustrates this transition. Photo by F.C. Pierce/Rockford Public Library*

The N.C. Thompson Manufacturing Company opened in the Water Power in 1859. It eventually became one of the region's largest producers of reapers, mowers, cultivators, and plows. Photo by F.C. Pierce/Rockford Public Library

Thomas G. Lawler, the head of the Rockford post, the oldest branch of the Illinois G.A.R. in continuous existence after 1877, assumed the duties of Commander-in-Chief at the national encampment in Pittsburgh in 1894. Shortly afterward, the national G.A.R. headquarters was established in Rockford's William Brown Building on South Main Street for the duration of Lawler's command.

ALBERT SPALDING AND THE FOREST CITY BASEBALL CLUB

The Rockford G.A.R. was not the only local fraternal organization to achieve national notoriety in the years following the Civil War. The other was its baseball team, the Forest Citys, which, in the words of its famous pitcher, Albert Goodwill Spalding, came into existence after a "volunteer private returned invalided to Rockford . . . in 1863. He saw the boys batting up flies, and he told them he knew a better game."

The game Spalding was thinking of had been played by soldiers, both North and South, to relieve the tedium of camp life. The evolution of baseball from the gentleman's game of cricket (which had a

limited following in Rockford) and the old roughhouse game of country ball, combining the rituals and techniques of one with the explosiveness of the other, reflected the changes in American society in the post-war period. Cricket was an English game, Spalding observed, and it could never really satisfy our "red-hot blood." Country ball, on the other hand, in all its crudeness, was no longer worthy of a civilized society.

Someone—the returning veteran perhaps or an insurance agent from Cincinnati named John Lewis (accounts of this vary)—produced a copy of Doubleday's rules, and baseball began in Rockford. According to one story, Lewis persuaded a local cricket club to lay out a baseball diamond on top of its playing field; a ball was manufactured from the sole of a rubber shoe, with a quartered orange peel serving as the model for its leather cover (in earlier days, balls had been made by winding woolen socks around pieces of cork); and a number of teams were organized with names like the Mercantiles, Sinnissippis, Pioneers, Forest Citys, and Unions. Spalding, who was then working as a grocery clerk in Rockford at $5 a week, had originally joined the Pioneers, a junior team, as a pitcher, but his fastball quickly attracted the attention of the Forest City Club, and he was asked to join that team. "Call it science, skill, luck or whatever you please," he wrote, "I had at that time, when only fifteen years old, acquired the knack of pitching winning ball."

It was quite a knack. In 1866 the Forest City team, reorganized with the addition of Spalding and Roscoe Barnes from the Pioneers, began to schedule a number of contests with other clubs in the region, such as the Badgers (Beloit), Clippers (Rochelle), Shaffers (Freeport), Mystics (Belvidere), and Cream Citys (Milwaukee). They were all nines composed of local amateurs, but Rockford was the only one that had Barnes and Spalding. "From the time Barnes and I became connected with the Forest City

Club," the latter remembered, "that organization had an almost uninterrupted succession of victories. No team in the Northwest was able to win from the Rockford nine until the tournament in July 1867 when the Chicago Excelsiors took two games by close scores—and these games were subsequently offset by a series, best two out of three, playing the following season for the championship of the Northwest, in which the Forest Citys were victorious by scores of 20 to 18 and 36 to 27, respectively."

Rockford could probably have laid claim to the American championship as well in 1867, since the Forest Citys defeated a touring all-star team from the East, the Washington Nationals, at Dexter Park in Chicago by a score of 29-33 (July 25). This was the only loss that the Nationals suffered, and in the words of their business agent, Colonel

Typical of the large, multistoried frame residences that were constructed along the river after the Civil War was the home of Henry Price on 607 N. Main Street. He was the president of four local businesses, including Rockford Watch Company, Rockford Silver Plate Company, Rockford Tack Company, and Manufacturers' and Merchants' Mutual Insurance Company. Photo by F.C. Pierce/Rockford Public Library

Churches dominated the Rockford skyline in this photograph of the east side taken in the 1870s. From such a rooftop vantage point, one could see the steeples of the State Street Baptist Church, Swedish M.E. Church, First Congregational Church, First Lutheran Church, First Methodist Church, and Westminster Presbyterian Church as one looked north to south (left to right) on the horizon. In its post-Civil War prosperity, Rockford retained many features of its earliest days: the limestone row houses; the three-story Rockford House Hotel (at the corner of State and Madison— then known as "Main Street" on the east side); and the Nettleton Grist Mill on the river, just south of the State Street Bridge. Nettleton's building, the barn-like structure at the center of this picture, was one of the last remnants of the 1845 mill race on the east side. Courtesy, Rockford Public Library

Frank Jones, Rockford "spoiled the whole trip."

The Nationals were generally considered to be the best team in the country. Their members had been recruited from throughout the East and assigned to a variety of "clerkships" in Washington, usually at inflated wages. The line-up included some of the most famous names in the game. In the absence of an organized league and a comparative accounting of wins and losses, a team like Washington had to prove its worth against any and all challengers. Every game it played was a game for the national championship.

After their shocking upset of Washington, the Forest City's returned to Rockford to a large reception and dance at Brown's Hall. The victory was widely reported in the Eastern press; the unknown "Country Boys" from Illinois had clearly become a force to be reckoned with in the new American sport.

The Forest Citys, playing their home games in the County Fair Grounds (present Fairgrounds Park), proved to be a popular attraction. Crowds numbered in the thousands, and betting was rampant in spite of local ordinances. Only the umpire, who was formally attired in a top hat and frock coat, was expressly forbidden by the rules from gambling. During the time of Rockford's so-called "public career" from 1866 to 1870, when it scheduled games against some of the best amateur and professional clubs in the country, its record of 51-14 was surpassed by only a handful of big-city teams such as the Red Stockings (Cincinnati) and Athletics (Philadelphia), and both of these teams on occasion were defeated by the Forest Citys.

In 1871 Rockford became a charter member of the National Association of Professional Base Ball, the forerunner of the National Baseball League, even though three of its best players—Spalding, Barnes, and Fred Cone—were hired away by the Boston Red Stockings. The 1871

This street-level view shows the intersection of South Main and Chestnut streets in the late nineteenth century. The William Brown Building (left) was the national headquarters of the Grand Army of the Republic, an association of Union Civil War veterans, in the 1890s.

Forest City team still included one future Hall of Famer, Adrian "Cap" Anson, but as the season progressed, it became evident that Rockford could no longer compete against its big-city opponents' considerable financial advantages. The team ended the season in seventh place, behind Philadelphia, Boston, Chicago, New York, Cleveland, and Washington, D.C. Unable to retain its best players and to meet its costs of operation, the Forest City club disbanded.

Spalding later led Boston to the championship of the National Association for four consecutive years, from 1872 to 1875. In 1876 he joined the Chicago White Stockings, bringing two other former Forest Citys, Barnes and Anson, with him, and once again pitched his team to the pennant. Rockford may not have really belonged in the big leagues, but a handful of its best players proved to be the equals of anyone on the field in the early years of organized baseball.

Farmers and Inventors

In the development of great baseball players, Albert Spalding once said, nothing was "more potent than the city just emerging from the chrysalis stage of village-dom." The new game "required the quality of young manhood which had been developed in the field and furrow, in combination with that which had come from cash desk and counter from forge and furnace," to reach its full potential. Spalding felt that the experience of living in a small town such as Rockford, at a time when its agrarian economy was changing to an urban industrial one, encouraged a basic inventiveness. This turned out to be as important to the achievements of its manufacturers as it was to those of its baseball players.

With an eye out for his own long-term business interests, Spalding not only helped to organize the new National League in the 1870s, but he convinced the League owners to adopt a uniform baseball (and then made sure that he received a kick-

back from the company that was chosen to manufacture it).

This kind of resourcefulness was natural to aspiring country boys like Spalding. Most of them were used to improvising and to getting by on their wits. In a society of home industries and subsistence farming, labor was usually so scarce that any kind of mechanical substitute was welcomed, and people spent their time working on ways to increase their productivity through the use of "novel devices." A few of these were fundamental, as we have already seen. The introduction of the water-driven iron turbine gave Rockford manufacturers an improved source of mechanical power. The reaper similarly liberated farmers from the drudgery of harvesting grain by hand. When seen in the perspective of the nineteenth century and its rapidly changing farm economy, these developments now seem as natural and inevitable as Spalding's National League.

The versatility of Rockford's early settlers was demonstrated somewhat amusingly by "Doc" Andrew Brown, a one-time proprietor of the Rockford House, who was so intrigued by the appearance of a locomotive in Boone County (the Galena & Chicago Union line was then being constructed westward) that he made up his mind to build one himself. We know little about Brown beyond that he was an experi-

Winnebago County newspapers in the nineteenth century served a variety of commercial and sectarian purposes. The Harvester was a journal of the Emerson & Company's farm implement business. The Golden Censer, a religious weekly with 18,000 subscribers at the peak of its operation, had a circulation that was larger than that of the rest of the city's newspapers combined.

enced hunter and wing shot and an occasional commercial peddler, but we do know that he did constructed a small engine that ran on a three-foot diameter track and was propelled by a "spirit lamp." He understood the dynamics of super-heated steam—he had undoubtedly seen his share of farmers' stills—and was smart enough to apply this knowledge to a rudimentary mechanical system. If one were to guess, he probably had little formal train-

ing, and only the experience of working in a handicraft tradition where ingenuity was prized above everything else.

The "farm arts," as they were called, were responsible for many kinds of practical inventions. South of Rockford, in Grand Detour, a journeyman blacksmith from Vermont named John Deere devised a revolutionary self-polishing plow by bending a broken saw blade over a wooden beam. Another farmer

St. James Catholic Church, shown here with the original deanery, was built in 1867 at a cost of $35,000. It was the city's oldest Catholic society, having been organized in 1850 by the Reverend John A. Hampston. Photo by F.C. Pierce/ Rockford Public Library

named William Worth Burson, who had moved to Illinois with his family from the East, invented a twine-binding mechanism for grain. Ralph Emerson recognized the commercial potential of Burson's device and offered to manufacture it for him on a royalty basis. This led to the opening of the Emerson Twine Works and brought Burson to the Water Power, where, with financial backing from several local industrialists, he continued his experiments. During his lifetime, he made mechanical improvements in areas as diverse as woodworking, harvesting, and textile manufacturing.

Few people were as fortunate as Burson, however, in being able to devote themselves to their inventions. Most found work wherever they could. Everyone farmed a little, including mechanics and city merchants, and everyone tinkered with mechanisms, especially farmers. Cabinetmakers like Alpheus Burpee made coffins along with furniture and sometimes conducted funerals. James Howell, an early miller, branched off into bookbinding and bookselling. Edmund Fish and Joseph Goundrey were Rockford blacksmiths who shod horses and

flattened plowshares and occasionally pulled teeth (both animal and human). Amos Woodward, a versatile mechanic and shop hand, repaired bicycles in his spare time. He also did "job work in hard wood and sheet metal" and developed a local reputation for the manufacture of custom pumps. Employed by N.C. Thompson as a practical machinist, Woodward invented a fly-ball speed-sensing mechanism to regulate the power of Thompson's factory's turbines.

Woodward was one of two Rockford inventors in the 1870s who eventually benefited from the start of his own business. The other was John Barnes, a native of New York and an experienced modelmaker who came here more or less by accident in pursuit of opportunities in the farm implement trade. He appeared in Rockford at the time of the Civil War and got a job making patterns for Ralph Emerson. In the course of carving his wooden models, Barnes devised a scroll saw which was pedestal-mounted and operated by a treadle, to help speed up production.

This shortcut was typical of a Yankee, and it is doubtful that any-

The 1868 First Presbyterian Church stood in the 200 block of North Main Street. It was erected at a cost of $40,000. Photo by F.C. Pierce/Rockford Public Library

thing of consequence would have happened to the machine it if had not attracted the attention of workers in the Water Power, who wanted scroll saws for themselves. What was Barnes to do? The manufacture of this tool in any quantity was beyond his existing resources. He started making a few saws piecemeal in 1868, then brought his brothers, Frank and William Fletcher, into the business and expanded production. The W.F. and John Barnes Company, one of the earliest Rockford machine tool manufacturers, was incorporated in 1872.

The Barnes scroll saw, it turned

This bird's-eye view of the Rockford skyline in the late nineteenth century was taken from the courthouse dome, looking east. In the center of the photograph (foreground) is the Hotel Holland. Immediately behind it is the Rockford Silver Plate Company. On the east side, at the river's edge (right), are some of the buildings of the W.F. and John Barnes Manufacturing Company. On the horizon are the spires (left to right) of the First Congregational, First Lutheran, and Centennial Methodist churches. Photo by F.C. Pierce/ Rockford Public Library

out, could not be mass-produced without the development of additional foot-powered equipment, such as a lathe, circular saw, and mortiser. So these, in time, were added to the line of Barnes commercial products. At the 1876 Centennial Exposition in Philadelphia, the company set up a booth to demonstrate the wonders of its jig saw, which turned out intricate wooden puzzles for the crowds of visitors. The Barnes expertise also extended to metalworking—the technical transfer between woods and metals was both natural and inevitable—and the company began to market a number of new tools

such as an open-frame, single-spindle drill press, an adjustable screw press, and a radial drill in the 1880s.

Like the Emerson Company that nurtured it, the W.F. and John Barnes Company was a breeding ground for other businesses and product lines. Levin Faust, the Swedish inventor and entrepreneur who launched the Mechanics Machine Company in 1890, worked at Barnes as a machinist, as did his three partners in the company, J. Forsberg, Frank Lindgren, and Gustave A. Dalin. Charles Ekstrom, who developed the drum sander and woodworking router for the domestic furniture trade and who founded Redin-Ekstrom & Company in 1904, worked as a mechanic at Barnes. With so many product lines, the Barnes brothers agreed to spin off their drill press operation into a separate business, the Barnes Drill Company. This was managed independently by Frank Barnes after 1907.

Much as been made of the commerical successes of companies like Woodward Governor and W.F. and John Barnes, but the truth is that these businesses were exceptions to the rule, and for every inventor who was able to take his products to market, there were dozens of others unable to exploit their designs. A good idea, even a great one, was no assurance of success. Ralph Emerson, N.C. Thompson, Wait Talcott, and Gilbert Woodruff occasionally provided capital for promising ventures, but most people who started a business bought on credit and then prayed that they could quickly earn enough money to satisfy their obligations.

Success was often a matter of timing and determination. Emerson admitted that he knew "little about

If Rockford warranted the title of the "Reaper City" in the 1870s, it was because of this concentration of farm implement manufacturers in the Water Power District. The rear of the N.C. Thompson Company is most prominent in the center of this photograph, as well as buildings belonging to Emerson, Talcott & Co., John P. Manny Mower Co., Knowlton Manufacturing Co., Rockford Plow Co., Skandia Plow Co., and Utter Manufacturing Co. Photo by F.C. Pierce/Rockford Public Library

mechanics" when he started building reapers ("I hardly knew a turning lathe for working iron from a plane to work wood, and had never spent five hours at a time in any machine shop"), but his instincts for managing his company were almost always right. Inventors were attracted to him because of his willingness to take risks. The Emerson Company made the first 1,000 grain binders ever manufactured in the U.S. and played a role in the development of the original self-tying attachment, one of the most important agricultural advances of the nineteenth century. Emerson was able to take advantage of the experiments of a farmer named Jacob Behel, who had solved the problem of automated binding with a flexible-jawed rotating shaft that wrapped twine around sheaves of wheat. Behel's greatest contribution to the entire process may have been an intricate little knot that was used to finish the binding, for of all the inventions that have been associated with Rockford, it is the one that has persisted the longest in its original form (farmers still use it in baling hay).

Behel lived in modest circumstances, and his lack of success in attracting financial backers other than Emerson eventually compelled him, in his own words, "to cease my

efforts in the grain-binding business." It was an irony of which he was no doubt painfully aware that the patent on his binder, the so-called "billhook" or "hawk bill" (its mechanical jaws resembled a hawk's head in profile), ran out at about the time that it began to be commercially popular. In a pattern that was to be repeated again and again in Rockford manufacturing, an inventor such as Behel would come up with an idea for a new implement or tool, patent the design, and then have it exploited, either through the sale of the patent or some other kind of technical transfer, by people with greater access to the marketplace and, inevitably, a better sense of market opportunities.

This was true not only of John H. Manny, who died of tuberculosis before he could realize even a fraction of the profits from the Northern Illinois Reaper, but also of his contemporary, Marquis Gorham, whose experiments in grain-binding were generously subsidized by N.C. Thompson in an organized research effort that involved a team of skilled mechanics and an investment of more than $150,000. According to Church, Gorham was visited in his workshop by an unidentified man who stole his ideas and subsequently incorporated them into a suc-

The drawing room of the Ralph Emerson mansion on North Church Street contained marble-topped tables, overstuffed chairs, gilt-frame paintings (including a half-length of Emerson himself), and life-size statuary. Courtesy, Rockford Museum Center

cessful commercial model, thereby depriving Gorham of the notoriety and Thompson of the anticipated return on his investment. Gorham died in 1876 from an illness said to have been "caused by worry and study over his inventions." Shortly afterwards, in an attempt to recoup some of his loss, Thompson sold the existing Gorham patents to Cyrus McCormick for $25,000.

Behel had the same hard luck as an inventor as Manny and Gorham, though he lived a much longer life than either man and was able to turn his mechanical experience to some account as a patent solicitor when he gave up his work

in grain binding. Originally from Pennsylvania, he settled in LaSalle County in the 1850s and tried to eke out a living by farming for the necessities of life and peddling his inventions to interested manufacturers. This took him to Rockford during the Civil War and made him acquainted with Emerson, who offered to purchase a "half-interest" in his grain binding inventions if Behel agreed to move his workshop permanently to the Water Power. The arrangement helped to make Emerson a national leader in the production of harvesting equipment, but it failed to improve Behel's economic situation very much. "Up to 1865 I had spent the whole of two years and nine months in my experiments and had exhausted all my means," he wrote, "and during my early experiments my two oldest sons (from whom I expected help), the younger between 18 and 19 years old, went at the call of their country to help defend the nation, which left me without help, and with a dependent family, consisting of a wife and eight children, the oldest an invalid (not including my two sons in the army)."

Behel was the prototype of the solitary inventor, chronically short of money and absorbed in his work sometimes to the exclusion of common sense. His experiments ranged over the entire field of mechanics. During his lifetime, he was awarded patents for things as various as a chain belt, window blind, fence-wire stretcher, electromagnetic engine, winnowing mill, whiffle-tree hook, burglar-proof lock, and clasp-mounted horseshoe. His portrait in old age shows a man with an enormous white beard and large saucer eyes that fill the lenses of his spectacles completely, a formidable intellectual. "He was always serious, thoughtful, his mind seemingly . . . resolving some intricate problem," the *Register* commented after his death. "He had no time for the froth and frivolities of life."

JOHN NELSON

As self-absorbed in his own way as Behel was the Swedish woodworker John Nelson. When he came to Rockford in 1852 with the first group of immigrants from Sweden, he was already an experienced cabinetmaker, and he was able to earn a living in this trade after he arrived. One measure of his early success was the planing mill for sashes, doors, and blinds that he

established in the Water Power in partnership with two other Swedes, Gust Hollem and A.C. Johnson. Occasionally he collaborated with inventors like Behel in the development of custom machinery (Behel's tennoning machine was designed for Nelson's mill). We know that William Gent, who built the first barbed wire machine, worked alongside him briefly as a pattern-maker.

Despite his facility with wood, Nelson's main interest was in mechanics. "He was always studying machinery," a contemporary observed, "and continually working out new plans to accomplish the same results. He also studied along the line of improvement and for many years was revolving in his mind plans for the manufacture of a knitting machine." The story has frequently been told of Nelson's fascination with a Lamm knitter which he saw on display at a trade show in Chicago. Nelson became convinced that he could improve the Lamm Knitter by redesigning the control mechanism. Inevitably, the task proved to be difficult. Nelson opened a workshop in the loft of his barn that was devoted to the project. He also sold his interest in the planing mill and did less and less work of any kind outside of his experiments. His wife was forced to take in others' washing, it was said, to support the family, even though both Emerson and Talcott were per-

John Nelson was the best known of Rockford's Swedish mechanics. His parallel-row knitting machine led to the development of the hosiery industry in the late nineteenth century. Courtesy, Rockford Museum Center

William Gent, who built the first barbed wire machine, is credited with improvements in the design of the steam engine, reaper, and knitting machine as well. Photo by A.S. Atchley/Rockford Public Library

suaded to invest in Nelson's machine. In 1866, probably at Emerson's suggestion, Nelson turned to William Burson for help. The company of Burson and Nelson, a sort of early Rockford research organization, was established as a result.

From the time that he saw the Lamm model in Chicago until the time that he developed a knitter to his satisfaction, Nelson spent ten years absorbed in the mechanics of hosiery production. His first ma-

chines were patented in 1868-1870; these were more technically sophisticated than the Lamm model, but they still required an operator to finish the heel of a sock manually, and they still contained a partial seam. A few years later, however, Nelson and Burson came out with a fully automated machine that knitted a double toe and double heel in an entirely seamless fashion. They had originally hoped to sell their knitter to families, following the example of the Singer Sewing Machine Company, which had captured a large market in the 1860s; but the size and weight of their machine— several people were needed to move it—eliminated this possibility. Nelson, who made a virtue of stubbornness, continued to experiment with ways to reduce the size of the knitter, while his son William and a friend named Frank Brown (the son of the Burson and Nelson Company financier, Judge William Brown) got permission to use the machines to manufacture a few men's cotton socks on an experimental basis. Once again, Emerson gave his blessing and his money to the project.

William Nelson's "Seamless Sock" proved to be a success. The Nelson Knitting Company, which was incorporated in 1880 to manufacture the sock, was joined in the

Looking north from the Chicago & Northwestern Railroad bridge in the 1880s, one could see the State Street bridge in the distance and the Rockford Mitten & Hosiery Company (left) on the west bank of the river. Photo by F.C. Pierce/ Rockford Public Library

field in 1881 by the Rockford Mitten and Hosiery Company, another user of the Nelson machine. After Nelson and Burson dissolved their partnership, Burson modified the mechanism to produce women's stockings and went into business for himself in 1890; the Burson Knitting Company chose Emerson for its president, no doubt acknowledging both his business acumen and the size of his investment. In some ways the entire Rockford knitting industry, including the Forest City and B.Z.B. companies, which were organized by the time of the First World War, remained an Emerson enterprise. His capital started it, his factories made its first machines, his knowledge of the marketplace helped it grow, his friends and family (William Hinchliff, his successor at Burson Knitting, was a son-in-law) directed its investments.

If Emerson was the presiding genius of the hosiery business, Nelson was its most representative

figure. His contribution to the industry was so decisive that it is impossible to imagine it without him. He was only one man, an inventor with a passing interest in actual manufacturing production and a curious indifference to making money, and he obviously needed Emerson to capitalize his company. Without Burson, moreover, he would have probably taken longer to perfect his invention, since it was Burson who came up with the idea of a flexible yarn carrier on the machine to change the yarns automatically. This was an important part of the knitter, an advance made possible by Burson's twine-binding experiments; but the really critical feature of the machine, the thing that permitted it to be automated, was Nelson's control mechanism, an 18-inch revolving cylinder that guided the needles' action.

Nelson grooved the surface of his wheel with tiny channels of varying lengths, and he positioned the needles along these openings in such a way that every point followed a channel, rising and falling as the wheel turned and the openings changed, its little teeth biting the yarn into place. The cylinder resembled the mechanism of an old-fashioned music box, except that its surface was free of pins. What was hard for Nelson to determine was the way that each needle should mesh with the yarn in each groove in order to permit a continuous knitting operation. It was a complicated

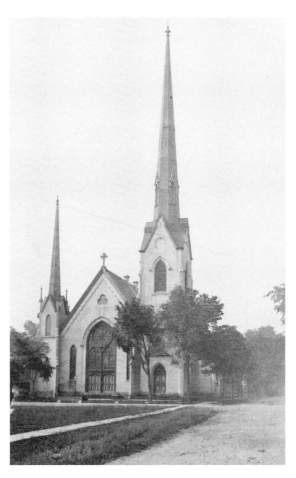

ABOVE: The First Congregational Church, which was the city's oldest religious organization in the nineteenth century, erected this handsome structure at the south end of the Kishwaukee Triangle in 1870. (Interestingly, its facade mirrored that of the State Street Baptist Church, which stood less than 100 yards away at the northern end of the Triangle.) Photo by F.C. Pierce

LEFT: The State Street Baptist Church was erected in 1868 at the corner of State and Third streets at a cost of $30,000. This view shows the old watering trough (foreground) at the intersection of State, Third, and Kishwaukee streets, the so-called "Kishwaukee Triangle." Photo by F.C. Pierce/Rockford Public Library

RIGHT: This view of the Water Power District in the 1880s shows the passenger depot (right) of the Chicago, Milwaukee & St. Paul Railroad. This building also served as an office for the reaper works of Emerson & Company. Other Emerson buildings are seen in the center of this photograph. Photo by F.C. Pierce/Rockford Public Library

BELOW: The Swedish M.E. Church was organized in 1861. This brick building on First Avenue was the congregation's second permanent home. After the church moved to a new location in the twentieth century, the building was converted into a Jewish synagogue. In the 1960s, it was converted into a coffee house and nightclub known as Charlotte's Web. Photo by F.C. Pierce/Rockford Public Library

bit of circuitry for its day, and it required ten years and a special kind of intelligence to formulate it for the first time.

The case of Nelson is illuminating not only because he embodies so many important aspects of nineteenth century manufacturing life—its handicraft tradition, its integration of different manual skills, and so on—but because he also foreshadows the twentieth century and Rockford's expertise in automated machining operations. His knitter was the predecessor of a whole line of later inventions, especially in the metal industries. Like the Barnes brothers and the Rockford manufacturer Howard Colman, who branched off from the production of hand tools into power-driven machinery, Nelson made the transition from model-maker to machine-builder in the course of his career because the state of the art in manufacturing called for new levels of speed and precision,

and this was only possible in a highly automated form.

The fact that he was a Swede and not a Yankee is all the more fitting in the case of Rockford, since many of the city's industries were to be shaped in the years ahead by Swedish entrepreneurial talents. Nelson was the first of his people here, in Faust's words, "to break through the American shell and become something other than a laborer or servant." When he patented his knitters, he was the best known of Rockford's Swedish mechanics, respected by Emerson and other Yankees for his ingenuity, but regarded with a certain amount of bewilderment by members of his own community as a result of his prolonged experiments. Faust believed that Nelson's knitter "became a fixed idea in his mind which held him prisoner and would not permit him freedom to undertake anything else." And it may have been that, given the difficulty of what he was trying to do, only this kind of concentration would have yielded the same results. Yet Nelson also paid the price, for the strain of his experiments is said to have ruined his health. He died in 1883, three years after Nelson Knitting was incorporated, leaving his sons to carry on his work.

THE ROCKFORD FURNITURE INDUSTRY

Swedish immigration in the nineteenth century had a major impact on Rockford. In sheer numbers alone, the Swedes were a force to be reckoned with as early as the 1870s, when their population was estimated to be about 3,500—or 25 percent of the city total. Every month after the Civil War they arrived by the hundreds. The first Swedes had lived in a makeshift tent city known as "Kohagen" (literally "cow pasture"). But once they had established a presence in Rockford and found more permanent lodging, the immigrants were able to care for their own new arrivals to a certain extent, and local merchants were attracted to the area to serve them. This was the beginning of a fairly extensive Swedish neighborhood along Kishwaukee Street, which, for many people in the Old Country, eventually had a level of name recognition surpassing that of the city itself. It is even alleged that letters and parcels addressed to "Kishwaukee Street, U.S.A." found their way to Rockford.

Because of its little colony here, Rockford had a particular attraction for Swedes coming to the U.S., and the flow of immigrants into Northern Illinois continued well into the twentieth century. When the Immigration Act of 1924 restricted the number of foreign nationals entering the country, the identification of "Swede Town" with the city as a whole was more or less complete. By then Rockford Swedes occupied the office of both mayor and chief of police. They controlled three national banks (Security, Commerical, and Swedish-American) and more than 50 of the largest industries here, as well as dominating a three-mile commercial corridor that ran from East State Street to Seventh Street to Broadway (Fourteenth Avenue) on the east side. According to the 1930 census, there were 10,088 people in Rockford who had been born in Sweden and another 12,243 people who had been born in America of Swedish parents. If we add to these figures the estimated number of third-generation Swedes who were then living in the city, the total was probably 35,000, or nearly 40 percent of the population.

The original western facade of the Swedish Zion Lutheran Church stood at the corner of Sixth Street and Fifth Avenue. Organized in 1883 by a splinter group from the First Lutheran Church, the congregation continues to meet in this structure today. Photo by F.C. Pierce/Rockford Public Library

For people of means, Victorian funerals were conducted with great style and elaboration. This hearse, photographed near the old Rockford College campus on Seminary Street, was available from the liveryman Ira E. Ginders. Courtesy, Laverne T. Ryder/Rockford Public Library

Why Rockford? It would be natural to think that the city's original attraction for the Swedes was the number of manufacturing jobs here in the 1850s or the availability of Winnebago County farm land, but the truth is that the first immigrants landed in Rockford more or less by accident, having decided to ride the train westward as far as it would go. When they boarded the Galena & Chicago Union in Cook County in 1852, the end of the line was Kishwaukee Street.

These were mostly country people, craftsmen and laborers and tenant farmers who had been dispossessed by crop failures in Scandinavia. Because of their provincial backgrounds, a Chicago minister named Erland Carlsson is said to have discouraged them from settling in Chicago, and to have directed

them to the rural areas of the state. Carlsson, we know, had never been to Rockford himself, and few, if any, of the immigrants on the train knew exactly where they were going. In fact, if the railroad had completed its line to Freeport in 1852 instead of halting at the Rock River, one suspects that Stephenson County would have gotten all the Swedes.

Whether it is true or not, Swedes are commonly supposed to be able to adapt themselves more easily to American life than other nationalities; and in the case of Rockford and its transplanted New England culture, they seem to have been quickly assimilated. They were really out of the same mold as the Yankees, despite superficial differences. They had developed a system of household manufacturing in

Sweden that was similar to the Yankee craft traditions. They were equally clever with their hands, and they had a knack for woodworking that was probably superior to that of the average Yankee farmer.

The Swedes who came to Rockford in the nineteenth century were eminently practical people who tended to reinforce the more conservative elements of this community. They founded a total of fourteen churches (seven of them Lutheran) and played a significant part in the city's temperance campaigns; the problem of alcoholism in Scandanavia, where whiskey was used as both an appetizer and a medium of exchange (servants often received it in pay), had made an impression on many of the immigrants and left them determined to escape its ravages in America. Yet in spite of their numbers, they had little actual impact on the Rockford economy before the 1870s. They worked as common laborers and domestics, and few took advantage of their mechanical resourcefulness. As in the case of Grand Rapids, Michigan, and Jamestown, New York, furniture making turned out to be the main vehicle of Swedish immigrant upward mobility.

Here the name of John Nelson surfaces again, since it was his planing mill in the Water Power that was the earliest Swedish woodworking venture. Nelson, as we have seen, sold his interest in the company in order to concentrate on his knitting experiments; but his partner Andrew Johnson took in other investors and continued the business, broadening his product line and organizing a new company, Forest City Furniture, with the help of the financier Gilbert Woodruff. The business was a combination of Swedish labor and Yankee capital, and it did not work very well for most of its employees, because

This view shows Rockford's near north side in the 1880s. The white-steepled First Baptist Church is seen at the lower left and the First Presbyterian Church at the center right. Photo by A.S. Atchley/Rockford Public Library

A rear view of the Forest City Furniture Company on Railroad Avenue shows the stacks of freshly cut lumber seasoning in the open air. Photo by F.C. Pierce/Rockford Public Library

Woodruff, who served as president and held the company purse strings (Johnson was given the title of "superintendent"), had the habit of cutting wages in order to meet expenses.

Worker unrest at Forest City led to the formation of the Union Furniture Company in 1876, the first Rockford business on a large scale to be owned and operated entirely by Swedes. It was the real start of the furniture industry here, and it showed the way for other Swedish ventures. A group of Forest City cabinet-makers and machinists had pooled their money to launch the business, and had taken in a few Swedish merchants as investors, while excluding Yankees. Union was organized on a cooperative plan, like the old European craft societies in which workers surrendered a portion of their wages each month as a means of paying expenses. (For this they received additional stock in the company.) It was a bootstrap approach that depended on the patience of its members. They signed the legal papers, joined hands on a Bible, and (sometimes) followed the Viking custom of pledging themselves in blood.

The Union Furniture Company

and other cooperatives also succeeded because they had the help of P.A. Peterson, an entrepreneurial genius who was the guiding light of the Rockford furniture industry. He was invited to join Union because he was known to have taken a business course, and among the Swedish workers, who were largely uneducated, this was thought to be important. Peterson started out as the Union bookkeeper, but he was soon forced to take over the management of its daily operations as well, since the company's capital stock of $12,000 was stretched to the limit by production. Rockford banks refused to risk much money on Union in the beginning, and Peterson turned to friends for assistance, trading on his family's reputation for honesty. "The day before each payday," he wrote, "I would go home early, hitch my horse to the wagon and drive out to the farmers for whom I had worked. From them I would borrow enough money to meet the payroll. My mother had a good credit, everybody took her word, and I had succeeded in winning a certain amount of confidence."

Peterson repaid every one of these loans on time, even when it meant borrowing additional money. His network of credit was maintained with great determination. He never showed uncertainty in his business dealings, conducting himself with the aplomb of a millionaire—he would throw his money on a banker's desk, he said, as if it meant only *'en spott styver for mig'* (a trifle for me)—and refuse offers of funds when he really needed them, because he thought it was necessary to keep up appearances: "I would say I did not have need for them for the moment, but that I might soon call for a loan since business was good, and it was getting necessary to expand."

Yet business was not very good in the first year at Union, and the company lost money, putting additional strain on its meager resources. Peterson called the workers together and admonished them for wasting time on the job, for standing and gossiping, and for not trying harder. The fact that they were shareholders gave them no excuse for idling, he said. He predicted the end of the company—and the loss of their investments—if things did not

change. It was from this speech in 1877 that we date the full emergence of Peterson, the entrepreneur, for the warning had its desired effect and productivity improved. Union declared a dividend, and Peterson's share, while only a few hundred dollars, seemed larger to him at the time (he later observed) than anything else he ever earned.

With the success of the Forest City and Union Furniture companies, Rockford entered a period of sustained business expansion lasting from 1879 through 1892, as groups of Swedes began to follow suit with other woodworking ventures. When John Nelson's old planing mill in the Water Power was destroyed by fire, its owners decided to rebuild a much larger structure on the site in emulation of the Forest City facility. Some 46 Swedish workers/ shareholders contributed $500 each to help finance the construction, and in 1879 the Central Furniture Company was incorporated.

Central, we should note, was the originator of the famous bookcase/ writing desk combination, the "side-by-side," the most popular piece of furniture ever manufactured in this city. (A Central employee named Robert Bauch designed it in 1882.) The demand for the "side-by-side" turned out to be

The Forest City Furniture Company was established in the 1870s on Railroad Avenue between Seventh and Eighth streets. Photo by F.C. Pierce/ Rockford Public Library

The Central Furniture Company, which was organized by L.D. Upson and E.L. Herrick, was one of the earliest furniture manufacturers in the city. It was located in the Water Power District at the mouth of Kent Creek. Photo by F.C. Pierce/ Rockford Public Library

a benefit to the entire industry, as Central's success produced a number of local imitators and Rockford established itself as the "Bookcase Town" in the eyes of the rest of the trade.

Peterson and some of the Union shareholders started a second business, the Rockford Chair and Furniture Company, in 1880, and hired a young Swede named Robert Lind as manager. The new company, which never got to the point of adding chairs to its line of products (or of removing the word "chair" from its name), ran into trouble almost immediately because of a lack of sales. Peterson saw that it would be necessary for him to take over the active management and for Lind to go on the road to drum up business if the company was going to survive. Thus, for several weeks, Peterson ran both Union and Rockford Chair single-handedly—this was the period of his life when he spent his entire work-

week in the factories, sleeping at his desk at night—until Lind returned to Rockford with enough orders to assure Rockford Chair's stability.

The owners of many Swedish woodworking companies sought out Peterson for financial help. According to Levin Faust, Peterson had established an "almost unlimited" network of credit in Rockford by the 1880s. So highly regarded was Peterson by bankers, in fact, that his endorsement of a company's note was enough to get it approved. He had a hard time turning down requests for assistance. If a company was still short of cash when the note was due, Peterson himself had to pay it off, acquiring shares in the business as his compensation. This turned out to be a very good arrangement in most cases. When the companies eventually prospered, Peterson, as a major stockholder, became a wealthy man.

A complete account of Peterson's business interests in Rockford would go far beyond the scope of this book, but a partial list will give us some idea of his influence: Union Furniture, Rockford Chair and Furniture, Rockford Mantel, Rockford Folding Bed, Skandia Furniture, Rockford Bookcase, and Rockford Steel Furniture. These he controlled as a stockholder. In addition, there were six furniture companies that he made significant contributions to as an investor/manager: Standard (later Rockford Standard), West End, Central, Mechanics, Rockford Miter Box, and Hanson Clock.

As opportunities presented themselves—and as the need to reduce production costs increased—he ventured into other areas of the furniture trade, such as pianos (Kurtz Action, Haddorff Piano), sewing machines (Illinois Sewing Machine), mirrors and glass (Rockford Mirror Plate, Rockford Glass Bending), varnish (Rockford Varnish), and hardware (National Lock). He purchased some of these companies outright; he established others by furnishing the capital; he joined still others as

an investor. We find that the majority listed him as a corporate officer— Faust believed that "the stockholders would unanimously elect him president, inasmuch as they needed somebody like Peterson to carry the brunt for them." In the twentieth century, he gave financial support to several Swedish machine shops at critical points in their development. One of these, Mechanics Machine Company, later became a founding division of the Borg-Warner Corporation. Two others, Rockford Tool Company and Rockford Milling Machine Company, eventually merged to form Sundstrand Corporation.

It is often surprising to learn how far Peterson's influence extended. Rockford's largest department store in the 1920s, Hess Brothers Company, was one of his enterprises, as was Rockford Drop Forge Company, Stonefield-Evans Shoe Company, and Rockford Life Insurance Company. He was a founder of the Swedish Building and Loan Association (afterwards Home Federal Savings and Loan).

The interior of the Thomas Butterworth home on 205 North Main Street in the 1880s was furnished with paintings, chromos, statuary, and overstuffed furniture in the popular style of the day, which emphasized massive forms and richly brocaded fabrics. Courtesy, Frances Porter

This panoramic view of Rockford's southwest side in the 1880s was taken from the courthouse dome by the photographer A.S. Atchley. The two railroad bridges in the distance are those of the Chicago & Northwestern (closest to the camera) and Milwaukee & St. Paul lines. In the right foreground, at the corner of South Church and Chestnut streets, is the Second Congregational Church. Courtesy, Rockford Public Library

He tried his hand at both farm implement and automobile manufacturing and only reluctantly abandoned these ventures after it became clear that the long-term prospects were unfavorable.

"Many have criticized Mr. Peterson for getting as rich and powerful as he did in later life," Faust wrote, "but the fact is that few persons are willing to pay the price that he paid for this power and riches." In view of everything that he achieved, this was probably an understatement.

Peterson's importance to the Rockford furniture industry—indeed to Rockford manufacturing as a whole—is impossible to estimate, but he was clearly the central figure in its expansion and diversification in the late nineteenth century. Without Peterson, we still would have had a furniture business of some sort in Rockford, given the success of the Forest City Furniture Com-

pany and the number of immigrants here who had a facility for working wood. However, it is doubtful that many of these companies would have survived very long without Peterson's help. Even with the abundance of cheap labor in Rockford and the availability of financing (always an uncertainty in the Swedish community), there remained an important entrepreneurial aspect of these early ventures, a feeling for markets and organization and an ability to make fortuitous judgments. Like Ralph Emerson, Peterson possessed this instinct to an exceptional degree, though his achievement was due equally to a strength of personality. Faust has characterized Peterson's gift in a wonderful line: "By his indomitable willpower he forced things to success, and as soon as success was made of one company, Mr. Peterson was ready for new conquests."

Portraits

Stephen Mack established an Indian trading post on the "Rocky River" in the early 1820s. He is generally credited with being the first white settler in this area, though there is some evidence that he spent his summers in Chicago and voted in its elections. Mack's ambition was to open the Rock and Pecatonica rivers to navigation, and he laid out the streets of a speculative settlement called "Pecatonic" on a bluff at the mouth of the Pecatonica River. Mack claimed that the site was "far better than Milwaukee." Nevertheless, he was disappointed in most of his plans. The rivers proved to be unnavigable; Pecatonic never grew beyond a few buildings. The female seminary that he had hoped to attract to his village was located in Rockford instead. In 1847 he endured the loss of his Indian wife Hononegah, who died from a high fever. In 1850 he was defeated by his rival Sylvester Talcott for the office of township supervisor. In April of the same year Mack died suddenly, giving rise to "dark rumors . . . that his death was caused by poison administered by a person . . . who materially benefited by his death." (These suspicions were never proved.)

Mack was buried next to Hononegah and two of his children in a small cemetery on the family farm. A picket fence was erected around their graves. Thirty years later, when the man who had purchased the farm threatened to plow up the cemetery, a group of old settlers from Rockton exhumed the remains of Mack and Hononegah and moved them to another location.

Courtesy, Winnebago County Forest Preserve District/Rockford Register Star

Major Isaiah Stillman was a "citizen volunteer" in the Illinois militia during the Black Hawk War and the namesake of the Battle of Stillman's Run, which took place on May 14, 1832, near the present town of Stillman Valley. Stillman had been put in command of an unattached battalion of 275 men by Governor John Reynolds, and he had marched them out of Dixon's Ferry (now Dixon) in pursuit of Black Hawk's band. In those days the state militia usually elected its own officers. Stillman's main recommendation seems to have been his brother's saloon in Peoria, where most of his men had been recruited, for he had no other evident qualifications. He had looked forward to the Black Hawk Campaign as a chance to prove his worth as a soldier. He promised his men "warm work" if they could catch up with Black Hawk and kept them marching throughout the day with the inducement of rye whiskey.

Black Hawk sent out a war party of some 40 braves on the night of May 14. He later said that he had expected them all to be killed; but the confusion caused by his surprise attack and the battalion's own whiskey suppers turned the fight into a rout of the Americans. The soldiers fired their weapons in every direction when the attack started. No battle lines were ever formed. Those men on horseback rode for Dixon's Ferry; the rest, on foot, retreated as best they could. In all, 11 volunteers were killed in the battle, though how many by the Indians and how many by the wild shots of their own comrades-in-arms it is impossible to say.

Stillman continued to serve in the militia for the balance of the

Courtesy, Illinois State Historical Library

Black Hawk Campaign. Always anxious for promotion and able to ingratiate himself with those in higher positions of authority, he was elected to the rank of brigadier general in January 1833.

Carrie Spafford was 15 years old when she met Elmer Ellsworth. She was the eldest daughter of a prominent Rockford banking family, and he was the drillmaster of a company of volunteer militia known as the Rockford City Greys. Despite a six-year difference in their ages they fell in love, and within a short period of time they became engaged. The engagement was conditional, at Spafford's father's insistence, on Ellsworth's pursuit of a more responsible career than soldiering. The young soldier agreed to become a lawyer.

Ellsworth eventually left Rockford to begin his legal studies in association with the firm of Abraham Lincoln in Springfield. When Lincoln was elected president in 1860, Ellsworth followed him to Washington. While he read for the bar, Ellsworth continued his military work, organizing a regiment of New York volunteers and training in intricate Zouave drills on the eve of the Civil War.

He took Carrie's photgraph with him wherever he went. The record of their correspondence shows that he intended to return to Rockford and marry her after he became a lawyer. "My own darling Kitty," he wrote in 1861 before marching his volunteers into Alexandria, Virginia, ". . . just accept this assurance, the only thing I can leave you—the highest happiness I looked for on earth was a union with you." It was a precautionary note, a soldier's farewell, even though hostilities had not yet broken out between the North and South.

But Ellsworth was tragically prescient. In Alexandria, he noticed a Confederate flag flying from the top of the Marshall House Hotel and climbed to the roof to remove it. Descending the stairs with the flag in his arms, he was confronted by the hotel's proprietor and shot to death.

Ellsworth was the first official casualty of the American Civil War, and news of his death created an enormous sensation in the North. At Lincoln's order, Ellsworth's body lay in state in the East room of the White House.

In Rockford, Carrie Spafford is said to have grieved over Ellsworth for years.

The first principal of the Rockford Female Seminary (later Rockford College) was a tall, ascetic easterner named **Anna Peck Sill**, who described herself as a humble servant of God and who felt her purpose in life was to win as many converts as possible to the Christian faith. From an early age, her greatest ambition had been to serve in the foreign missions; when she had been unable to find work abroad (missionary assignments were given almost exclusively to men in the nineteenth century), she turned her attention to education and to the idea of establishing a training school for women in the "wild northwest."

Sill believed all her life that the purpose of a seminary was the building of character. In 1849 she advertised her fledgling institution in

Rockford as a comprehensive English and classical school, and insisted that her students learn hygiene and deportment along with arithmetic and grammar. They were being prepared for a Christian life, she said; a girl's character should be strengthened for the condition of motherhood.

Sill had little time for idle amusements. She initiated a system of regular devotional exercises at the Seminary that included daily prayer meetings and the examination of Scripture. Students were expected to observe an hour of silence every night. They were also expected to report any infraction of the rules, such as whispering, during these periods. Each girl kept a private "report book" for recording indiscretions, both her own and other students', and these journals were regularly examined by teachers and the violators punished.

Sill never doubted that her actions were guided by Providence or that she would ultimately succeed in winning the hearts and minds of the girls in her custody. She provided her trustees with a regular report on the number of religious conversions at the Seminary, and she prayed openly at chapel meetings for the souls of the girls who refused to be converted.

Courtesy, Rockford College

Shy in public but with an obvious flair for business, **Ralph Emerson** manipulated his investment in the reaper company of John H. Manny into a controlling interest by the late 1850s. Through hard work he nurtured the company, which he renamed Emerson & Company, into a manufacturing giant.

For more than a half century Emerson dominated Rockford's farm implement industry. Though he was seldom out of debt, he withstood lawsuits and recessions to emerge as the epitome of business success in Rockford after the Civil War. He built an elaborate three-story Italianate mansion on the city's northwest side. Emerson contributed generously to the Rockford Female Seminary, Rockford Hospital, and the Second Congregational Church, as well as to the Emerson Institute in Mobile, Alabama, which provided for the education of emancipated slaves. Both Abraham Lincoln and Booker T. Washington regarded him as a friend.

Emerson's many public achievements masked uncertainties, however. He never entirely overcame his reserve; as financial pressures mounted, he isolated himself from Rockford society. Trusting his instincts to make the right decisions, he admitted that his tendency throughout life was to "build a tower or castle in the air without sitting down first to count the cost thereof." Had he been less religious, he might have chosen a different profession, since Emerson had once spent several months studying law before becoming a manufacturer. In his autobiography, he describes how he had begun to have serious doubts about the ethics of his chosen profession, and how he had been compelled to bring the problem up to Lincoln himself one day while they were taking a walk in Bloomington. "Was it really possible for a man to be both a lawyer and a Christian?," he had asked. He remembered that Lincoln had "almost stopped" in his tracks and had uttered a "long sigh...then suddenly his chin projected forward and we walked on in silence. No word came but I had got my answer."

Courtesy, Winnebago County Public Safety Building

One of the smallest soldiers at Rockford's Camp Fuller in 1862 was a private from Belvidere by the name of **Albert D.J. Cashier**. Only five feet tall, he was sometimes referred to in later life as a "drummer boy," though all available evidence indicates that he served in the Union Army (95th Illinios Volunteers) with distinction, fighting in the Battles of the Red River Campaign, Brice's Crossroads, Spring Hill, and Franklin. He was mustered out in the summer of 1865.

Thereafter Cashier is said to have moved to the village of Saunemin in Livingston County and to have been employed as a truck gardener and general handyman. In 1911, when he was in his sixties and working in the garage of State Senator Ira M. Lish, he fractured his leg in an automobile accident. During the course of what seemed to be a routine examination, the physician inadvertently discovered that Cashier was a *woman*. She admitted that her name was Jennie Hodgers. She had been born in Ireland, she said, and had come to this country as a stowaway. She had disguised her real sex for more than 40 years and had passed as a man even in the close quarters of Civil War infantry life.

Cashier—or Hodgers—was subsequently admitted to the Soldiers' and Sailors' Home in Quincy, but her real sex was kept secret from all but the facility's superintendent and physician. She continued to wear men's clothing. Records show that she remained in Quincy until 1914, when her deteriorating mental condition caused her to be moved to the state insane asylum in Watertown. She died in the asylum, in a woman's dress, on October 15, 1915.

Jonas Peters, who came to this country from Sweden at the age of 10, was orphaned by the deaths of his parents in a cholera epidemic in 1854. As a boy, he worked in the Rockford furniture store of A.C. Burpee, and at the age of 17, he enlisted in the Union Army (he said he was 21), satisfying the minimum weight requirement by wearing three pairs of underwear and the heaviest shoes that he could find.

After the Civil War Peters went to work as a salesman for several Chicago furniture companies. When the Chicago Fire destroyed their facilities in 1871, he returned to Rockford to work in the planing mill of Andrew C. Johnson. Peters' background and training qualified him to be a cabinetmaker, but he hated the drudgery of shop work and preferred to go on the road as an agent instead. With his knowledge of furniture markets in the Midwest, he persuaded Johnson to begin manufacturing a small cabinet that later became one of the staples of the Rockford furniture industry. (He also persuaded Johnson to send him on the road to market it.) The success of this venture eventually led to the establishment of other product lines. Along with men such as John Erlander, P.A. Peterson, and C.F. Blomberg, Peters helped to found the Union Furniture Company, Rockford's first cooperative, in 1876.

The **W.B. Reynolds' Consolidated Shows, Circus, Menagerie, Egyptian Caravan, and Trained Animal Exposition** was organized in Rockford in the winter of 1891-1892 by a local alderman and livery stable owner. Though modest in size by modern standards, the circus contained at least 9 tents, 34 wagons, 150 horses, 10 ponies, 2 camels, and one very large elephant. It was a traveling show, and everything had to move overland, often on dirt roads that were little better than Indian trails, and across streams without bridges. Will Reynolds, the owner, employed some 175 people as managers, trainers, performers, and laborers. He customarily rode in the bandwagon during parades and operated its brakes.

The circus, which had its winter headquarters in Rockford, lasted from 1892 through 1896 and traveled as far away as New York and Texas (it moved by rail in later years), suffering through a variety of natural and man-made disasters that included railroad accidents, cyclones, mob attacks, and graft. In Ohio, Reynolds's employees once seized the circus equipment itself in order to demand their back wages; and old "Wash" Reynolds, the owner's father, was forced to go there from Rockford with enough money to recover the equipment.

It is hard to characterize Rockford's **Elisha C. Dunn**, who at various times in his life and in various places was a physician, statesman, traveler, author, lecturer, politician, collector, showman, prohibitionist, rationalist, dog fancier, and automobile enthusiast.

Born in New York, Dunn is said to have studied at the University of Michigan, University of Pennsylvania, and the American Eclectic College of Medicine in Philadelphia, and to have practiced medicine abroad in New Zealand and Australia. While still a young man, Dunn fell under the influence of Dr. J.M. Peebles, the American counsul to Turkey, who became his benefactor and saved him from becoming a profligate, personally supervised his education, and took him on his travels around the world.

Dunn arrived in Rockford during the Civil War. He quickly established himself as a sage and raconteur, holding forth for friends on topics in science, history, and religion. His "fund of information" was said to have been "inexhaustible." His medical practice in Rockford was frequently interrupted by visits

From Charles Church, Historical Encyclopedia of Illinois: Winnebago County, *1916*

to other countries and by conferences with some of the world's leading political and scientific figures. Queen Victoria presented him with a family portrait; the Prince of Wales gave him a Masonic apron. He became fluent in several languages in order to lecture more effectively abroad on human anatomy and contagious diseases. He considered himself a free thinker and liberal philosopher, but on a trip to Palestine to gather evidence for his lectures against organized religion, he experienced a sudden conversion to Christianity and joined the Methodist Church. He listed his profession in the 1877 Rockford City Directory simply as "capitalist."

In old age Dunn devoted himself to the study of the so-called "lower animals," especially dogs, and spent increasing amounts of time with his collection of rare coins, curios, and Indian relics. He also published an illustrated book entitled *The Sagacity of Dogs.* As a sign of his affection, he adapted a new one-cylinder Cadillac to include a special riding platform for his favorite pet, a spitz.

After Dunn's death in 1914, a controversy developed in Rockford over the authenticity of some of his rare coins, since molds were found among his personal effects that matched the coins exactly. It was also discovered that his much-celebrated collection of nooses, which supposedly had been saved from different hangings in the Midwest, had actually been taken from the same fragment of rope.

Courtesy, Rockford YMCA

There is probably no one in the history of Rockford who contributed more to the development of the city's major industries and who was directly responsible for the creation of more jobs and more general prosperity over the years than **P.A. Peterson**.

If Jonas Peters was the father of Rockford's furniture trade, Peterson was its benefactor. His contemporary Levin Faust called him "Rockford's greatest citizen," and certainly if greatness is measured in terms of economic influence, Peterson had a legitimate claim to that title. When the financial panic of 1893 shut down Rockford's factories, it was Peterson who, working with the banks, helped many of them to recover.

To say that he was an uncomplicated man is not to disparage him in any way, because only someone with the same kind of single-mindedness could have accomplished what he did. His capacity for work was truly phenomenal. Rising sometimes as early as 3:30 in the morning (he actually started work at 4:00 A.M. during World War I), he rarely left his office before evening, and then usually for business meetings and negotiations that lasted several hours. As a young man he managed the Union Furniture Company by day and the Rockford Chair and Furniture Company by night, sleeping at his desk between jobs and becoming a virtual 24-hour inhabitant of his factories. As well as he knew the mechanics of business, he knew people even better. He had the kind of cool feline intelligence that measured strangers at a distance and sensed a potential adversary in a weak handshake or exaggerated politeness. He received salesmen during his own lunch hour in order to combine two necessary but (to him) relatively unimportant obligations.

Peterson never drove a car, partly because he did not want to depend on one, and partly because he walked so fast. In fact, he walked everywhere, in all kinds of weather, seldom bothering to wear an overcoat and gloves despite the cold. A quiet, buttoned-up, formal man, he was the least pretentious of people. He made it a point to know the names of all his workers and to listen to their complaints; his meetings were conducted as often on the wood piles in his factories as they were in the company boardrooms.

By middle age, Peterson had become a kind of public commodity in Rockford, entirely the creature of his own business enterprises. His name had the authority of an institution; his signature on a scrap of paper was enough to guarantee a loan. Almost on a daily basis, people visited him with requests for assistance. He believed in God, in the essential goodness of human beings, and in the Republican Party. He was deeply religious, yet he distrusted religious extremism, shunned revivals, and would not tolerate long services. Once, in his impatience, he brought a prayer meeting to an end, saying "You will have to quit now, because I am going to turn out the lights and lock up. I have to get up in the morning and go to work."

James Henry Breasted, who was born in Rockford in 1865, was one of the best-known archaeologists of his day, the discoverer of King Solomon's stable at Armageddon, the temples of King Sargon the Great of Assyria, and the palace grounds of Alexander the Great. He was one of the first people to explore King Tut's Tomb, and it was his research that actually deciphered the hieroglyphics on the walls of the tomb and confirmed the identity of its occupant.

Breasted showed an early interest in semitic languages while studying for the ministry at the Chicago Theological Seminary, though he later withdrew from the Seminary and transferred to Yale after his researches into Hebrew convinced him that certain passages in the King James Bible had been translated inaccurately. In 1894 he received a Ph.D. from the University of Berlin in Egyptology. A year later he returned to the Midwest to become Professor of Egyptology and Oriental History at the University of Chicago, the first person to hold such a chair at an American university.

Because of his association with King Tut's Tomb, his death in 1935 from a throat infection was subject to intense scrutiny, and an elaborate post mortem examination was conducted, in the words of the *New York Times*, "to eliminate any possibility that Dr. Breasted's death might be attributed by superstitious persons to the widely circulated and oft-discredited story of the curse of 'Tut-ankh-amen'." Three doctors signed the post mortem statement. Breasted's ashes were buried in the family plot in Rockford's Greenwood Cemetery beneath a granite marker that had been presented by the Egyptian government.

Courtesy, The Oriental Institute, University of Chicago

Anthony Marchesano was a proud, compassionate, demanding individual, harder on himself perhaps than anyone, a scholar of classical theology and an old-fashioned believer in the absolute primacy of family, church, and state. Ordained as a priest in 1906, Marchesano came to the United States in the same year to visit some members of his family in Chicago. When he realized that there were few Italian-speaking priests in the immigrant neighborhoods, he requested permission from his own diocese to stay in America and minister to their needs. Three years later he answered a call from Bishop Muldoon of Rockford to organize a new parish among the Italian immigrants here, already numbering more than 300 families and then being served by English-speaking churches. With initial pledges of $45, Marchesano undertook an ambitious building campaign, overseeing the construction of a new church, school hall, and gymnasium—the nucleus of a thriving Italian-American community on the city's southwest side that eventually numbered in the thousands.

Until his death in 1929, "Father Tony" was the virtual shepherd of his flock, meeting new arrivals at the train station, arranging for housing and jobs, intervening in quarrels, interpreting American customs to his parishoners and Italian customs to everyone else, visiting the sick, celebrating Mass, drilling English lessons into the heads of sometimes unwilling students, and supervising a rigorous program of Americanization for anyone hoping to be a citizen. There was no one more patriotic, no greater Rockford booster. A familiar and lovable character in his dark suit and straw Panama hat, Marchesano set high standards for his parishoners and thundered fire and brimstone from the pulpit. He could see the gates of hell, he said; he wanted his people to be ready for Judgment.

John T. Haight was a native of Rockdale, Wisconsin, who answered an advertisement for a teaching position at Rockford's Central High School in 1907. He was hired as an instructor of physiology and mathematics at an annual salary of $800.

Haight had been the principal of both a grammar school and high school before moving to Rockford, but his experience had also evidently extended to music, since one of the things that he did after assuming his new duties at Central High was to organize a school band—the first of its kind in the United States. Along with a teacher named Arthur C. Norris, Haight scheduled tryouts in the spring of 1908 for 18 positions. More than 50 boys responded. Each was tested for rhythm and finger dexterity on a mechanical apparatus that Haight devised out of a block of wood and steel pins, the latter having been driven in at various lengths so that they produced different pitches when plucked by the fingers. Haight raised money in the community at large for instruments and uniforms, and he worked with the boys throughout the summer.

In the fall the band made its first appearance in public, performing at high school football games and braving the jeers and rotten fruit of opposing fans who found the spectacle amusing. Haight nevertheless persisted. In the course of the next decade he had the satisfaction of seeing many of his skeptics converted as one after another of Rockford's athletic opponents established bands themselves.

Sammy Mandala learned to box from his older brother Joe, who arranged fights for him in schoolyards and in a natural amphitheater at Camp Grant. He was slender, only five feet, six inches and 130 pounds at maturity, but fast with his hands and extremely agile. Spectators used to make bets to see if they could count his left jabs.

What distinguished him from other boxers was his discipline. He studied boxing in the same way that a dancer prepared for a performance: patiently, analytically, rehearsing his moves. The comment was made that Mandala was too handsome to be a fighter—he had the Latin good looks of Rudolph Valentino—and because of this was given the nickname, the "Rockford Sheik." Yet he prided himself on the fact that he was a scientific boxer and not a slugger, and that his quickness in the ring kept him from taking many punches. The late

Billy Celebron called him "the man they couldn't touch."

A professional at 16, Mandala fought most of his early matches on the east coast. In New York, the Rockford Sheik turned into plain and simple "Sammy Mandell," his last name changed by Brooklyn mispronunciations. He adopted "Mandell" as his professional name because of its popularity with fight crowds there. But he returned to his own state for the most important match of his life. On July 3, 1926, in the first legalized fight in Illinois history, Mandell won the lightweight boxing championship of the world in a ten-round decision over Rocky Kansas. "The lad who boxed for nickels in grade school and fought in the preliminaries at Camp Grant," the Rockford *Register-Gazette* commented, "has climbed the hill." He was world champion from 1926 until 1930, one of the longest reigns in lightweight boxing history.

Courtesy, Richard Mandell

Bert Hassell got the nickname "Fish" from his days as an exhibition pilot before the First World War. He had been performing for friends by flying as close to the surface of Lake Michigan as possible and had crashed his plane. After he had been pulled from the lake, which he later remembered as "liquid ice," he heard a voice say: "Anyone who can swim in that water must be a fish!"

Hassell continually rebelled against the system. His parents had wanted him to become a Lutheran

minister, but he succeeded in getting himself expelled from Augustana College after only four days as a result of "student foolishness." As a civilian flight instructor in the 4th Aero Squadron, he helped to train many of America's aces in World War I, but he hated the monotony of teaching and later resigned his $700-a-month position to enlist in the Army as a private. Once there he rubbed manure in his vaccination to escape to the hospital, slept in class, and neglected to salute a captain. He said that he felt

hemmed in by regulations.

During Prohibition he worked for what was called the Lincoln (Nebraska) School of Aviation, in truth a sophisticated bootlegging operation between the United States and Canada. His nighttime whiskey runs were made without the benefit of radar, his only navigational aids being a compass on the floor and a simple plumb bob on a string. In his barnstorming days, he used the trotting tracks of county fairs as runways and repaired his engine in the open. When he got lost, he flew over railroad stations to read the names of towns or simply put his plane down in a field and asked a farmer directions. Sent to the Museum of Science and Industry in Chicago to dismantle a single-engine Bellanca on display at an air show, he decided to save time and fly it out instead, using the museum parking lot as a runway.

From his days as a bush pilot in Canada, Hassell's greatest ambition had been to pioneer a commercial air route over the Arctic Circle. On August 16, 1928, after crashing his plane on an earlier attempt, Hassell and his co-pilot Parker "Shorty" Cramer flew out of Machesney Field (now the Machesney Mall) for Stockholm in a Stinson Detroiter named the *Greater Rockford*. After 24 hours and 12 minutes they ran out of gas on a polar ice cap in Greenland; but their efforts earned them headlines around the world, and they were honored at the White House by President Coolidge. During World War II, Hassell commanded an Air Force Base in Goose Bay, Labrador, and after the war he was instrumental in developing the Distant Early Warning (DEW) radar line across the Arctic Circle.

In 1968, a few years before Hassell's death, the *Greater Rockford* was retrieved from Greenland. It is now exhibited at the Rockford Museum Center.

It is one measure of **Julia Lathrop**'s humanity that Jane Addams chose her as a subject of a biography (*My Friend, Julia Lathrop*, 1935). Both grew up in the same area of northern Illinois, both attended Rockford College (though Lathrop only for one year), and both worked in Chicago's Hull House in the early days of the project. Yet where time has magnified the reputation of Addams, the Nobel laureate, it has dimmed that of her able colleague, the first head of the U.S. Children's Bureau, and the first woman ever to be given an important federal post.

Julia Lathrop learned her politics at home. Her mother was a suffragette, and her father, a lawyer and one-time Republican Congressman from Rockford, an early activitist for women's rights. When she went to work at Hull House after college, Lathrop already sympathized with the problems of the tenement populations. Her involvement in relief work there, and her investigations of conditions in the hospitals and insane asylums as an official "county visitor," confirmed her choice of a vocation.

She was appointed to the Illinois Board of Public Charities in 1893 (she was the first female member of the board) and later helped to establish the Chicago Institute of Social Service, the Illinois Institute for Juvenile Research, and the Cook County Juvenile Court, which was the first of its kind in the world. She was a vibrant, witty woman with a "roguish sense," according to Addams, of the "tragi-comedy of American politics." She fought the spoils system in government and adopted, partially in self defense, a view of the world that combined idealism with a quiet acceptance of the limitations of human enterprises. This made her sensitive to hypocrisy, but it also gave her the courage to begin things that other people, less inclined to be philosophical, hesitated to undertake. "This doing things that we don't know how to do is going too far," Addams once told her after Lathrop had started a new service in midwifery at Hull House. Lathrop replied that Addams herself was being naive at a time when so much was already being done on faith. "If we have to begin to hew down to the line of our ignorance," she said, "for goodness sake don't let us begin at the humanitarian end."

One of the most colorful and intriguing Rockford personalities of the twentieth century was a tobacco merchant and philanthropist named **Fay Lewis**. Edgar Lee Masters, who knew and admired him, portrayed him as "Lewis Fay" in the *New Spoon River Anthology* (some of the book was actually written in Lewis' house); and Alice Beal Parsons, whom he befriended after her arrest in the Palmer Raids of 1920, based the character of Ray Whittlesey on him in her autobiographical novel, *The Trial of Helen McLeod*. Clarence Darrow called Lewis his "friend of a life-time." When Parsons and others were put on trial here, Lewis persuaded Darrow to come to Rockford to take over their defense. Similarly, when Darrow had been arrested in Los Angeles at the time of the McNamara Trials in 1912, Lewis had left his business in Rockford to be at his friend's side.

Among Lewis' talents was an ability to balance the interests of a small-town businessman and social reformer. He enjoyed the confidence of Darrow, Lincoln Stephens, and Elizabeth Gurley Flynn; he contributed regularly to the Public Ownership League of America and maintained open trade union loyalties, but he was also a 20-year Kiwanian and the president of the Rockford Park Board.

Lewis, who had gone to work in a Rockford cigar store at the age of 17, was widely recognized as the largest wholesale distributor of tobacco in the Midwest outside of the city of Chicago. He was independently wealthy and free to indulge his special interests, which included the Anti-Capital Punishment Society of America and the Winnebago County branch of the Illinois Humane Society (he was the founding president). With a characteristic blend of politics and pragmatism, he marketed a five-cent cigar named after one of the leading exponents of the redistribution of wealth in the United States (Henry George), and put paroled convicts to work in his stores as laborers.

Courtesy, Rockford Park District

Courtesy, Rockford Register Star

Janet Lynn, they used to say, helped to put Rockford on the map. She was one of the most popular American athletes of her time, perhaps the greatest free skater in the history of the sport in terms of sheer artistry, and just about everyone who followed her career knew where she was from. Chicago newspapers routinely referred to her as "Rockford's Janet Lynn." Politicians liked to have their pictures taken with her. *Newsweek* put her photograph on its cover, and Rockford rented a huge billboard to brag about her skating. The television networks flashed the name of her hometown at the bottom of the screen whenever they showed her on the ice. It was virtually impossible—though a visiting journalist once tried—to find anyone here who did not recognize her name.

She was indeed something of a skating phenomenon: a gold test skater at 11 (one of the youngest ever, even to this day), the junior national champion at 12, a five-time senior national champion and six-time member of the U.S. World Team, an Olympic competitor in 1968 and 1972, and eventually, when she joined the Ice Follies in 1973, the highest-paid female athlete in the world.

Courtesy, Associated Press/Rockford Register Star

The Secret Service gave him the code name "Stardust." His colleagues in Congress called him "St. John the Righteous," though never to his face, and usually with a kind of grudging respect. Gerald Ford said he was one of the most capable legislators he knew; and Bob Dole described him as the "brightest" of all the Republican candidates for President. To millions of Americans in 1980, **John Anderson** was an unknown Congressman from Rockford, Illinois, who had projected himself into the national spotlight with a maverick campaign for the presidency that was distinguished by a willingness to speak his mind regardless of the circumstances. He was a shooting star in the political heavens, the newspapers said, an "unguided missile" that was as likely to attack the policies of his own party as those of the Democrats.

People had seldom seen anyone like him. In Iowa, Anderson defended the grain embargo of the Soviet Union and recanted his earlier support of the war in Vietnam. In New Hampshire, he lectured gun owners on the need for greater handgun controls. In Michigan, he attacked the Chyrsler bailout and announced a radical new plan to tax gasoline to support the Social Security system. In Oklahoma, he suggested that oil revenues from the state be shared with the rest of the country. Ronald Reagan was a prisoner of the past, Anderson said, a star of "Eighteenth Century Fox," and Jimmy Carter "the apotheosis of failure;" they offered voters "not a choice, but a dilemma." When asked during a nationally televised debate how he would balance the budget and increase defense spending at the same time—a proposition advocated by the leaders of his own party—Anderson delivered the best throwaway line of the campaign: "That's easy. You do it all with mirrors."

He was the epitome of the anticandidate, an old-fashioned moralist who ridiculed campaigning as a "dehumanizing, degrading, debilitating and almost, sometimes, a disgraceful way of choosing the chief magistrate of the United States." His stump speeches were more like legal briefs than popular addresses, with few punch lines and a heavy larding of polysyllabic words that sent his listeners running for their dictionaries. His dark oversized glasses made him seem gnomic, and his great head of white hair gave him the look at the podium of a political guru. Not surprisingly, college audiences loved him. His campaign for the presidency—what *Newsweek* described as a "traveling seminar in hard truths"—became the last Magical Mystery Tour of the Vietnam War era, and Anderson himself, for a few months in 1980 at least, a cult figure on American campuses of Beatles-like proportions. He said the right things; he attacked all the sacred cows of insider politics, the big-money maneuverings and manipulations, which (he felt) had contaminated the elective process. When he committed the ultimate political heresy and left the Republican party for good in favor of an independent candidacy, his ascension to the status of a celebrity was complete.

Playboy interviewed him at length. "Doonesbury" spoofed him good-naturedly in its panels. NBC's *Saturday Night Live* featured him in a cameo spot.

The high-water mark of Anderson's National Unity Campaign came in the early summer of 1980, when opinion polls showed that nearly one in every four Americans supported his candidacy. After that, his legal difficulties in getting his name on the ballot as an independent, his financial problems, and lack of a bona fide party mechanism began to take their toll. He was all but overwhelmed by the media blitzes of Carter and Reagan. Though he eventually succeeded in raising $12 million in contributions and collected enough signatures on petitions to get on the ballot in every state, he never really had a chance. As the conventional wisdom went, he was too smart, too honest, and too conscientious to be the President of the United States. How in the world could you ever trust a person like that?

Rockford's association with the **Olympic Games** goes back to 1896, when Francis Lane, a Princeton student, was one of 15 athletes on the American team in Athens. Lane, who failed to win a medal in the 100 meter dash, was not at that time a Rockford resident, but he later went to Camp Grant as a captain in the medical corps, met and married a member of the local Barnes family, and settled down. When he died in 1927, his remains were entombed in Rockford's Forest View Abbey.

Since the Olympics were revived in 1896, athletes from Rockford representing the United States were: Bob Packard, 200 meter dash in 1936 (Berlin); Janet Lynn, figure skating in 1968 and 1972 (Grenoble

and Sapporo); Debbie Genovese, luge, and Sandy Lenz, figure skating, in 1980 (Lake Placid); Ron Merriott, diving, in 1984 (Los Angeles); **Kenny Gould**, boxing, in 1988 (Seoul); and Jenny Spangler, marathon in 1996 (Atlanta). Lynn, Merriott, and Gould were all bronze medal winners. Another bronze medalist, in the 1988 Winter Games in Calgary, was a one-time Rockford resident and Guilford High School graduate, Peter Oppegard, who skated in the pairs.

Kenny Gould, Rockford's popular boxing champion, held the U.S. Amateur Title in 1985-1987 and the World Amateur Title in 1986. He also won a silver medal in the 1987 Pan American Games.

Courtesy, Rockford Register Star

CHAPTER

Civilizing the City

R ockford had trouble keeping up with its booming industry after the Civil War, as factories seemed to sprout faster than prairie corn and new workers arrived constantly to fill the waiting jobs. In the last quarter of the century, in fact, Rockford's rate of growth was greater than that of any other city in Illinois, with the exception of Chicago. Fifth in population, Rockford had become the state's second-largest manufacturer. Yet there were housing shortages here, material shortages, and problems of sanitation. The introduction of gas lights and telephones could not disguise the fact that municipal services were primitive at best and zoning an idea whose time was still to come. Alongside of the Holland House, the finest hotel in the city, were sheds, privies, and livestock pens. The Winnebago County Courthouse stood opposite a row of unpainted livery barns on Elm Street which looked as though they had been mainly put together from the odds and ends of other buildings.

Even State Street, with its storefronts of plate glass and cast-iron gingerbread, which fashionably reflected the high style of the period, contained plank sidewalks that were so dilapidated that baby carriages could no longer be wheeled on them safely, causing one local newspaper, the Winnebago County *Chief*, to wonder whether Rockford mothers would eventually stop having children altogether if conditions did not improve.

For years Rockford residents had drawn their water from the Rock River and private wells; but the need for some kind of water service to deal with fires in outlying areas of the city led to the creation of a series of public cisterns. These proved to be only a limited success, however, since people used the cisterns for other things, such as washing laundry, and regularly depleted the contents. In 1874 Rockford hired the Holly Manufacturing Company to lay mains from a central well to 125 hydrants throughout the city, distributing a yellowish liquid which was said to have resembled water but which most people refused to drink. Even after a larger well was dug in 1881, people complained that the city water left a filmy residue on glassware and smelled a lot worse than the river. The drilling of an artesian well in 1885 might have solved this problem, but the city embarked on the development of a

rudimentary sewage system at almost the same time, thereby disrupting the water service. Inevitably, the pressure on the city wells increased after this, and officials resorted to turning river water into the mains as a way of preventing shortages. In view of the fact that the river continued to serve as one of the city's main vehicles of waste removal, the outbreak of a serious typhoid epidemic in 1912 was not at all surprising.

The City Council took the necessary measures to change Rockford's country habits. It banned nude bathing in the river and insisted that livestock be tethered within the city limits (any animal doing damage to property was impounded). The half-wild shoats that fed on Rockford's refuse piles were killed, captured, or driven off. People were encouraged to be more responsible in the disposal of garbage and, if possible, to empty their waste in the river *below* the city dam. Sparrows and pigeons became the targets of bounty hunt-

ers because they soiled the courthouse steps. Ordinances were also enacted to insure that saloon owners expelled human undesirables, such as "black-listers, habitual drunkards, and women of ill repute."

No municipal issue ever provoked such intense debate among Rockford voters as the sale of liquor. After 1865, the temperance movement emerged as a significant force in local politics, and more than a few public officials saw their careers rise and fall on their support of the "liquor traffic." Rockford elected temperance mayors in 1876 (Levi Rhoades) and 1879 (S.B. Wilkins) and only grudgingly submitted to the state's regulatory system for dram shops in 1883, limiting the sale of liquor with a $600 licensing fee. By 1888, this fee had been increased again to $1,000, a large sum for most saloon-keepers to raise, but a necessary tariff in the eyes of the City Council. In fact, when the issue of the $1,000 fee was brought up

for debate a second time by opponents of the license, Mayor S.C. Scovill and seven temperance aldermen retaliated by abolishing saloons entirely.

The Rockford temperance movement, which began as a kind of Yankee moralism, drew much of its later support from the Swedish immigrant community. Charles Church noted that the majority of the Drys on the 1892 City Council, for example, were from the "Swedish wards." Moreover, when Rockford women were given a chance to voice their opinion of dram shops in special referendums in 1881 and 1914, they voted overwhelmingly against them. Rockford men had wavered between licensing and outright prohibition for a half century, voting wet one year and dry the next, until the referendum of 1914 seemed to settle the

matter for good. After this, Rockford gained the reputation of a hard-core temperance town, and drinkers bootlegged liquor from places like Afton, Wisconsin, while waiting for less sober-minded aldermen to win seats on the Council. Local option laws, similar to the one that created Rockford's "anti-saloon territory," effectively banned liquor from most of the region by the time of America's entry into the First World War. Abstinence became a patriotic virtue. Then, with the passage of the Eighteenth Amendment in 1919, America hardened its resolve against the liquor traffic, outlawing its manufacture, sale, and distribution. Rockford drinkers did not taste another drop, legally, until 1933.

Everything that people consumed was subject to increasing governmental regulation. The new

ABOVE: Members of the Rockford Boat Club used the decks of the riverboat (left) as a viewing stand during the club's annual canoe races on the Rock River in the early 1900s.

FACING PAGE, TOP: Fire destroyed the Rockford Wholesale Grocery Warehouse on October 28, 1910. This is a view of the fire from the west end of the State Street bridge. Courtesy, Rockford Museum Center

FACING PAGE, BOTTOM: The riverboat Illinois sits docked at the foot of Mulberry Street not long after the construction of the Carnegie Library (1903). Courtesy, Rockford Museum Center

Rockford Board of Health, formed in 1885, established standards for the bottling of milk and outlawed both its bulk sale and the frequent practice of watering. Dairy workers themselves were required to take physical examinations. The Board ordered library books to be fumigated, created "fresh-air departments" in the schools to counter the threat of tuberculosis, and tested the air in public meeting places for its carbon dioxide content. With a growing appreciation of the dangers of bacteria, Rockford also did away with the common drinking cup in public restrooms.

Health care was institutionalized when the city's first hospital opened in the former downtown residence of Dr. W.H. Fitch on Court Street in 1885; the Rockford Hospital staff included six physicians and surgeons and a head matron. Fourteen years later the Sisters of the Third Order of St. Francis founded St. Anthony's Hospital on the old east-side Sanborn Estate, incorporating the Sanborn mansion into a large turreted Italianate building of three stories

FACING PAGE, TOP: *In an era of colder weather and fewer environmental contaminants, the Rock River was a favorite place for winter games. This impromptu hockey match took place behind the Rockford Public Library in the early twentieth century. Courtesy, Rockford Museum Center*

FACING PAGE, BOTTOM: *The east side YMCA building at the corner of State and Madison streets was erected in 1888 at a cost of $50,000. Its architect, Robert Rae of Chicago, was the designer of the Farragaut Boat Club. Courtesy, Rockford Museum Center*

LEFT: *The 1872 Winnebago County Jail formerly stood on the southeast corner of the courthouse square (intersection of Church and Elm streets). The sheriff and his family lived in quarters on the second floor of the main building. Prisoners were confined in the "bastille" at the rear. Photo by F.C. Pierce/Rockford Public Library*

BELOW: *Rockford police confiscated these homemade stills during Prohibition. Courtesy, Rockford Museum Center*

that commanded the summit of the East State Street hill. Rockford's Swedish community organized a Swedish-American Hospital Association in 1911 after an appeal for funds in the *Svenska-Posten,* an immigrant newspaper, pointed out the need for a local sanitarium. The hospital was eventually erected in 1918.

Rockford, like most American cities, was inundated by a variety of processed foods and patent medicines in the late nineteenth century, as merchants here advertised their wares with an almost circus-day excitement. The newspapers regularly announced the "Fresh Arrival of New Goods" and "Grand Exhibitions of Natural and Artificial Curiosities . . . Received from New York by Express." Indian-doctor remedies offered help for cancer, tuberculosis, asthma, catarrh, rheumatism, and lost manhood. Liver and kidney balms promised to reduce fat and purify the blood, and anodyne mixtures to cure "colds, coughs, and croup." For five cents, you could buy a wild cherry and pepsin phosphate in an eight-ounce bottle or a handful of junket tablets that turned to pudding in water. For those interested in the newer therapies, Rockford listed several institutes of

magnetic healing—a kind of hypnotism combined with "oxygen exhiliration" (inhaling pure oxygen)—such as the Gordon School of Medicine in the Stewart Building, the Shiner-Gray Institute on East State Street, and the Hyland Institute on North Church.

There are a number of magnetic forces in nature, however, and the one that proved to be the most intriguing to people was the myste-

A Rockford grocery store is filled with canned food, fruit, vegetables, and more in this late nineteenth century photo. Courtesy, Rockford Museum Center

rious "fluid" electricity. Edison's carbon filament lamp appeared in Winnebago County in the mid-1880s when the first generating stations opened for business here, the pioneering Forest City Electric Company on Market Street later absorbing the rival Rockford Electric Power Company on the west side to form the Rockford General Electric Power Company in 1896. An exhibition of electricity at Chicago's World Fair, which was said to have "turned the night into day" with the power of a thousand torches, convinced Rockford visitors that they had seen the city of the future; William Fletcher Barnes was so taken with a demonstration of an experimental launch named the *Electra* that he purchased the boat at

the conclusion of the Fair and brought it back to Rockford.

After struggling for nearly a decade to attract enough passengers, the Rockford Street Railway made the decision to abandon its horses in favor of electric traction, and gradually extended services to Belvidere, Beloit, Janesville, and Freeport. The new lines spurred the development of outlying areas of the city, particularly the West End between Central and Bayliss avenues (R.N. Baylies, after whom the latter was named, was a president of the traction company), and encouraged commerce between the major cities of the region. At the high point of the system in the early 1900s, the Rockford & Interurban Railway, as it came to be known, carried

600,000 passengers annually.

The steam railway also increased its services in the last years of the century. The virtual monopoly that the Chicago & Northwestern Company (the successor to the Galena & Chicago Union) had enjoyed in both freight and passenger traffic for many years in Rockford was finally broken by the arrival of the Illinois Central in 1888. A contemporary called the new line "the godfather" of Rockford's boom: "It cost the company something like a million dollars, but when the work was completed, the city began to put on its good clothes and to swell." The Illinois Central became the city's most direct route to Cook County. Alderman Edward W. Brown, the company's general agent in Winnebago County, laid out a belt-line on the southeast side—much of it on his own land—with the dual purpose of creating a new industrial district and of blocking the anticipated entry into Rockford of a rival railroad, which was then in the process of laying a track northward through Ogle County. In the end, the Illinois Central belt-line denied the rival company direct access to the city and forced it into receivership, its tracks being purchased by the Chicago, Milwaukee & St. Paul Railroad.

The Illinois Central is often thought to be the reason for the large Italian immigration to Rockford at the turn of the century. Like the Irish in the 1850s, it is said, the Italians were hired as track hands on the railroad, working their way westward to the Rock River; and while this may be true, it is important to note that the majority of the Italians who came to Rockford between 1900 and 1920 entered the United States through the port of New Orleans and then traveled north along the Mississippi.

Rockford's R.S. Sanborn erected this home at the crest of the hill on East State Street near the intersection of Summit Street. Later it was owned by the family of Leonard Schmauss (shown here on the grounds of the estate in the 1880s). After St. Anthony Hospital was constructed on this site in 1899, the building was adapted for nursing quarters. Courtesy, Rockford Public Library

The railroad (both steam and electric), in any event, was part of a revolution in transportation that gradually reduced Americans' dependence on horse-power and changed the way that they lived and did business. The increase in commercial service locally—by 1905 there were four companies operating in Rockford (the Burlington Route, Chicago, Milwaukee & St. Paul, Illinois Central, Chicago & Northwestern) in addition to the interurban—helped to overcome the city's sense of regional isolation and made it conscious of its place in a national manufacturing economy. If some people were skeptical of the railroads and not quite ready to abandon the horse, it was because the

ABOVE: The ornate soda fountain of Porter's Drug Store at the turn of the century reflected the jutting bric-a-brac qualities of the finest Eastlake residential interiors in the city. Courtesy, Frances Porter

RIGHT: Porter's Drug Store (John R. Porter & Co.), which stood at the corner of State and Main for more than a century, looked this way in the 1870s, its shelves lined with patent medicines, tobacco, perfumes, paints, oils, glass, and art goods. Porter, like other Rockford druggists, sometimes dispensed whiskey for medicinal purposes, even though it was widely believed that his "prescription" was more potent than the whiskey served in local saloons and hence greatly prized by certain customers for the wrong reasons. Courtesy, Frances Porter

What was needed, of course, was a mechanically-propelled vehicle that ran on the street. A preliminary answer seemed to be the bicycle, a vehicle whose commercial introduction in the 1880s resulted in a huge national fad (4,000,000 were sold by the turn of the century). Rockford organized a local branch of the League of American Wheelmen, the principal association of sport cyclists in the country, and packs of wheelmen or "scorchers" appeared on the streets testing their speeds. Harlem Avenue residents complained that cyclists regularly frightened their horses, riding against traffic and ignoring the right-of-way of horsedrawn vehicles. North Main Street, on weekends, was taken over by the League's "practice runs." Cyclists, in turn, complained that local streets were unfit even for horses, and said that Rockford could hardly be called civilized so long as these conditions existed.

The cyclists had a point. Although Rockford had erected a new courthouse, opera house, and post office in the last quarter of the century, as well as a number of substantial commercial buildings, and

latter still offered them the greatest convenience in short-range travel, and Americans valued their independence above just about everything else.

although it had replaced the old State Street bridge with a steel-girder unit and put up new bridges at Morgan Street, Chestnut Street, and Fifteenth Avenue, it had ignored the roadbeds. Exactly 1,730 feet of East State Street were planked with cedar in 1889—the equivalent of only about two and a half city blocks. Rockford added 1,735 feet of planking the next year to West State Street, and similarly improved 3,770 feet of South Main Street leading to the Illinois Central station, but it left the rest of the roadbeds alone, perhaps because the hardwood surface proved to be little better than the road it replaced. Planking, in fact, was mostly cosmetic. The cedar, which was covered with a petroleum compound to seal the cracks, soon shifted under the weight of horses and wagons, developing bumps and depressions just like the old roadbeds, and mixing dirt and horse droppings with the tar-like adhesive.

If cyclists found Rockford roads impassable in bad weather, they were no different than other travelers, who learned to trim their weight in carriages to keep from sinking in the mud, leaning left or right as the wheels dug in, and who occasionally rode their horses on the sidewalks to avoid problems in the street.

AUTOMOBILES

Given the interest in mechanical locomotion in the late nineteenth century, it was inevitable that sooner or later someone would mount a boiler on a bicycle or experiment with an electric motor on a four-wheeled chassis. Road locomotives, such as Hiram Maxim's motor tricycle and Lucius Copeland's steam-powered penny-farthing bike, began to appear in American cities, mostly on the East Coast, and scores of bicycle

mechanics applied their knowledge of gear trains and turning pivots to the next logical step in mechanized travel, the self-propelling buggy or carryall. Electricity and high-pressure steam both had early adherents—the first "auto-motor car" in Rockford was an electric phaeton purchased by William Fletcher Barnes in 1898—but internal combustion, the revolutionary new process that drove a piston with fire inside the cylinder, finally conquered the industry because of its greater efficiency. Gas engines were lighter, more portable, and cheaper to manufacture. Henry Ford, who had introduced the "quadricycle" in the late 1890s by connecting a pair of bicycles with a motorized platform, returned a decade later with the first Model T, the so-called "Universal Car," and the Automobile Age was born.

Rockford's "automobile colony," which was said to have consisted of 216 vechicles in 1908, was, by local estimates, one of the largest of "any city of its size in the country." Its leading figure, Fritz Ulrici of the

ABOVE: One measure of the permanence of the ice on the Rock River 80 years ago was the fact that the city placed electric lampposts and wooden changing benches on the surface during the winter. This photograph, which was taken from the State Street Bridge looking north, shows some of the people who gathered on the river to skate, fish, race horses (and later automobiles), and play hockey. Courtesy, Rockford Public Library

FOLLOWING PAGE, TOP: At the peak of the Rockford and Interurban Railway, in the days before the First World War, the company served an area as far west as Freeport and as far north as Janesville. Car 129, which was constructed by the St. Louis Car Company in 1903, ran mainly on the Freeport line. It was fitted with reversible rattan seats and a mahogany interior. The "cow catcher" on the front (known also as a pilot) was useful for sweeping the tracks in both summer and winter. Courtesy, Rockford Public Library

FOLLOWING PAGE, BOTTOM: This group of laborers on South Main Street at the turn of the century appears to be occupied with the laying of track for the Rockford Street Railway. Courtesy, Rockford Museum Center

Ulrici Paper-Box Company, drove a twelve-horsepower, two-cylinder Olds, and led expeditions of local autoists on "long-distance road runs." Ulrici's newspaper articles advised prospective autoists to drive a car of at least two cylinders in order to "save the concussions on your back," and to avoid engines mounted under the car's body "or you will have to lie in the dirty road on your back to fix it." Mechanical problems were expected, and the mark of a good autoist was to take them in stride. It was considered good form to ask ladies in the tonneau to get out of the vehicle and sit on the grass when repairs were being made.

Rockford's interest in these new "auto-motors" went far beyond their use as vehicles, however. More than a few mechanics here investigated the possibilities of making cars

themselves, producing line drawings and miniature models in order to attract investors and, failing that, building full-sized prototypes. It is estimated that there have been as many as 3,000 new car companies in the United States at one time or another, and to this total Rockford contributed perhaps eleven bona fide ventures of its own. The majority of these companies were stillborn by a lack of capital and engineering expertise, but one, the

Tarkington Motor Car Company, was a very serious effort with a large factory building, an authorized capital stock of $500,000, and a working pilot model that was praised in the national press.

The earliest Rockford automobile was the M'Arthur, an 1895 entry in an auto-making contest sponsored by the Chicago *Times-Herald* and probably never intended for production. Its designer was said to have been A.W. M'Arthur, an

Blacksmithing was a part of Rockford life for more than 115 years. The smith in this photograph, James Jensen, worked on Second Avenue in the early 1900s. The city's last blacksmith, Gust Djupstrom, closed his business on Fifth Avenue in 1952. Courtesy, Rockford Public Library

officer in a Rockford foundry. In 1900 the Gittings-Stevens Motor Vehicle Company was organized by two mechanical engineers who developed a two-cylinder prototype for the Chicago Auto Show. This roadster, one-seated with an open carriage, was described by its builders as a "success in every way except for a few minor details." The details, it seems, were the undoing of the company. The next year two Chicago mechanics, R.K. Swift and M.H. Detrick, founded the Rockford Automobile Company to perfect an experimental model that they had been working on. The company came to Rockford because local investors were said to have pledged $100,000, but no record exists of the Rockford Automobile ever reaching the actual stage of production.

Another vehicle of the same name, the "Rockford," was constructed in 1903 by J.J. Cole and his son, H.L. Cole, the proprietors of a small bicycle shop on East State Street. Like the previous Rockford ventures, this, too, was a failure, but the Coles evidently learned something from their experience, because their bicycle business soon became a sidelight in the Cole & Son Automobile Garage. In the same year, the *Cycle and Automobile Trade Journal* listed a new "Cotta Steam Car" that was being made by the Cotta Automobile Company of Rockford, Illinois. This vechicle was the invention of a Lanark nursery-man named Charles Cotta, who had moved to Rockford to begin mass production. The Cotta Steam Car had a four-wheel drive, six-horsepower engine, and 30-inch wire-spoke wheels. Like the Coles family, Cotta turned his failed enterprise into a profitable spin-off, the Cotta Transmission Company, which began manufacturing

operations in 1909.

There were several other notable ventures: the Rockford Automobile and Engine Company, founded in 1907, which assembled the "Federal" for one year before moving to Elkhart, Indiana; the Joslyn Motor Company, formed in 1908, which was capitalized for $5,000 but never started production; and the Comet Automobile Company, founded in 1916, whose owner, H.R. Sackett, issued a prospectus in an effort to raise money and then abandoned the attempt when he failed to attract investors. The Mechanics Machine Company experimented with a prototype of the "Rockford Truck" in 1913, but the venture was not a success. A few sources have listed Rockford as a manufacturing site for the Reliable-Dayton automobile and the Pontiac Motor Buggy—both of which are normally associated with other cities—as well as for the peculiarly-spelled "Rockoit," an awkward combination of the words "Rockford" and "Beloit," which obviously was some kind of local venture. Companies waited for signs of interest in their prototypes, a favorable review in a trade journal perhaps, or the indulgence of a wealthy investor, and most companies waited in vain.

An exception to this was the Tarkington Motor Car Company, an enterprise of P.A. Peterson's which not only seemed to be adequately financed compared to most automotive start-ups, but which offered a pilot model with a number of striking mechanical innovations. The *Standard Catalog of American Cars* has called the Tarkington "one of the most poignant failures in the history of the American automobile." Years ahead of its time in many ways, the car was the product of J. Arthur Tarkington, a former plant manager for the Kissel Car Company in Wisconsin and an experienced automotive engineer, and Carl Swenson, Rockford's inventor of the oil-lubricated universal joint. The vehicle contained a straight-lined aluminum body, running boards of laminated wood, leather upholstery, a walnut instrument panel, and a lightweight, overhead-valve, six-cylinder engine. The real surprises were said to have been in the transmission, whose aluminum housing enclosed gears of nickel steel riding on annular ball bearings, and in a 126-inch wheelbase chassis which, the *Catalog* says, "bristled with ingenuity."

According to Faust, when Peterson made up his mind "to go into the automobile business," he recruited Tarkington with a promise of complete freedom in designing an "ideal car," while also offering him his continued financial backing and the considerable manufacturing resources of the Mechanics and Rockford Drop Forge companies, both of which Peterson controlled as a stockholder. Tarkington came to Rockford with a large portfolio of automotive drawings, but he leaned heavily on the ideas of Swenson and others in working out the details of the car's mechanical system. "A successful and large organization of fine machinists and drop forgers, long making precision tools and forgings for the best automotive manufacturers," the company's advertisement said, "have developed a new motor car. They have set forth in tangible form their principles and ideas of simplicity, lightness, and sturdiness . . ." The Tarkington was meant to appeal to "the man who can own a good car but who loves to drive and care

for it himself," the independent autoist often found in "towns under 25,000 population."

The Tarkington made its official debut at the Chicago Auto Show of 1923, and critics praised its design. *Motor Age Magazine* hailed the "new car in the six-cylinder field." Yet investors in Rockford evidently got cold feet when more money was required to begin mass production, having already spent more than $250,000 in the development of six prototypes, and rather than go forward, the corporation was dissolved. According to the *Standard Catalog of American Cars*, "J. Arthur Tarkington was devastated. After failing to secure another position in the automobile

ABOVE: This view of the downtown riverfront in the early 1900s shows the barn-like exterior of the Grand Opera House, which concentrated its decorative details on the Wyman Street facade and on the inside of the theater itself. Courtesy, Rockford Museum Center

RIGHT: Rockford's Romanesque post office building was constructed at the corner of South Main and Green streets in 1895. Courtesy, Rockford Museum Center

industry, and after refusing a job at the Rockford Drilling Machine Company, he left his home in Rockford one day and was never seen again. All six of his Tarkington automobiles were scrapped."

Despite such disappointments, Rockford became an important vendor of machine tools and components to the automobile industry. The drills, lathes, and saws of the W.F. and John Barnes Company achieved a national reputation, and many found their way into the workshops of inventors such as Henry Ford. The Mechanics Machine Company was given a contract for transmissions by Chevrolet, whose demand rose so sharply in subsequent months that Mechanics was forced to abandon its less-profitable machine tool business—the rights were sold to another company—in order to

The Morgan Street Bridge was erected in 1917. This view from the southeast shows the outline of the Water Power industries in the distance. Courtesy, Rockford Museum Center

keep pace. Carl Swenson's perfection of a water-tight seal in the universal joint, allowing it to use oil as a lubricant instead of grease and thus extending its working life by thousands of miles, revolutionized the industry. In 1928, when the company became one of the four founding divisions of the Borg-Warner Corporation, it had changed its name to Mechanics Universal Joint.

The Rockford Drilling Machine Company, another breakaway venture of Barnes machinists, likewise

An unidentified military parade passes the Church of the Christian Union (right) on North Main Street, probably at the time of the Spanish-American War. Courtesy, Rockford Museum Center

shifted its emphasis from the production of horizontal drills to automotive clutches, joining Mechanics in the Borg-Warner Corporation as the Rockford Clutch Division in 1929.

A steady increase in car sales in the early decades of the twentieth century spurred new demands for iron and steel, bigger and better production machines, and improved automotive components. Rockford companies took advantage of opportunities in this ever-widening market. Alex Forbes' Rockford Malleable Iron Works, which had

been in the foundry business since 1854 as a farm-implement contractor, began to turn out iron transmission castings for both cars and trucks. Rockford Drop Forge, originally a foundry for Mechanics Machine Company, won contracts for caterpillar tractor parts. The Emerson-Brantingham Implement Company (formerly Emerson and Company), Cormack and Company, and National Gas Engine Company produced tractor gas-engines, though the latter eventually concentrated on the manufacture of machine tools after receiving a large contract for custom machinery from a Chicago business. National Gas Engine changed its name to Rockford Machine Tool.

Entry into the automobile market was sometimes inadvertent, the matter of a lucky hunch or a makeshift invention. James and Seth Atwood, the owners of the Atwood Vacuum Machine Company, developed an adjustable door bumper, a kind of small rubber shock-absorber, to silence an annoying rattle in one of their cars. They recognized the commercial potential of the bumper, developed additional models, and put them on the market. Like the early Chevrolet contract at Mechanics, the bumper's popularity changed the Atwood Company's orientation, and by 1919 it had abandoned the vacuum cleaner business and directed all its resources towards the development of automobile hardware (then commonly referred to as automobile "sundries") such as latches, brackets, hitches, and locks.

The list of Rockford companies that profited from the automobile trade is long, and this superficial survey cannot begin to do justice to it. The F.A. Bingham Company introduced the "Bingham Perfect Spark

Plug" and Redin-Ekstrom, the machine-tool builder, offered the "Perfect Seal Piston Ring."

Roy Burd, a salesman for the Burroughs Adding Machine Company, founded the Burd High Compression Piston Ring Company here in 1914 and later manufactured a successful hot-water car heater. The Hess and Hopkins Company, Rockford's giant tannery on the west side overlooking Fairgrounds Park, made gaskets, valves, clutch leather, and upoholstery; the smaller Rockford Leather Works produced gaskets and hydraulic packings.

NEW COMPANIES ARRIVE

Rockford promoted itself as the "New Industrial City of Illinois," while pointing to its improved rail services, abundant land for development, and skilled labor force. Business syndicates, such as the fledgling Chamber of Commerce founded in 1909, actively solicited companies from other cities in the Midwest. Though the majority of new manufacturers continued to be homegrown—bloodlines and family relationships were nearly as important as the availability of investment capital in the start of businesses here, especially in the furniture and knitting industries—the city's reputution as a low-cost jobbing center was probably responsible for attracting more companies to Rockford than anything else.

George Roper, a one-armed amputee of aristocratic bearings and unusual determination, bought a half-interest in the Van Wie Stove Company of Cleveland and moved the business to Rockford in 1888 to take advantage of what he considered to be a better labor market. The company nevertheless failed two years later, and Roper, under an arrangement with its creditors to repay the outstanding obligations in exchange for full ownership, took over the day-to-day management. Roper succeeded in paying all the company's debts by 1894; but ten days after satisfying the last creditor, the Van Wie factory was destroyed by fire.

Roper proceeded to rebuild the factory, purchasing castings and other parts from Rockford companies until his business was back in operation. His new facility on South Main Street, which he renamed the

This rare photograph shows a Tarkington Motor Car that was assembled from parts in the 1920s by P. Joseph Peterson of Rockford after the failure of the Tarkington Company. Courtesy, Jane P. LaGrande

Eclipse Gas Stove Company, was said to have been the largest manufacturing plant of its kind in the United States. Roper opened his own foundry in 1901 and acquired the Trahern Pump Company in 1906 in order to diversify his holdings. To these businesses he eventually added the Rockford Vitreous Enamel Manufacturing Company, the producer of the Eclipse stove's trademark porcelain enamel finish. The George D. Roper Corporation, which consolidated his interests in

ABOVE: The Alex Forbes mansion on North Main Street was the epitome of elegance in the 1880s. It contained six bathrooms, 10 marble fireplaces, and an elaborate dining-room wooden mosaic of cherry and maple. Photo by F.C. Pierce/Rockford Public Library

RIGHT: The $100,000 City Hall building, which was constructed between 1904 and 1906, was the center of a political controversy over the thickness of its walls. A petition presented to the city council claimed that Rockford had paid for eight-inch stone walls in the building but received four-inch walls instead. A subsequent investigation led to the dismissal of the architect and subcontractor. Rumors of graft in city government led to the election of a labor candidate for mayor, Mark Jardine, in 1907. Courtesy, Rockford Museum Center

1919, marketed a new and technically-sophisticated "Roper Range," a stove with a so-called "college education," and the range became a national sales leader.

Another important business that moved to Rockford in the late nineteenth century was the Ingersoll Milling Machine Company, a Cleveland manufacturer of metal cutting tools, which was attracted, in the words of its owner, Winthrop Ingersoll, by the city's outstanding "class

of mechanics" and a $29,000 loan from local investors. Beginning with a small shop of 19 employees in Rockford's north end in 1891, Ingersoll concentrated on the development of heavy-duty equipment for railroads and steel mills, and in 1903 received a contract from General Electric for the construction of a 315,000 pound milling machine, the largest of its type ever to be designed. The G.E. mill established Ingersoll's reputation for precision work and led to other contracts with the manufacturers of steam and gasoline engines, such as Ford, Olds, and Continental Motors. When the Model T was built, in fact, a huge Ingersoll mill made its main bearings and panrail. (This machine is now the most prominent piece of metalworking equipment in the Henry Ford Museum in Dearborn.)

Ingersoll's list of tool-building accomplishments is noteworthy. It made the first in-line transfer machine for the automobile industry, allowing engine blocks to move automatically from one metal-cutting

station to the next during manufacturing, and it constructed some of the largest general-purpose milling machines in the world. A modern Ingersoll mill that was designed for the Cummins Engine Company turned out to be 700 feet long, another for Babcock and Wilcox some 60 feet high; still another for General Electric was wide enough to allow two full-sized freight trains to pass side-by-side between its vertical supports.

Manufacturers were attracted to Rockford for different reasons. Howard Colman, a young Wisconsin inventor of something called the

Swiss watchmakers), and he rented the loft of their building to work on several inventions.

To prime the pump, so to speak, to raise enough money to undertake the costly mass production of the warp drawing-in machine, Colman organized the Barber-Colman Company in Rockford in 1900 (Barber, now long-forgotten except for his association with Colman, was a Wisconsin lumberman who invested $100), and began manufacturing small quantities of two other tools: a "check-controlled liquid deliverer" (a device for extracting butterfat from milk)

This three-story Italianate structure on South Madison Street was the home of the Rockford Watch Company in 1874. It was later occupied by the Rockford Board of Education, W.F. and John Barnes Company, and most recently the Ingersoll Milling Machine Company. Photo by F.C. Pierce/Rockford Public Library

"warp drawing-in machine"—an apparatus that he believed would automatically draw the threads on an industrial loom into the eye of the loom harness and greatly speed up textile production—came here to find a metalworking shop to build a prototype for him. His own models were made from wood, and he needed to demonstrate a working machine before anyone would buy it. Colman chose the Spengler Brothers Company in the Water Power, a small contract manufacturer of "metal specialties" (George and Charles Spengler were formerly

and a pliers-like "hand-knotter" for joining textile threads. Both sold well enough for Colman to launch both his warp drawing-in machine and a new line of gear-cutting tools. With subsequent ventures into the development of small motors, temperature and humidity controls, and aircraft components, Barber-Colman became one of the most diversified of Rockford's large manufacturers.

The Ingersoll and Colman companies were small-scale enterprises that were built from the ground up; but the Greenlee Brothers Company of Chicago, which moved its manu-

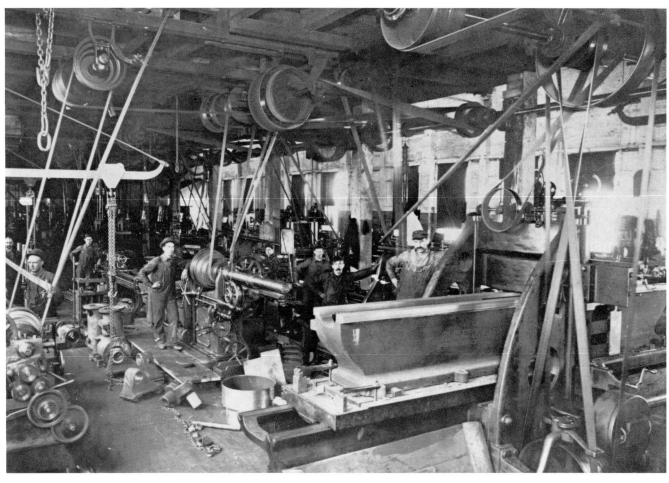

Ingersoll Milling Machine Company employees paused from their work to be photographed in the early twentieth century. Ingersoll concentrated on the development of heavy-duty equipment for railroads and steel mills.

facturing facility to Rockford in 1903, was already a mature industry, with a successful product line of woodworking and hand tools. The Greenlee Brothers, who were identical, bearded twins and virtually inseparable (people referred to them in jest as "the friendly team of oxen"), had achieved notoriety at the 1876 Centennial Exposition in Philadelphia with the invention of a hollow chisel that bored square holes in wood, an amazing technical advance at the time, and they had profited from a big demand for woodworking machines in the aftermath of the Chicago Fire, as the city began to rebuild, and in the great era of American railroad expansion in the last quarter of the nineteenth

century. Greenlee specialty machines that trimmed and bored railway ties were mounted on box cars and hauled up to the railheads by construction crews.

Greenlee's growth had caused it problems, however. Its Chicago factories, which were hemmed in by other buildings and lacked railroad sidings, had become overcrowded and increasingly inefficient. A long teamsters' strike in 1895-1896 had nearly paralyzed the company and had exposed its vulnerability. Rockford, on the other hand, was in the process of constructing a new industrial belt-line track (Illinois Central) on the southeast side of the city. It had a history of stable labor relations. And it was the home of a large number of furniture manufacturers who were already Greenlee customers.

After moving to Rockford, Greenlee expanded its production of hand tools, primarily hollow chisels and auger bits, and manufactured a number of custom woodworking machines for the automobile industry that were used to finish door pillars and crossbars in the car bodies. In 1915, recognizing that wooden components were being phased out by the railroad and automobile industries, Greenlee made the decision to enter the metal working business and purchased the Modern Machine Tool Company of Cincinnati. This gave it the rights to the Modern Machine turret lathe, a recognized market leader, and eased its transition into metalworking design. Greenlee became a pioneering manufacturer of automatic transfer machines, both electrically- and hydraulically-powered, and eventually served customers in the automotive, aircraft, and farm implement industries.

Like Greenlee, the Mattison Machine Company of Beloit was an established manufacturer of woodworking tools when it moved to Rockford in 1917. Chris Mattison, the company founder, had left Beloit's Yates Manufacturing Company in order to develop a turning machine on his own in 1896. Two decades later, Rockford offered what Mattison felt was the best opportunity for factory expansion. After it constructed a facility here, Mattison Machine entered the metalworking field with a variety of grinding and polishing tools, while continuing to produce turning and shaping lathes, moulders, sanders, grinders, and saws for woodworking.

Mattison moved to Rockford in the same year that the United States became involved in the First World War, a time of greatly-increased industrial production in this country, as manufacturers were called on to support the American Expeditionary Forces in Europe. The payroll of local industry tripled between 1917 and 1918, and companies proved their adaptability by manufacturing parts for engines, tanks, airplanes, machine guns, artillery projectiles, fuses, uniforms, and military instruments. Even the furniture factories were engaged in the production of wagons and rifle stocks for the Armed Forces, as well as of fixtures for the city's newly-established military training center, Camp Grant. "Without exception," the anonymous author of *Manufacturing and Wholesale Industries of Illinois* wrote in 1919, "Rockford has almost absolutely ceased its production of manufactured goods for the open market . . . Nearly every factory in the city has been engaged to a greater or lesser extent in the fulfilling of government contracts of war materials."

The assembly line of the Emerson Carriage Company is pictured at the time of the First World War. Courtesy, Rockford Museum Center

CHAPTER

6

Machine City

B y the time of the First
World War, the commercial and
mechanical resources of Rockford's
traditional manufacturing families—
furniture, knitting, and farm implements—had reached a stage of
development where the normal inter-
play of business activities was resulting in ever-greater company and
product diversity. The huge Emerson-
Brantingham Implement Company
complex in the city's West End,
which employed 1,700 people and occupied more than 50 acres of factory
space and "proving ground" for the
"E-B Line of Farm Machinery," was
Rockford's largest, though the remainder of the once-dominant agricultural implement business locally had
shrunk to a handful of small repair
shops, jobbers, and dealers. By itself,
however, Emerson-Brantingham accounted for nearly 18 percent of the
industrial work force and steadily increased its assets with an ambitious
program of business acquisitions that
included nine different companies in
the United States and Canada.

Rockford's five knitting factories employed 2,100 workers and were credited with being the largest producers of hosiery in the country. Furniture, with 26 factories and more than 3,000 workers, was approaching the peak of its development, and Rockford was asserting its claim to the title of the nation's "Second City of Furniture" after Grand Rapids. Rockford fixtures were sold with great fanfare to royalty and Hollywood film stars. The city justified its place in the forefront of the woodworking industry when it presented a large cedar chest, filled with candy, to the wife of the President, Mrs. Calvin Coolidge, in the 1920s.

Yet P.A. Peterson himself, Rockford's acknowledged "Furniture King," foresaw the trade's eventual decline because of the difficulty in obtaining raw materials here—the hardwood forests of Wisconsin and the upper Midwest, the nearest sources of Rockford lumber, had been depleted by the turn of the century—and because of steady wage pressure from the local metal trades, which were attracting the furniture industry's employees. Metalworking, he believed, was the way of the future. Continuous product innovation characterized the American marketplace, as the country's car-makers were demonstrating with their regular model changes (even Henry Ford would be forced to give up his Model T in 1927); and the consumer demand for iron and steel products was increasing at a tremendous rate. Metals had the advantage over wood of both a more abundant supply and greater durability. They were thus best-suited to high-volume, standardized manufacturing, which was the basis of the nation's wealth.

Because of the size of the industry and the number of machinists, model-makers, wood-finishing jobbers, millwrights, and general mechanics that depended on it for their livelihoods, furniture actually gave a start to many Rockford metalworking businesses. Charles Forsberg's Rockford Machine Company, the earliest Swedish-owned contract metalworking shop, made knife blades for furniture carving machines. Nels J. Billstrom invented a gluing-clamp carrier for furniture assembly that was later marketed by the Greenlee Brothers Company (Billstrom also designed a barbed-wire manufacturing machine). The Anderson Brothers Company, which was to become one of the nation's main producers of ice cream packaging equipment, originally manufactured a pneumatic rubbing machine for furniture. Swan Anderson, one of its founders, had worked with two other toolmakers, Levin Faust and Elmer Lutzhoff, to design a metal drill-chuck for cutting tools in furniture carving machines and a belt-sander for furniture finishing operations. The chuck and sander had been distributed by the Rockford Tool Company in 1905, which, like most small machine shops, did a variety of contract work in order to stay in business.

Metalworking jobbers served a variety of masters. They built specialty machines, tools, dies, jigs, and fixtures for larger companies and did secondary operations, such as drilling, milling, and grinding, when other businesses had trouble meeting production deadlines. Most jobbers could do repairs and millwright work when they were needed, and most were willing to undertake, on demand, the fabrication of certain furniture trimmings (hinges, handles, and locks) and fasteners. They also produced sheet metal and wire products. It was a fact of life in most shops that outside orders would always be limited and somewhat sporadic, that machinists would have to mix the jobs they did and make constant engineering changes—to develop new setups and reconfigure their machines—as a price of doing business. For some shops, this was acceptable, even desirable; for others, the flexibility that jobbing demanded and the long-term uncertainty of orders made them look seriously at manufacturing ventures of their own.

The Andrews Wire and Iron Works went into the production of window guards, railings, and trellises in the 1890s and later, as the Washburn Company, accounted for nearly 50 percent of the bicycle baskets made in the United States. The National Lock Company, begun in 1903, drew upon the jobbing instincts of Faust, Peterson, and F.G. Hogland, initially marketing only Faust's patented mortise lock to the furniture industry, but soon adding butts and hinges to its product line and then, in rapid succession, brass and wood knobs, escutcheons, screws, bolts, nails, tacks, and "sheet metal and wire goods to order." National Lock called itself the nation's "all-from-one-source hardware manufacturer," and it eventually became the all-from-one-source originator, too, of a series of independent hardware ventures.

In the early years of woodworking here, Rockford furniture companies ordered most of their metal fixtures from manufacturers in the East, though records show that local businesses such as Redin-Ekstrom, Spengler-Loomis (formerly Spengler Brothers), Rockford Metal Specialty, and Illinois Screw, in addition to National Lock, supplied some hardware to the industry. Contract shops had occasionally been called on to do "novelty jobbing" in hardware, especially for experimental product lines and short manufacturing runs, but National Lock was the first Rockford business to devote extensive resources to this field. Its success in winning contracts, both locally and nationally, spawned a number of imitators in Rockford industry, and it dominated the skyline of the southeast side with a large six-story factory (its corner tower was eight-stories high) that occupied some 25 acres of manufacturing space.

There were many notable Rockford ventures in hardware after the founding of National Lock, but for the purposes of this history, we will mention just the four best-known ones. The earliest was called the Elco Tool Corporation, and when it was established in 1918 it manufactured cutting tools and not hardware. Evar Lagerholm, a Barber-Colman representative in Chicago, had been asked by a Rockford business syndicate to direct the sales of their new tool company. Lagerholm had agreed and given his name (or at least his initials) to the enterprise; but later, when Elco consolidated with Illinois Screw and shifted its emphasis to the production of fasteners, he resigned from the company, saying that the change of direction was a mistake.

Elco was followed by the Aldeen Manufacturing Company, which was organized by a group of

former National Lock employees in 1928 to manufacture cabinet hardware. Among the founders, Gedor and Reuben Aldeen were the guiding forces of the new business. They were both immigrant Swedes, trained as mechanics before coming to this country as young men and rising through the ranks at National Lock to positions of responsibility: Gedor to vice president of engineering, Reuben to superintendent of tool, machine, and maintenance. The Aldeen Company, which changed its name to the American Cabinet Hardware Corporation (and later to Amerock), occupied the twelfth floor of the Ziock Building on South Main Street in the heart of the knitting district. By 1942 the company's business had grown to the point that it occupied the entire structure.

Rockford Screw Products Company was founded in 1929, at the start of the Great Depression, by another group of industrialists with ties to National Lock, the chief of

The stacks of gear-drive castings in the foreground of this photograph suggest that this unidentified Rockford metal-working company may have been involved in the production of agricultural implements. The size of this department and the structure of the building itself suggests the Emerson-Brantingham Company.

them a one-time foreman of the screw department, Swan Hillman, a jack-of-all-trades who had previously worked as a farm hand, day laborer, tinner, locksmith, electrician, and vaudeville strongman. Largely uneducated, Hillman had indomitable willpower and an unwillingness to recognize either his own limitations or the odds against starting a successful business during a time of national emergency. Rockford Screw Products owed its resilience to Hillman's pluck and the confidence of a few local investors who, in Hillman's words, "came to my help with capital."

The last important hardware company to be founded in Rockford was the Camcar Screw and Manufacturing Corporation. Founded in 1943, "Camcar" is an amalgamation of two of the founder's names, Bob Campbell and Ray Carlson. Camcar made a reputation for itself in the fastener industry after designing a special metal linkage—called a terminal—for the B-24 bomber. From an initial investment of $16,000, Camcar earned $1,180,000 in its first year of operation and went on to become one of the country's largest manufacturers of customized metal screws.

Success in the metal trades was sometimes a matter of sheer persistence, of staying in business until the right products and the right customers were found. The Mechanics Machine Company, which started on a $1,000 shoestring in the basement of one of the founder's houses, operated for six years at a break-even level and never generated enough revenue during this time for any of the founders to draw a salary. (None could afford to give up jobs elsewhere.) They conducted a repair and contract business at night with an old

foot-powered lathe and a reconditioned steam engine that had been salvaged from the wreckage of a burned-out Rockford factory. By the time that the company received its first substantial order for machines, two of the original founders, Charles Forsberg and Gustav Dalin, had been forced to withdraw from the business. When he left, Dalin sold the rights to his friction-driven drill press to the remaining partners, Faust and Charles Lindgren, who were able to "perfect and complete . . . the machine and to market it" through Hill, Clark and Company of Chicago.

Dalin was indirectly responsible for the success of another small Rockford shop, the National Machine and Tool Company, which purchased the design of one of his smaller hand mills. This machine, after certain modifications by Edwin Cedarleaf and Oscar and David Sundstrand, the company owners, was put on the market as the "Rockford Miller." Once again, Dalin's model proved to be a commercial success, and demand for the machine was strong enough to warrant a considerable increase in production and an issuance of capital stock. After Hugo Olson was taken into the business as an investor and financial adviser, its name was changed to the Rockford Milling Machine Company.

David Sundstrand, who was the company's chief engineer and a chronic tinkerer with mechanisms, devised a new ten-key adding machine that simplified the logic of the popular twelve-key model and swept the domestic market at the time of the First World War. The Sundstrand Adding Machine Company was subsequently formed as a subsidiary of Rockford Milling Machine, and an "all-window" factory of structural steel and reinforced concrete, four stories high, was erected on Eleventh Street to mass produce the Sundstrand model. The "Sundstrand Figuring Machine" continued to be a national sales leader well into the next decade, with corporations such as Sears and Standard Oil making regular volume purchases. In 1926, however, after Rockford Milling Machine merged with Rockford Tool Company to form the Sundstrand Machine Tool Company, the rights to the adding machine line were sold to Underwood-Elliot-Fisher.

The Sundstrand Company decided to concentrate its resources in the machine tool business—its sales personnel were oriented to this market—while exploring new methods of power transmission in the manufacture of metal parts. The development of Sundstrand's first hydraulic machine tool in 1932-1933 led to other applications of fluid power in the succeeding years, such as fuel oil pumps, automatic lathes, and hy-

draulic transmissions for aircraft.

Sundstrand's interest in hydraulics was typical of Rockford industry in the 1930s and 1940s, as fluid power became the state of the art in machining operations. Ernest Svenson, a Swedish engineer who had been employed by the Sundstrands after arriving in this country in 1919, experimented with gear and plunger pumps for the John S. Barnes Company, a subsidiary of W.F. and John Barnes, and designed a number of intricate hydraulic circuits for vertical drills. The variable-displacement plunger pump was his best-known invention, but his more than 200 patents for electrical, mechanical, hydraulic, and metallurgical structures attest to his versatility. Svenson, who lived for years on three hours of sleep a night and who never married until he was 65, found his greatest enjoyment in life in his work and referred to his patents as his "chil-

The commercial anchors of the west end of the Chestnut Street Bridge in the 1920s were the Nelson Hotel and the William Brown Building, which housed both the Security Insurance Company and the People's State Bank. Courtesy, Rockford Museum Center

Four months before the end of the First World War, the troops of the 86th Infantry Division at Camp Grant staged this Independence Day Parade on East State Street. Company F of the 341st Infantry is seen passing the reviewing stand in front of the State Street Baptist Church. Courtesy, Rockford Public Library

dren." He maintained a library of thousands of working drawings to which he repeatedly referred. A throwback to the Rockford mechanical men of the nineteenth century in his single-minded preoccupation with his inventions, he described himself as a "faithful exponent and exemplar of the traditional principles of the American dream." He had the honor, in the 1950s, of helping to design the hydraulic system in the Nautilus submarine.

Fluid power technology was in-

corporated into Greenlee transfer machines, Barnes honing machines, Ingersoll mills, and Rockford clutch transmission controls. The Rockford Machine Tool Company substituted its own "reciprocating hydraulic drives" for electric motors in the construction of high-speed shapers and planers—special cutting tools that moved back-and-forth in a straight path over stationary pieces of metal—and captured nearly half of the American market. Woodward Governor perfected new control systems for diesel engines and hydraulic turbines. The Hydro-Line Manufacturing Company became a leading producer of hydraulic and pneumatic cylinders. Ted Brolund, a young engineer at W.A. Whitney in the 1950s, applied fluid power to the company's line of hand tools and discovered a new market for hydraulic shears and presses.

Rockford's expertise in the manufacture of hydraulic equipment, its interest in the dynamics of liquids and gases under pressure, went back to the beginning of its industrial development—its first foundry and machine shop, in fact, made lift pumps for the Galena lead mines—and experiments in fluid mechanics were more or less a continuous aspect of its manufacturing life. "Doc" Andrew Brown's early steam locomotive, Howard Colman's check-pump cream deliverer, and the Rockford Tool Company's air-operating rubbing machine were all antecedents of the machine tool industry's modern fluid power systems.

In a city with so many varied industrial resources, it was inevitable that businesses would develop specialty products that were unrelated to their existing commercial activities. Some of these, like Faust's door-equalizer and razor-blade sharpener, would never see the light of day. Some would come and go as fashions changed and newer technologies emerged; some would give rise to new product lines and entirely new company configurations. David Sundstrand's adding machine was the result of six years of patient research and a financial success as soon as it was marketed; but after the owners of the Sundstrand Company (including David Sundstrand himself) decided to concentrate their resources in the development of machine tools, the adding ma-

chine became expendable. Joe Ness, a plant superintendent for Spengler Brothers, likewise invented a pencil sharpener that sold well on the market, attracting the attention of the Automatic Pencil Sharpener Company of Chicago, one of the nation's leading vendors. In 1911 the two businesses consolidated under the name of Spengler-Loomis and located their manufacturing facility in Rockford. Spenger-Loomis went on to capture 75 percent of the domestic trade; but pencil sharpener production also made other metal specialty work at the Rockford plant impossible, and George Spengler decided to leave the company to go into jobbing again.

New product development was unpredictable. Garnet McKee, the founder of the Eclipse Fuel Engineering Company, started in business as a manufacturer of a little metal bar for hanging gas meters on a wall. Albert Brearley was a wholesale distributor of knitted goods before venturing into the production of bathroom scales. Ny-Lint Tool and

Rockford held a number of public celebrations at the end of the First World War to honor its returning veterans. These residents gathered for a barbecue in Blackhawk Park on Arbor Day, April 19, 1919. Courtesy, Rockford Museum Center

Manufacturing made kitchen wares before it began designing metal toys.

In 1904 John Lewis Clark, an east-side hardware dealer, and Fred Truesbury, a local tinsmith who was known for his work on dust collectors for furniture factories, collaborated on the design and manufacture of a tin insert for stovepipe holes called the Gem Flue Stopper. In time, this modest business venture led Clark into the mass production of lithographed tin cans and a leading place in the field of metal packaging. The J.L. Clark Company referred to itself as the "unspoken household word" because of the virtual invisibility of its products: "You'd be hard pressed to find an

American home that didn't have many Clark products on hand. But you'd find it equally difficult to find our name on these products . . ." The low-profile, workmanlike metal fixture was a Rockford tradition that was entirely in keeping with the city's image of itself.

"THE MOST PROSPEROUS COMMUNITY IN THE NATION"

The strength of Rockford's manufacturing economy was clearly demonstrated in wartime. Payrolls and profits reached record levels, and many factories scheduled multiple work shifts. Colonel Don Anderson, the executive officer of the War

It is impossible to date this gathering on the east end of the State Street Bridge with any degree of certainty, but we know that the trolley car (number 613) at the right of the picture was not constructed by the Birney Company until 1920. We also know that the policeman in the background (standing to the left of the lamppost with the patrolman's rounded-crown hat) was Henry W. Doebereiner, a long-time member of the Rockford Police Department who was assigned to this "beat" in the 1920s. Courtesy, Rockford Public Library

A clamming boat passes through downtown Rockford at the time of the First World War. Courtesy, Rockford Museum Center

Department's Chicago Ordinance District, said that he considered Rockford to be the most important city of its size in the country in terms of national defense; and although this was said during the Second World War, it was no doubt appropriate to the city's industrial activities during the First World War as well. At that time local leaders, encouraged by the continuing high level of industrial orders here and the liberal provisions of commercial credit, predicted that Rockford would emerge in peacetime with a greater diversity of manufacturing resources than ever before. Roger Babson, the famous business and financial statis-

tician, said soon afterward that he regarded Rockford as the "most prosperous community in the nation" on the basis of its per capita income.

One of the reasons for Rockford's wartime prosperity in both 1918 and 1945 was Camp Grant, a huge military installation on the southeast side of the city that served as a training center for thousands of enlisted men. Just about every physical relic of the camp is gone now—the Rockford Airport was built on the site in the late 1940s after most of the barracks were dismantled—but the impact of Camp Grant on Rockford is unmistakable. "It is quite the biggest thing that ever happened in Rockford," John Camlin, head of the chamber of commerce, was quoted as saying in 1917, after he learned of the city's selection as a national army training site. It would possibly mean, he said, "another Rockford as big as this city was ten years ago . . ." When the camp population swelled to 50,000 men in July 1918, Camlin's prediction turned out to be true.

Camp Grant contained more than 1,100 buildings, 22 miles of macadam and concrete roads, water reservoirs of 550,000 gallons, and

endless stables, corrals, and infantry grounds. Due to high turnover, the Bates and Rogers Company of Chicago, which supervised the camp construction, was said to have directed the activities of perhaps 50,000 workers in all.

The economic effects of this were considerable. It is estimated that the camp added as much $1,000,000 a month to Rockford business. Restaurants and barber shops developed regular queues. Movie theaters, such as the Palm and Midway, played to packed houses. The

West State Street in the 1920s was Rockford's principal commercial thoroughfare. The newly renovated Rockford National Bank building on the southeast corner of State and Main, which had added four stories to its original seven-story structure in 1922, was one of the city's best examples of the modern Chicago-Style architecture of glass walls and structural-steel scaffolding. Courtesy, Rockford Museum Center

Grand Opera on Wyman Street, which at one time featured the greatest actors of the nineteenth-century stage, turned to offerings from the Columbia burlesque circuit. The Harlem Amusement Park on the northwest side finally repaid the investment of the electric traction company, which had opened it to promote ridership on its lines, and a new amusement center farther north near the intersection of Auburn and Central began to compete for the serviceman's dollar. Although Mayor Robert Rew asked for strict enforcement of the city's local option laws and established a ten-mile "sanitary zone" around the camp to control the sale of liquor, authorities were unable to eliminate a substantial contraband business.

Camp Grant succeeded in doing for Rockford what the bicycle and automobile had been slow to initiate: improve the roads. "Macadam improvements" were carried out to such an extent, in fact, that the city treasury was threatened with bankruptcy. Taxi traffic, which increased to as many as 500 vehicles before the war was over, gave Rockford the feeling of a major urban center. On July 4, 1918, in a farewell parade, the 28,000 soldiers of the camp's 86th Division marched through the center of the city. When the head of the procession passed the reviewing stand in front of the State Street Baptist Church, the end of the line was still marching out of the camp, more than four miles away. Nearly 100,000 spectators witnessed the parade.

Camp Grant altered the scale of Rockford life (and Rockford thinking). Though residents here had experienced serious outbreaks of disease before, they were overwhelmed by an outbreak of Spanish influenza at the camp during the last months of

the war. In September 1918 some 4,000 soldiers became ill with the virus, and by early October the death rate exceeded 100 a day. When the influenza was finally brought under control, 1,400 servicemen and 323 civilians were dead. This number did not include the acting commander of the base, Colonel Charles B. Hagadorn, who committed suicide at the height of the epidemic because of the apparent futility of the measures taken to curb it.

In the course of two decades, between 1900 and 1920, Rockford's population grew from 31,051 to 65,651,

The elaborate stone exterior of the Manufacturers National Bank building was photographed not long after its completion in 1926.

stimulated by immigration, a healthy
economy, and the creation of Camp
Grant. During the 1920s, a period of
unprecedented commercial and residential construction, Rockford's population continued to increase by an
average of 2,000 people a year.

Like many Midwestern cities,
Rockford tended to measure its ur-

RULE PRINTS

*The Midway Amusement Center (left) was the larg-
est motion picture theater in northern Illinois at
the time of its erection in 1918. The $2.75 mil-
lion Faust Hotel, which was constructed nine
years later, made this portion of East State Street
one of the city's leading entertainment areas for
more than three decades. Courtesy, Rockford
Museum Center*

ban sophistication by the height of
its commercial buildings. Its earliest
"skyscrapers," the Ashton and Rockford National Bank buildings, had
been put up shortly after the turn
of the century in a new "Chicago
style" that emphasized the use of
glass and weight-bearing walls, but
other important construction downtown did not take place until after
the First World War. The first noteworthy effort was the thirteen-story
Ziock Building, an indication of the
knitting industry's continuing prosperity and a challenge to the civic
pride of the rest of the business community. In 1922, the Forest City
Bank built a new seven-story structure on the corner of State and
Church, and the neighboring Rockford National Bank increased the
height of its existing building to
eleven stories by adding four new
floors. The Security, Commercial,

and Manufacturer's banks all built
new structures in the mid-1920s, the
last company laying claim for a
brief period to having the tallest
building on the east side. In 1927
this was surpassed by the 400-room
Hotel Faust which occupied an entire city block and rose to twelve
stories. The west-side Talcott Building, also built in 1927, matched the
height of the Ziock Building to its
south and laid claim to being the
tallest office building in the city.

In a single year, 1927, Rockford
issued 2,117 building permits for
new commercial and residential
construction, and in the course of
the decade more than 4,000 private
residences were built here with a
value of $15,305,065. The city's
aggressive Labor League mayor,
Herman Hallstrom, a journeyman
bricklayer and one-time Socialist,
pushed a zoning plan through the
City Council and initiated a program
of new street improvements.
The grande dame of Rockford's
movie houses, the Coronado Theatre, opened in 1927 to much excitement. Its exotic interior details
were duplicated to a lesser degree
by two other theaters on South
Main Street, the Rialto and the Capitol, both built in 1928. On the eve
of Bert Hassell's first attempt to fly
his Stinson-Detroiter plane to Stockholm, the Chamber of Commerce authorized his starting point north of
Rockford as the official city airport,
though no amount of speech-
making could change the grassy
fields of the former William Ziock
farm into surfaced runways.

Nearly ten years to the day after
the outbreak of Spanish influenza
in the city, Rockford suffered a new
natural calamity—a devastating tornado that struck the southeast side
and caused property damage of
more than $2,000,000. Fourteen peo-

ple lost their lives in the storm, and 360 houses were totally destroyed. Among the five factories demolished was the Rockford Chair and Furniture Company's Factory B. The Mechanics Machine Company, Elco Tool Company, and Union Furniture Company all suffered considerable damage.

A disaster of a different kind struck Rockford the following year—the stock market crash of 1929. At first the effects of the crash were comparatively mild here, signaled mainly by a decline in new construction. Encouraged by a decade of prosperity and not quite ready to give up the ghost of industrial expansion, Rockford business leaders organized a Mardi Gras celebration for the week of June 15, 1931, as a gesture of good faith; parades, fireworks, and outboard motor races would apparently undo the negativism in the national press. Yet in an ironic coincidence, three Rockford banks failed on the very morning of the celebration, causing a rush of anxious depositors to line up outside to withdraw their money. The parade took place as scheduled in spite of the general confusion, which was intensified by the appearance of several groups of heavily-armed men. "Armored trucks rumbled through the streets of the city . . . loaded with hundreds of thousands of dollars," the *Register-Gazette* reported, "guarded by squads of police detectives, state policemen, deputy sheriffs and private detectives armed with shotguns, revolvers, and tear-guns . . ."

The collapse of the local economy was mirrored in the almost total failure of the Rockford housing industry in the early 1930s. Five years after the city had issued an average of 17 new residential building permits a day, it issued only 11—in

a 12-month period. By 1934, this number had fallen to two, and Rockford was experiencing the full force of the Depression. Factory closings and lay-offs led to the listing of 8,102 families on work relief in 1935. During a decade of economic turmoil, business initiatives were rare: the Illinois National Bank opened in the old People's State Bank Building, the Twin Disc Clutch Company of Racine, Wisconsin, established a small manufacturing operation in a shop that had been part of the Emerson-Brantingham works, and the Rockford Screw Products Company moved into the former Forest City Phonograph fac-

tory on Railroad Avenue. The handful of new commercial structures—the News Tower, Gas-Electric Building, and Federal Post Office—contrasted with the long list of public projects that were conducted by the Works Progress Administration.

Despite an exhausted city treasury, Mayor Hallstrom continued to

Flags and other patriotic emblems festooned the Masonic Temple building on North Main Street, probably for the Fourth of July. Courtesy, Rockford Museum Center

Artwork lines the walls of a Rockford school-room, probably Central High School, in the 1920s.

oversee a number of municipal improvements, including the widening of Wyman Street and the extension of the city's water and sewer lines. His particular brand of Labor League politics emphasized low taxes and basic city services, not exactly a radical manifesto, and rumors circulated from time to time that he had sold out to the chamber of commerce and the utility companies. One person who apparently thought so in 1933 was his one-time Socialist colleague, C. Henry Bloom, who organized a broad coalition of disaffected Labor Leaguers, Swedish evangelicals, and business interests

to end Hallstrom's ten-year tenure in office. Bloom nevertheless continued Hallstrom's policy of enlightened pinchpenny government, forging a later alliance with Frank Ditto of the People's Coalition Party, a Fifth Ward Democratic organization, that kept him in office—with the exception of a single four-year term between 1937 and 1941—until 1953. Bloom intended to take over the gas and electric companies, at the very least to regulate their charges, but during his term out of office his conservative opponent, Charles Brown, turned the tables on him and sold the city's lighting system to the Central Illinois Electric and Gas Company for $100,000.

The gradual recovery of the American automobile industry in the late 1930s and the advent of compulsory military service on the eve of the Second World War were two things that helped Rockford emerge from the Depression. Car sales stimulated machine tool orders here, and military conscription led to the reestablishment of Camp Grant as a training facility. The Griffith and Sons Construction Company of Chicago directed the rehabilitation of the base in the fall of 1940, erecting 365 new buildings. With the outbreak of the Second World War, Camp Grant became the largest reception center in the country for U.S. Army personnel.

As in every other period of national conflict since the Civil War, Rockford industry benefited from orders for military equipment. The city's population, which had actually declined by 1,397 people during the 1930s, began to grow rapidly once again as unfilled wartime jobs attracted people from outside the area. Annexations of new neighborhoods adjoining the city, the successful peacetime conversion of Rockford manufacturing to a consumer market centering on the automobile, and the beginnings of a local "baby boom," evident for the first time in 1946, were all important factors in the city's increase to 105,438 people by 1952.

The 1950s, like the 1920s, were prosperous times in Rockford, as demonstrated by the increased activity in the construction trades and a steady rise in the median standard of living. Commercial television was becoming the dominant form of mass entertainment, replacing the cinema, and advertisers were learning how to exploit this medium with a

much greater sophistication than was evident on the radio. Less than four years apart, Rockford gained its first television stations, WTVO and WREX, and dismantled its old vaudeville house, the Palace Theatre, to make room for a dime store. Within a decade, the majority of the city's movie houses would also be gone, converted to other uses or moved to outlying neighborhoods where they were accessible to the automobile.

The mobile American car culture of the 1950s influenced many aspects of Rockford life. More than any other factor, perhaps, it was responsible for the gradual dislocation of the central business district and the shift in population to the east side of the river. It spurred continuing real estate speculation in subdivisions outside the city's corporate limits. It helped to transform the general appearance of the area by making popular a new kind of California roadside architecture, the drivein, and it eventually led to the development of large shopping center clusters, such as Meadowmart in 1953, High Crest in 1955, and Rockford Plaza and North Towne in 1956.

Like the rest of America, Rockford turned from Main Street to

The west side commercial district was photographed in the 1920s from the east bank of the rock river below the Chestnut Street Bridge. Courtesy, Rockford Museum Center

This panorama of the east side, evidently taken from the Ziock Building in the 1920s, shows afternoon traffic on the Chestnut Street Bridge. Courtesy, Rockford Museum Center

the countryside, and it gave priority to every road improvement scheme that offered to speed up the flow of traffic. City taxes paid for better highways, which carried city residents out of the older commercial neighborhoods and allowed them to spend their money in places which paid no city taxes at all. Traffic congestion in the downtown, increasingly an irritant, was solved by the introduction of parking meters, but these discouraged shoppers and hastened the exodus of merchants from the downtown.

The costs of redevelopment in the built-up portions of the city in the 1950s were high in comparison to those in outlying areas, and most businesses chose to undertake their new construction on farmland. The American Chicle Company (later Warner Lambert) erected a new $5,000,000 facility on the far northeast side in 1955, and at least five major Rockford corporations—Elco, Amerock, Sundstrand, National

Lock, and Rockford Clutch—made plans for new facilities away from their existing locations. Both Rockford Memorial and St. Anthony hospitals moved out of the downtown. Rockford College announced in 1956 that it was giving up its century-old riverside campus for a new complex on East State Street. Anticipating future population trends, the private and public school systems hurried to buy land in the country, offering yet another incentive for the movement out of Rockford. In 1958, Governor William Stratton dedicated the new Northwest Tollway ten miles east of the city limits. This was to prove to be the greatest future shock to Rockford's center of gravity, as a highly developed commercial strip formed along East State Street leading to the tollway. The later establishment of the Rock Valley College Campus in 1965 and the Cherry Vale Regional Mall in 1973 on east-side farmland solidified an inevitable urban pattern.

By 1960, when Rockford's population had reached 126,706 people, it had passed Peoria as the second-largest city in Illinois. John Anderson, in the April elections, became Rockford's first congressional representative from the 16th District since John Buckbee in 1927. After more than a decade of economic expansion, marred only by the closing of the Roper Company here in 1957, the city enjoyed the notoriety of several national studies which showed it ranking unusually high in its average level of disposable income. The chamber of commerce would claim, without revealing the exact source of the information, that Rockford had more parks, churches, color televisions, privately-owned homes, and millionaires per capita than any other city in the United States. Rockford welcomed the new Chrysler Assembly Plant in neighboring Boone County in 1965, confident that this addition would enhance the area's prosperity.

Yet it was a changing world, and the 1960s would mark the end—or at least the beginning of the end—of Rockford's status as one of the nation's great centers of family-owned corporations. The high costs of competing in a global marketplace, especially the demands of research and development, and the difficulties in staying liquid in an often volatile durable goods industry forced many manufacturers here to seek outside sources of capital, and subsequently outside ownership. The gasoline crisis of the mid-1970s and the massive invasion of corporate America by Japan led to a downturn in Rockford manufacturing, followed by lay-offs and plant closings. Between 1979 and 1987 the percentage of manufacturing jobs in Winnebago County declined from 45 percent to 34 percent, with a corresponding increase in the number of low-paying service sector jobs during the same period. In July 1982, during a national recession, Rockford's unemployment rate of 19.2 percent was the highest in the United States, peaking at 25.5 percent in January 1983. Although the local economy rebounded significantly in the late 1980s and manufacturing continued to account for the overwhelming majority of the community's wealth, more than half of the 100 largest corporations in Rockford had become "non-local and public interests," responsive to corporate decisions—and corporate pressures—elsewhere.

In a community that had always been slow to change and sometimes regarded by outsiders as a company town, this may have been a welcome development, resulting in an infusion of new ideas and energies. Yet it was also probably true that many of the things that distinguished Rockford manufacturing life in the past, its independent business initiatives and level of general community involvement, were increasingly at risk.

This early numerically controlled drafting machine was designed by Ekstrom-Carlson & Company in the 1960s. Courtesy, Ekstrom-Carlson & Company

7

Rockford's Heritage

R ockford reveals its past in unusual ways. Though there's not much left now from the first few decades of its history, the street patterns in the oldest sections of the city are a reminder of Rockford's early habit of doing things on its own. Germanicus Kent and Daniel Shaw Haight platted their settlements with little regard for either the compass or the developments on the opposite side of the river. After the Kentville and Haightville areas were incorporated into the city of Rockford, moreover, they attached themselves to adjoining areas in an equally haphazard fashion, leaving us today with one of the most fantastic road schemes of any city of its size in the continental United States.

"Streets crisscross at odd angles and run afoul of cemeteries, rock quarries or factory yards at places least expected," a WPA guidebook to Rockford warned in 1941,

Small triangular plots, landscaped by the park department, bob up where

PROCLAMATION BY THE MAYOR!

By authority in me vested, I, Levi Rhoades, Mayor of the City of Rockford, do issue this, my Proclamation. enjoining all good citizens that,

WHEREAS, on Thursday, the 22d day of June, 1876, public ceremonies are to be held in laying the corner stone of the new Court House, and military and civic processions are to parade the streets, and it being deemed prudent and necessary that the streets should be free from all obstructions on the line of march,

NOW THEREFORE, all persons are forbid hitching any teams on the following streets from 1:30 o'clock of the afternoon of said day until said processions have completed their line of march on said streets as follows:

LEVI RHOADES,
Mayor of the City of Rockford.

Rockford, Ill., June 20, 1876.

streets converge or change courses. What appears to be a most reliable thoroughfare sometimes abruptly changes its name and numbering system. Little courts and avenues that were formerly alleys or private driveways are scattered throughout the city. It is doubtful if there is another municipality in Illinois in which so many fine streets run smack into dead ends.

Does the history of a place like Rockford really make any difference to its residents? Ask people here, and they will probably say no . . . until you remind them of the streets. Sometimes, in fact, it takes a visitor to point these things out, for as difficult as this city is for a local to understand, it is even more puzzling for an outsider. Consider that there are more than 120 duplicates of street names in Rockford, and many that are reproduced three or four times. Park Avenue in the downtown, for example, must be distinguished from Park Street on the northwest side and Park Court on the southeast side, to say nothing of two other Park Drives, a Park Ridge, Park Terrace, and Park-er-Woods. There are also, predictably, three Parksides, two Parkviews, a Parkwood, and a Parkway. Five streets here are called Orchard (not including Orchard Park), five River, and four Fairview. More than 20 take their name from some derivative of "Wood" (Woodbine, Woodfair,

Woodhill, Woodlake, Woodland, Woodlawn, etc.). There's no shortage of examples.

As if the duplication of street names is not enough, Rockford has long adhered to what its City-County Planning Commission called an "unsystematic system of . . . numbering individual properties," —in other words, no system at all—and left it up to property owners to choose for themselves. Thus, odd and even numbers have been assigned to opposite sides of the street according to whim, sometimes to one side, sometimes to the other, and the sequence of property numbers established without much consistency. Occasionally, Rockford's lack of regulation has led to the ultimate contradiction: different properties, on different streets, with exactly the same address.

Pat Cunningham of the *Rockford Register-Star,* who has raised most of these points in his weekly column, offered the following theory: "The decisions on street names and address numbers are made in city and county government buildings in downtown Rockford—and downtown Rockford, you'll notice on the map, is off-center. Downtown is tilted. It throws off our sense of direction and heaven-knows-whatelse . . ." How did the downtown get tilted? Cunningham might have laid the blame on the shoulders of Kent and Haight, who platted their streets in the 1830s according to the irregular channel of the Rock River instead of aligning them to the true magnetic north.

Imagine a group of strangers, who have somehow been dropped into the heart of downtown, trying to judge the actual size of the city from the appearance of West State Street: no more than a dozen commercial blocks of any consequence,

nine or ten large office buildings (the tallest only thirteen stories), a civic center, several parking structures and surface parking lots, and— hardest of all to judge—street parking without a single parking meter. What would they guess? 20,000 people perhaps?

Even in 1941 the WPA guidebook observed, "One of Rockford's most distinctive aspects and one that frequently deceives visitors about the city's size, is the decentralization of its commerical area.

FACING PAGE: The so-called "Cobblestone House" on Broadway, which was erected by E.F. Herrick in the 1840s, is not Rockford's oldest existing structure, as is often supposed, although it is one of a handful of cobblestone (or rubblestone) buildings still standing in Illinois. Photo by Steve Pitkin

BELOW: The Rockford Museum Center frequently stages historical reenactments such as this to give visitors a sense of earlier customs and social habits. This photograph was taken in the old schoolhouse in Midway Village. Photo by Steve Pitkin

Rockford's Graham-Ginestra House was constructed in 1857 by Freeman Graham, a prominent local businessman who opened the first sour mash whiskey distillery in Illinois. The house has a slate gable roof and one-foot walls made out of limestone block. Photo by Steve Pitkin

Unlike most cities of similar population, Rockford's business districts are separated. Instead of the ubiquitous business core—the downtown or Main Street of 'Middletown'—Rockford has five large business districts, each surrounded by residential or industrial areas."

The truth is that there has never been a single Rockford "downtown," even in the early days, but always at least two, an east side (Haightville) and a west side (Kentville), with the majority of its public buildings concentrated in the latter—the semi-official heart of the city and the focus of most visitors' atten-

tion. This was fine for the west side and its promoters but discouraging for the east side, which chose to develop its own commercial district away from the Rock River.

Rockford history confirms that this was only the beginning. After the Swedes arrived in the 1850s, they too established a business district. Seventh Street (*Sjunde Gatan*) on the southeast side became a self-contained Swedish commercial area of some 11 city blocks, with a variety of stores, churches, and ethnic associations. It developed away from East State Street just as East State Street had developed away from the

Rock River, and it extended Rockford's business corridor into the immigrant neighborhood.

When the Illinois Central Railroad opened its industrial belt-line on the southeast side in 1905-1906 and set off a wave of commerical speculation in that part of the city, the fourth of Rockford's "downtowns," the so-called "Broadway Business District," came into being, crossing Seventh Street at Fourteenth Avenue and extending east and west for seven or eight blocks.

At almost the same time, the arrival of hundreds of Italian immigrants in southwest Rockford led to a fifth "downtown" along South Main Street.

As the WPA guidebook explained, "The character of Rockford's population is probably as responsible for this dispersion of commercial activity as any chance quality of site or accident of settlement"—the high degree of "national compactness" among its various ethnic groups having a lot

The John Erlander Home (1871) on South Third Street contains a number of examples of early Rockford furniture, including a combination desk and bureau made from wild cherry and the first Haddorff piano produced by the company here. The Erlander Home is operated by the Swedish Historical Society. Courtesy, Rockford Area Convention and Visitors Bureau

to do, in the book's opinion, with the strength of its neighborhood businesses.

Obviously a lot has changed since 1941, and the old-time Rockford neighborhoods are not what they were. The younger sons and daughters of the Italians of St. Anthony's parish and the Lithuanians of St. Peter and Paul have moved on; the Seventh Street Swedes, the few that remain in business, now live mostly outside the old sixth ward. There are Laotians in "Swede Town" and blacks and Hispanics in southwest Rockford. The Swedish-American Bank of Seventh Street has evolved into the AMCORE Financial Plaza, with a metallic eagle above its front entrance. Box's Bar-B-Q, the family business of Rockford's first black mayor, operates on the same street as one of the city's oldest Italian businesses, the Roma Bakery. The complexion of the neighborhoods may have changed, but the neighborhoods themselves persist in a way that still gives some meaning to the generalization about the "character of Rockford's population."

It helps to keep in mind that Rockford, as it grew, absorbed a number of small, de facto company towns, such as the Woodruff Addition on the southeast side and B.A. "Boomer" Knight's Addition ("Knightsville") further north in the vicinity of B, C, and D streets, which had been platted in the 1880s to provide an area of inexpensive housing for the workers at the old Skandia and Rockford Desk factories. These little "towns" were usually the result of special land syndicates or manufacturers' associations—Knight happened to be an officer of Skandia as well as a real estate agent—and located outside of what were called the "built-up portions of the city."

Gilbert Woodruff, a Rockford mayor from 1873 to 1875, not only sold lots on his farm to the employees of his nearby furniture factory (Forest City), but he helped them finance the purchase of the property through his own bank (Rockford National). The Woodruff addition was the beginning of a considerable commerical and residential development along Railroad Avenue known as "Furnitureville" or "Furniture Row," the first great concentration of woodworking businesses on the east side. The area was solidly Swedish, and most of the men who lived there were employed by the "Row" factories.

"Possibly because of the predominantly Swedish element," Herman Nelson wrote in *Americans of Swedish Descent* in 1948, "Rockford does not have the usual appearance of an American industrial city." This is possibly true, as far as it goes. Each American city impresses us with its peculiar urban images, and among the most enduring ones of Rockford are those of certain blue-collar neighborhoods on the Swedish east side that really do not look very much like blue-collar neighborhoods. As John Alexander noted in a 1949 survey of the city's "New Furniture Row" along 18th Avenue: "The residential areas marginal to this Southern Industrial Area are surprisingly clean and well kept . . . Houses are well maintained . . . Lawns are neat and frequently landscaped with shrubbery. There is room for a large garden plot behind each house. Streets are lined with trees."

This was typical of Rockford in general. One would have found the same thing in the St. Stanislaus parish near the old Forest City Knitting Company and in those parts of southwest Rockford that were then adjacent to the Barber Colman plant.

ABOVE: The circular stairway of the Tinker Swiss Cottage is said to have been steamed and shaped over several years from a single piece of walnut. Courtesy, Rockford Area Convention and Visitors Bureau

FACING PAGE: The library of Rockford's Tinker Swiss Cottage (1865-1878), which is said to have been inspired by Sir Walter Scott's library in Abbottsford, Scotland, contains five different kinds of wood. The rustic furniture in this photograph is part of a large collection of handmade benches, chairs, tables, and fixtures that Tinker distributed throughout his dwelling. Photo by Steve Pitkin

LEFT: The Tinker Swiss Cottage dining room is pictured with the family's formal tableware. Photo by Steve Pitkin

ABOVE: The Rockford Museum's "Midway Village" contains a number of restored and replica buildings in a re-created turn-of-the-century midwestern setting. Photo by Steve Pitkin

FACING PAGE: The Amos Catlin Spafford House (circa 1863) possesses some of the most finely elaborated exterior details of any residence in the city. Erected by the president of Rockford's Third National Bank, it has been occupied continuously by Spafford family members for seven generations. Photo by Steve Pitkin

RIGHT AND BELOW: The Emerson & Company Farm Implement Works used these posters to advertise its wares. The posters were preserved in the cornerstone of the 1878 courthouse and uncovered during the building's demolition in the 1960s.

FACING PAGE: The Zion Lutheran Church, organized by a group of Swedish immigrants in 1883, was the last Rockford congregation to hold Swedish-language services. The city's changing demographics are reflected in the current membership of the church (1989), which includes more than 60 families from Southeast Asia. Photo by Steve Pitkin

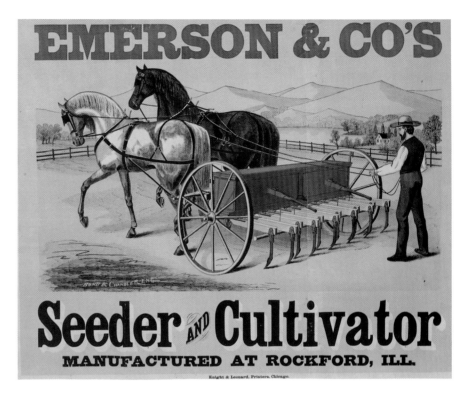

One of the most conspicuous landmarks in the Rockford downtown is the 10,000-seat Metro-Centre (1981), the site of concerts, trade shows, exhibitions, and sporting events. Courtesy, Larson & Darby, Inc.

The J.L. Clark Company (now CLARCOR) reminded Alexander of the "administration building" on a small college campus, its central Gothic tower actually concealing the factory's water tank. The Ingersoll Milling Machine Company, which was located in one of the city's most exclusive residential areas on the northwest side, had grounds that were suited to a "country club." (Rockford Country Club, of course, was right across the street.)

What impressed Alexander about these places was not just that they intermingled houses and factories, but that they apparently did so without serious detriment to either. If there were blighted areas of the city, they were located as often as not where factories had closed, and they were certainly no more heavily concentrated in industrial areas than in other sections. Rockford might have used a company-town approach to some of its industrial development without much regard for the rules of good city planning, but it had also ended up producing a pleasant kind of urban environment that was usually found only in smaller communities.

For better or worse, Rockford has always prided itself on being independent. The patchwork of little neighborhoods, the scattered business districts, and the strange street grids and numbering are all expressions of this; and if it's sometimes tempting to see these things as accidental aspects of a place that has merely had difficulty in governing itself, the evidence of the past is clear that, within Rockford's long-standing tradition of *laissez faire*, the decisions of a few key people have shaped the community.

In the beginning, Rockford had little enough to recommend it as a manufacturing site over other cities in the region. We can talk today about water power and trading routes and the proximity to certain markets, but the truth is that there were many river towns above and below Rockford with the same advantages. The fact that manufacturing developed here on a large scale, instead of, for instance, in Byron or Oregon downriver, had much more to do with the presence in Rockford of men like Ralph Emerson and John Manny than it did with any kind of natural resource. Emerson originally came to Rockford to manage a hardware store, not to make reapers. Manny came to make reapers, but only because he had run out of money in Waddam's Grove. One way to gauge the importance of these men is to ask ourselves what would have happened to the Water Power (and Rockford manufacturing) in the 1850s if Emerson for some reason had decided to remain in Beloit, where he had been a bookkeeper, and if Manny had found his financial backers in Freeport instead of in Winnebago County.

What, for that matter, would have happened to Rockford if the Galena & Chicago Union Railroad had completed its line to Freeport in 1852 instead of halting at the Rock River? One answer is that furniture and knitting would very likely have become Freeport industries instead of Rockford ones, for during the time it took to build a railroad bridge across the Rock, John Nelson and P.A. Peterson and a group of other Swedish immigrants got off the train at the east side station.

In the last analysis, the Rock River figures most prominently in Rockford history not as a trade route or a source of hydraulic power, but as an *obstacle*. In the 1830s it slowed the movement of settlers to the West—long enough at

least for a small town to develop here as a stopping place along the way. Later, it slowed down the construction of the railroad line to Freeport. Despite the belief of Germanicus Kent and other early settlers that the river would someday prove to be an important commercial highway, it turned out to be too shallow for navigation, and repeated dredging only served to destroy limestone beds like the old Rock ford. Yet even if the river had been deeper and the flat boats able to use it, it is doubtful that the Rock would have lived up to Kent's expectations. As a writer for the Madison *Argus* observed in 1844, the river would probably "not admit of this kind of navigation to any advantage . . . The business of the territory naturally extends east and west, and any attempt to turn it north and south into the channels of our shallow river must be an up-stream undertaking."

Simply put, the river ran the wrong way. Rockford's manufactur-

FACING PAGE: The Gothic Revival Lake-Peterson Home on East State Street was erected by Rockford lumberman John Lake in the 1870s and later occupied by well-known furniture tycoon, P.A. Peterson. It now houses the administrative offices of the Swedish American Hospital. Courtesy, Rockford Area Convention and Visitors Bureau

LEFT: The Rockford Time Museum houses one of the world's largest collections of timekeeping pieces. Courtesy, Rockford Time Museum

ing markets, with the exception perhaps of the ones for the farm implement industry, were located to the east—Chicago, Philadelphia, and New York—while the largest ports down-river on the Mississippi, such as St. Louis and Memphis, to which the Rock River led, were agricultural markets and therefore unlikely outlets for Rockford's durable goods.

A trip to Chicago in the days before the railroad was said to have taken a week or more and to have frequently been hampered by the wet prairies; one farmer estimated that the cost of hauling his wheat to market each year was equal to "all other expenses of plowing, sowing, harvesting, and threshing." If Rock-

ford had never been industrialized, and if an extensive dredging and widening operation had actually been conducted along the river south of Rockford, the river might well have been used to carry the county's surplus grain to St. Louis. But the river was dammed in the 1840s, the railroad came, and Rockford turned away from farming.

For all its impracticality, the idea of a river route to the Mississippi took a long time to die. The Galena & Chicago Union Railroad never completed its line to Galena, as originally planned, but instead constructed a second track south of Rockford that eventually (in 1855) connected Chicago with the Missis-

A Woodward Governor machinist sets up a computer-controlled machining center. Courtesy, Woodward Governor Company

sippi River at Fulton. This left Rockford on a less-important branch line and contributed to what many manufacturers here thought were excessive rail charges. People grumbled about "freight tariffs," and there was a popular movement on more than one occasion to raise money for some kind of interstate waterway as an alternative to the railroad, preferably a shipping channel that linked the Rock River and Lake Michigan. River conventions were held in Rockford in 1865-1866 and again, in 1899, to rally public support.

Rockford attracted settlers during the early stages of the great American westward migration because it was strategically located on the road to Galena, and it was similarly well-situated on the railroad to take advantage of the arrival of the Swedes in Illinois in the 1850s; but it was otherwise unfortunate as a manufacturing site because of its distance from both markets and raw materials.

Not even the Forest City could provide lumber for its fledgling furniture industry in the 1870s. Rockford quickly exhausted the available hardwood in the Pecatonica Bottomlands and had to haul in stock from central Wisconsin and, at the turn of the century, from as far away as Mississippi and Arkansas. The Illinois coalfields near LaSalle kept Rockford supplied for much of the nineteenth century, but steel had to be shipped from Chicago and even Pittsburgh. Pig iron, cotton, wool, and leather also came to Rockford by rail.

When we take away the advantages of convenient markets and raw materials, what is left? Only labor, the work force here, and perhaps the advantage to that work force of living in a community where a reasonable standard of living can be achieved in an industrial trade.

Rockford had no business being in furniture manufacturing at all, except for the Swedes. It could not compete with the lower freight expenses of Chicago companies and the access that those places had to major markets, but it could compete on the basis of labor, and it did so very well until the higher wages of the metal trades began to attract its workers. The obstacles that manufacturers faced in organizing and getting their goods to market made them anxious to exploit the resources

Rockford Mayor Charles Box stands next to the sign of his family's restaurant on Marchesano Drive. Box, who served previously as Rockford city attorney and city administrator, carried all 14 wards in Rockford in the April 1989 elections and won 63 percent of the popular vote. He became the first black mayor in the city's history. Photo by Steve Pitkin

they had, and it made them unusually inventive. We should also remember that P.A. Peterson worked a 90-hour week and that men like Manny, Gorham, and Nelson literally worked themselves to death.

"Because the Rock Valley's primary endowment is its labor supply," Alexander wrote, "the industries which have developed to the highest degree are those which make the most use of this resource, i.e., the industries in which labor represents a high proportion of production costs." This would have been in the skilled mechanical trades, in farm implements, furniture, hardware, machinery, and machine tools. It would probably not have been in knitting, however, which

was highly automated in Rockford and no more than a semi-skilled industry. Like furniture, knitting declined here when competing companies elsewhere had significantly cheaper labor costs as well as greater access to raw materials.

The "character of Rockford's population," we could say, has been responsible for both the appearance of the place, its neighborhoods and little company towns, and for the resilience of its economy. Rockford industry learned to make the most of its workforce. And it prospered because the workforce was skilled enough in the past to overcome whatever limitations these manufacturers might have had as a result of their location.

ABOVE: Situated on the Rock River 85 miles northwest of Chicago, Rockford is primarily a manufacturing community with more than 1,000 factories. Chief manufactures include precision machinery, fasteners, machine tools, hardware, adhesive, paints, and chewing gum. This view of the west-side downtown looks northwest. Photo by Steve Pitkin

FACING PAGE: The Rockford Park District's 154 park areas and six miles of paved pathways for walking, biking, and jogging are today among the city's principal assets. Photo by Steve Pitkin

8

Changing Fortunes

O ne of the reasons that Rockford has a hard time defining itself is its reflection of the national norm. Its demographics are almost perfectly in line with the American average. To look at the city's vital statistics - levels of income and education, median age, people per household, percentage of home ownership, voting patterns, and ethnic distribution - is to experience a cross-section of the country itself. Over the years Rockford's "average-ness" has turned out to be one of its main claims to fame, and it has struggled to find another identity.

Anyone who knows the history of Rockford since the Second World War will tell you that the city's business fortunes have always followed those of the country's middle class. The post-war decades were one of the great eras of American industrial expansion, and Rockford was in a good position, as a result of its manufacturing, to take advantage of the huge new domestic market that emerged in the

Rockford's Fourth of July celebration is one of the city's largest annual festivals. Here a crowd at the corner of State and Madison Streets watches as the Phantom Regiment's Drum and Bugle Corps perform in 1989. Photo by Eddy Montville, Rockford Register Star

1950s. When hostilities ceased, military spending changed to the support of new technology. Gas rationing came to an end. Cars went back into full-scale production. Within a few years, everything was soaring: wages, investments, stock values, corporate profits, consumer confidence, and birthrates. Most importantly, the country's new prosperity was being shared across the board. The market gave workers a fair return on their labor and offered the possibility of upward mobility. Most people thought that wages and living standards would go on rising indefinitely. Like many manufacturing cities, Rockford was transformed by the post-war boom. Its industrial job-machine provided steady employment for nearly half of the city's workforce; and its per capita levels of disposable income were among the highest in the nation for communities of its size.

When W. Lloyd Warner and his group of "roving, note-taking experts" from the University of Chicago arrived in Rockford to do research for a book on social systems, they found a city where the middle class was expanding and the "process of mobility" was working well ("A Sociologist Looks at an American Community," *Life*, 1949). At the time Rockford depended on a network of railroads and a downtown depot that served seven daily passenger trains. The city's main roads branched out from its historic nineteenth-century core, and the better residential neighborhoods along them were intermixed with lower income homes, reflecting a pattern of gradual development. There were no slums. To get a glimpse of poverty, Warner had to search out a few small unincorporated areas at the edges of the city, and even these places were as much a reflection of the people's rural lifestyles as they were of a lack of money.

A trip to Chicago in those days took more than an hour by train and three hours by car. Local businesses wanted to find faster ways to get their goods to market without the costs and inconvenience of the railroad freight system, and without having to truck them through every village and four-way stop along the way.

Relief appeared, in the mid-1950s, in the form of the Interstate Highway System; and cities like Rockford, which had previously been isolated from regional markets, were soon to become part of a 40,000 mile network that spanned the entire nation. The Northwest Tollway arrived on the outskirts of Rockford in 1958, one year after Sputnik, when the city limits were still defined in most people's minds by the Edge-o-Town Restaurant four miles to the west at the corner of East State and Alpine. The decision to build the Tollway on farmlands east of the city instead of running it through the downtown has often been identified as one of the reasons for the west side's decline. We know that an earlier study of the so-called "Chicago-St. Paul Expressway" had recommended bringing the road into Rockford along Woodruff Avenue on the southeast side and eventually

Illinois Governor William G. Stratton (left) shakes hands with Wyman Austin, Chairman of the Toll Roads Commission, at the 1956 groundbreaking for the Northern Illinois Tollway. The construction of the highway along the eastern edge of Rockford influenced the city's later geographic development more than any other single event. Courtesy, Rockford Register Star

connecting it with either North Second Street or Huffman Boulevard to the north; but property values in these areas were high, and people were in a hurry, and the planners, in all their wisdom, decided otherwise.

The country's road-building programs provided extra incentives for business expansion, since inexpensive land was available along the developing roadways. The gradual drift of Rockford towards the Boone County line, which started in the 1950s with the Tollway and the normal expansion of east-side neighborhoods, picked up steam in the 1960s with the relocation of St. Anthony Hospital and Rockford College to land along Route 20 and the construction of Rock Valley Community College on Mulford

Road. The smart money in Rockford was finding its way to the eastern edges of the city. The opening of a regional shopping mall in Cherry Valley Township, in 1973, merely confirmed what everyone was already saying: things would never be the same again downtown.

From 1947-73, Census figures show, family incomes in Rockford - and elsewhere in the nation - rose an average of 2-3% each year and virtually doubled between the beginning and end of the period. Eisenhower's claim that personal earnings in the U.S. grew by more than 40% during the eight years of his presidency was not just empty rhetoric; it was confirmed by the Census. What is also amazing is the fact that this income growth was

When the Northern Illinois Tollway opened in 1958, the eastern edge of Rockford was Alpine Road, shown here at a stop at State Street. Thirty years later, this corner had become the city's busiest intersection, with more than 60,000 cars a day passing through it. The Edge-o-Town Restaurant in the background had turned into a Godfather's Pizza outlet. Courtesy, Rockford Register Star

shared more or less equally by all levels of society. The lowest income groups made gains at roughly the same rate as the other groups above it. "The two fundamental propositions of the American Dream," Lloyd Warner told a *Life* reporter in Rockford, "are that all of us are equal and that each of us has the right to climb to the top." What better illustration could there be of this kind of social equity than the steady wage expansion of the entire workforce?

After 1973, the situation changed, and the optimism of many Americans began to fade. Family

incomes did not expand, but instead leveled off and declined slightly over the course of the decade (in constant, non-inflationary dollars). At the same time, higher prices drove down family purchasing power. The cost of living, according to the Consumer Price Index, increased an astounding 92% in the 1970s, while installment debt rose by $42 billion.

The initial culprits were the Arab Oil Embargo and the decision by the federal government to let the dollar float against other national currencies; but there were also the

This view of the downtown was taken in the early 1970s from the Rockford News Tower, looking northeast. Photo by Don Holt, Rockford Register Star

subtle inflationary pressures on the economy of the war in Vietnam and a whole series of not-so-subtle shocks to the American collective consciousness of things like the Kennedy assassinations, the murder of Martin Luther King, riots in Watts and Detroit, My Lai, Charles Manson, Attica, and

speed limits imposed. Christmas lighting was banned. Airline fuel prices quadrupled. President Nixon resigned from office to avoid being impeached. The year of the Bicentennial witnessed the largest trade deficit in U.S. history, massive job layoffs, a falling dollar, Saigon's surrender, and widespread

Watergate. The country had faced challenges throughout its history, but seldom since the Depression had the news been so dispiriting and so threatening to its faith in the social order. America seemed to be coming unhinged. Gas was rationed and new

discussions about the possibility of an ex-president being hauled before a grand jury.

In Rockford, the Board of Education announced that it was strapped financially and canceling sports. Merchants continued to

The city's "miracle mile" retail development, which began in the 1960s along East State Street, eventually extended several miles eastward to the Illinois Tollway, creating one of the largest concentrations of national franchises in Illinois outside of the Chicago area. Photo by Don Holt, Rockford Register Star

Rockford tried to reinvigorate its older commercial districts with the installation of powerful street lights in the late 1960s. The dedication ceremonies drew more people downtown, according to one contemporary account, than any other event since V-J Day. The classic rock band, Johnny and the Hurricanes, played at the corner of State and Main. Civic boosters claimed that Rockford had become the "world's brightest city". This photograph was taken on Seventh Street in 1976. Photo by Tom Clift, Rockford Register Star

leave the downtown in spite of—or perhaps because of—a new pedestrian mall that closed State and Main Streets to automobile traffic. Amtrak ended its passenger service to Chicago. Commonwealth Edison dynamited the old smokestacks at the Fordham Dam and turned its attention to the construction of a nuclear power plant in Ogle County. Despite higher gasoline prices, developers erected more new buildings than ever in the wide open spaces near the Illinois Tollway, while urban renewal bulldozers created new open spaces in Rockford's downtown. "Homesteading" was now a term that the federal government could legitimately use for housing programs in the city's West End, where rising crime rates and abandoned buildings contributed to a frontier mentality.

For the first time in 45 years, a Rockford police officer was killed in the line of duty. There were strikes, sometimes bitter ones, against the Board of Education, Sundstrand, National Lock, Illinois Bell, the City of Rockford, and the Rockford Newspa-

pers. Women boycotted meat and coffee as a protest against higher prices and entered the workforce in ever-increasing numbers. By the end of the decade, they accounted for 40% of all local employees, an increase of 10% since the 1960s. "I grew up being told and believing this nation was the richest nation in the world, and it always would be," Rockford Mayor Bob McGaw said in 1979. "Now we've learned that America is no longer the rich uncle" ("Are We Better or Worse for the '70s?", Rockford *Morning Star*). During the decade, the city experienced three of its five coldest winters on record, the worst one, in 1979, resulting in 74.5 inches of total snowfall and 100 straight days of freezing temperatures.

After the Arab Oil Embargo, Rockford's unemployment followed a roller-coaster course: rising to 14.7% in 1975; falling to 7.2% at the beginning of the 1980s; rising again to 19.2% two years later; and rising still further to 25.5% at the beginning of 1983, when temporary layoffs for retooling at the Chrysler plant made

Mayor John McNamara, with his defiant bumper sticker "Keep the Lights ON! I'M STAYING", is shown in the City Council Chambers in 1982, when Rockford's unemployment level was the highest in the U.S. Photo by Don Holt, Rockford Register Star

the city's numbers look like the beginning of a depression. John McNamara, who had followed McGaw as mayor in 1981, tried to rally public opinion with the bumper sticker "Keep the Lights ON! I'M STAYING". (He applied the sticker to the front of his desk in the City Council Chambers.) In 1984 local officials admitted that the downtown mall had probably been a mistake and made the decision to tear up the State Street portion. The huge steel sculpture, "Symbol", which had been erected at the Wyman Street intersection when hopes were still high for urban renewal, was cut into pieces with an acetylene torch. Too bulky to be moved easily and much too valuable to be destroyed, the sculpture —or what remained of it—was stored for months on the west bank of the Rock River, in full view of everyone crossing the State Street Bridge. The arrangement struck many people as being appropriate, given the condition of downtown.

During the 1980s Rockford lost more than 8,000 jobs, a devastating turn-of-events for a community of its size, since the majority of these positions were in manufacturing

businesses that offered a living wage and the possibility of upward advancement for their employees. The machining and machine tool industries here were hit particularly

The clock tower of the National Lock Company was a Rockford landmark for most of the twentieth century. When the business moved to South Carolina in the 1980s, the city lost one of its largest employers. Photo by Brad Burt, Rockford Register Star

Professional sports came to Rockford in the 1980s. The city's Continental Basketball Association franchise, the Lightning, made its debut in the Metro Centre in 1986. Two years later, the Rockford Expos, a farm team of the National Baseball League's Montreal Expos, inaugurated the Rockford Park District's new Marinelli Field. The Expos were eventually replaced by minor league teams of the Kansas City Royals (Rockford Royals) and Chicago Cubs (Rockford Cubbies). Photo by Don Holt, Rockford Register Star

hard. Declining sales, competition from overseas, and the high costs of developing new product lines led to layoffs, divestitures, and plant closings. W.F. and John Barnes, one of Rockford's earliest machine tool makers, was sold by the Babcock and Wilcox Company to Acme of Detroit. In the same year, Greenlee closed its subsidiary Rockford Machine Tool and began to phase out its own machine tool division. White Consolidated Industries, which had purchased Sundstrand's machine tool business in the 1970s, sold the company to DeVlieg-Bullard. Barber-Colman followed suit by divesting itself of its machine tool lines in order to concentrate on more profitable areas, such as its small motor and temperature

control divisions. There was bad news from other manufacturing sectors as well. The city's fastener pioneer, National Lock, one of the area's largest employers, moved to South Carolina because of continuing labor problems; and the Quaker Oats Company, with excess capacity in its pet foods division, decided to close its Rockford facility.

THE GLOBAL ECONOMY
One way of understanding Rockford in the 1980s is to see it in the context of an emerging world economy. Advances in information technology and telecommunications had given manufacturers everywhere the ability to participate in global production networks and to solicit bids from around the world for

literally every phase of their business. New products could be designed in one country, manufactured in another, and assembled in still another, with the financing put together from all three or perhaps from an entirely different group of nations altogether. Money crossed borders electronically in search of the best earnings, as trade barriers fell and American financial institutions purchased new high-growth stocks in overseas markets. The transfer of money occurred in even the most routine daily transactions. A person in Rockford would buy life insurance or contribute to a pension plan, and this money would find its way into the hands of a professional fund manager, and some of it would eventually be invested in stock shares and factory equipment outside of the country because of the high return on the dollar.

The importance of this for a Rockford company in the 1980s was not only the threat of foreign competition, but the fact that the rules of the game had changed: short-term profits had become a critical measure of success. The value of an investment in a business here had to be measured against the potential value of that investment elsewhere, not just locally, but anywhere in the world. Machine tool builders needed to be heavily capitalized for research and development, since new technology was vital to their success; but whereas a privately-owned company like Ingersoll could pursue a longer development strategy and reinvest a high percentage of its earnings, a publicly-traded company had to satisfy its shareholders first. Its product cycles had to be shorter. A company could not afford to run the risk of sluggish earnings over an extended period of time, unless it was

willing to risk the company itself. Investors would simply find better options for their money.

Rockford's business climate improved in the early 1990s, though a mild recession in 1991 held new hiring back well into the following year. Local unemployment, which had dipped to 7.2% in 1988, hovered around 10% through the middle of 1992. During the following year,

Ingersoll engineer Jim Sharp works on the company's new Octahedral Hexapod, a machine tool that represented a revolutionary advance in manufacturing in the 1990s. Ingersoll, which survived the collapse of the local machine tool industry a decade earlier, was one of Rockford's most successful global competitors at the end of the twentieth century. Photo by Pete Kendall, Rockford Register Star

Zeke Giorgi in the Illinois House of Representatives. Courtesy of Barbara Giorgi Vella.

Edolo J. "Zeke" Giorgi was a 28-year veteran of the Illinois Legislature and the Dean of the House of Representatives at the time of his death in 1993. The son of Italian immigrants from the Fifth Ward, Giorgi was an old-fashioned, straight-talking political pragmatist, who never called a press conference in his life and seldom minced words. He was a master of the legislative process, the most effective Representative that Rockford ever had. No one could match his ability to move new bills through the Illinois House, and few could rival him in his knowledge of human nature. "Zeke knew what people were about, who they were, where they were coming from...," the Speaker of the House, Mike Madigan said. "Up in his brain, he had a book on everybody."

Giorgi's legislative accomplishments were legion, from the Illinois Lottery to the Chrysler loan bill and Northern Illinois University Law School; but he was proudest of his day-to-day efforts on behalf of the working families of Rockford, the "little people" of the area, the poor and dispossessed. He helped everyone who came to him, regardless of background and party affiliation. "Zeke was the only politician I ever met," former U.S. Senator Adlai Stevenson said, "whose highest ambition in life was only to serve the residents of his own district."

Lynn Martin at a Rockford press conference in the 1980s. Photo by Fred Hutcherson, Rockford Register Star

Rockford's Lynn Martin, who began her professional career as a teacher at Guilford High School, was elected, in succession, to the Winnebago County Board, Illinois House of Representatives, and U.S. Congress (replacing John B. Anderson). During the Bush Administration, she was chosen to be U.S. Secretary of Labor.

however, a surge in national consumer spending triggered a dramatic increase in industrial production across the U.S., as domestic manufacturers regained some of the market share that they had lost to foreign competition in the previous decade. *Fortune* compared this surprising comeback to MacArthur's return to the Phillipines in the Second World War and Richard Nixon's political resurrection at the end of the 1960s, and said that American industry had succeeded because of a "steady, relentless drive to raise productivity, improve quality and boost competitiveness". What was even more remarkable was the fact that this recovery was being led by the nation's rustbelt region, rather than by either coast, and that an area once known for its chronic unemployment was in the midst of a labor-market boom.

No area of the rustbelt rebounded more swiftly than northern Illinois, and no city in this part of the state gained a greater percentage of new jobs than Rockford. Analysts pointed out that it had been one of the first places to hit bottom in the 1980s and to go through the pain of layoffs and business restructuring, and that this had worked to its advantage, in a perverse way, by forcing it to adjust

to the realities of a world economy a lot sooner than other manufacturing cities in the country.

Despite its plant closings and divestitures, Rockford had retained an important competitive asset: a large number of people who were skilled in the production of durable goods. Company failures might make headlines, but the area still had a dozen manufacturers with at least 1,000 employees, as well as some 800 small and medium-sized companies that were engaged in the production of durable goods either as prime manufacturers or as engineers, designers, jobbers, and suppliers for other industrial businesses. This wealth of experience - economists called it "human capital" - was the real source of Rockford's recovery in the 1990s, though the city benefited financially from the number of national discounters who set up their big-box superstores along East State Street. The value of Rockford's airport, with its considerable freight and cargo capacity, should also be taken into account, since it was this asset above all others that convinced the United Parcel Service to establish its Midwest Air Sorting Hub here and

Despite the closing of National Lock, Rockford has retained its status as a world leader in the production of metal fasteners. Here a Camcar-Textron employee checks bolts in a roll-threading machine. Photo by Fred Hutcherson, Rockford Register Star

One of Rockford's enduring family traditions is the downtown Kiwanis Club's Annual Pancake Day in the Metro Centre. The event, which is billed as the "world's largest pancake day", raises money for nonprofit organizations. Photo by Don Holt, Rockford *Register Star*

attracted a new Motorola service and repair plant.

Employment continued to be a critical issue for Rockford in the 1990s as it had been in both of the previous decades, but this time the issue was not a shortage of jobs but a lack of people to fill them. Factories were operating around the clock to fill orders, and managers were requiring overtime as a matter of course to prevent a loss of production. "It is sort of ironic, I know," Elco's John Lutz told a British reporter, "but we would welcome a slowdown in the economy; we would really like to strike a happy medium" ("Jobs Boom Puts a Shine on the Old Rustbelt", *The Independent*, 1995).

If Rockford was everyone's leading candidate for comeback

honors, it was also attracting plenty of attention from the press as a bellwether of American public opinion. The *New York Times*, in a front page article, called Rockford one of the ten most typical cities in the nation demographically; and the *Wall Street Journal* identified it in a headline as a "Microcosm of the U.S." while sampling voters' attitudes towards the two political parties. NBC Television visited the city twice to prepare reports on the country's health care system. Peter Jennings' "World News Tonight" was broadcast from the steps of Memorial Hall downtown because ABC wanted to gauge people's reactions here to President Clinton's State of the Union Address. In the country's continuing partisan debate over family values—initiated by Dan Quayle and later co-opted by Clinton—PBS decided to examine some of the issues in a hour-long "Citizens '96" documentary. According to the executive producer, Kathy Bissen, PBS wanted to provide a profile of families in "a community that everyone could relate to". Eventually, after considering several possibilities, it chose Rockford, Illinois.

Yet not everyone in PBS's audience—and particularly the readers of *Money* magazine—could relate to this community. An amusing footnote to Rockford's perennial status as a meat-and-potatoes town was the fact that *Money* ranked it at the bottom of its annual listing of the best places to live in the country. This raised a number of interesting questions about: (1) *Money* magazine; (2) Rockford; and (3) the state of affairs in Middle America. Chuck Sweeny of the *Rockford Register -Star* probably put it best: "If Rockford is supposed to be a cross-section of the U.S. and the median point demographically, and if *Money* ranks it last, then most of the country is in a lot worse shape than anybody realized."

Census figures show that the downward pressures on American family income, which were evident in the 1970s, continued into the following decades. While manufacturing output increased in the 1980s and 1990s, most of the growth in earnings was distributed to the richest and most highly-educated segments of the community. The average weekly wage of a man in Rockford, in inflation-adjusted dollars, actually *declined* by 10% from 1979-95. Family incomes may have been partially sustained by the entry of women into the workforce, but Census data indicates that most people had to work longer and harder just to keep up with inflation. If the

wages of women increased by an average of 9-10% during this period, it's important to remember that they were still considerably less than their husbands' earnings and generally not enough to compensate for the slow erosion of the family's purchasing power. The news was worse the further one went down the educational ladder, for the wage rates of high school dropouts declined by as much as 20% here in the last quarter of the twentieth century.

Had Lloyd Warner returned to Rockford in the 1990s to update his book on social systems, he would have found a much different city from the one he visited in 1949. He would have discovered a more ethnically-diverse community, with a significant black population and three times as many Hispanics as the rest of the foreign-born residents combined. He would have learned that the steady middle-class wage expansion of the post-war years had given way to an income gap between the community's richest and poorest families. The top quarter of the population, the richest households, now controlled half of the area's wealth, while the bottom quarter accounted for less than 7%. The city's job-machine, which once had provided hundreds of unskilled and semi-skilled manufacturing positions, was continually upgrading its entry-level standards. To say that there were more jobs in Rockford in the 1990s than people to fill them might be technically correct, but the real point was that there were more jobs than *qualified* applicants. There was an oversupply of unskilled workers and an undersupply of skilled ones. If the American economy was never again going to generate enough unskilled jobs of value to support the families of the lower income classes, then there

Rockford is the home of one of only two Laotian Buddhist temples in the U.S., east of the Mississippi River. According to a Rockford Board of Education census, families from 45 different language backgrounds were enrolled in the public schools in 1989. Courtesy, Rockford Register Star

was only one thing to do: raise the skills of these classes so that they could compete for the available jobs.

The prescription was simple in theory but enormously complicated in practice. No other issue was more vital to Rockford's future as a community, and no other issue bedeviled it so long

as the question of its school system and its treatment of low-income and minority students. In 1969, an ad hoc group of parents and west-side residents known as QUEFAC ("Quality Education for All Children") had sued the Rockford Board of Education for discriminating against blacks; and this lawsuit, which dragged on in the courts for most of the 1970s, resulted in the city's first court-supervised desegregation plan (1978). Eleven years later, another group of west-side residents calling themselves the "People Who Care" was back in the U.S. District Court leveling the same charges. After five years of legal action and millions of dollars in legal fees, the Rockford schools were once again found guilty. Eventually, after more court trials and a welter of charges and counter-charges, the schools were placed under the supervision of a court-appointed master.

Complicated by the opposition of the school district's unions and (frequently) by the school board itself,

A young volunteer at the Downtown Kiwanis Club's Annual Pancake Day takes a break from his duties as a pancake batter carrier. Photo by Wendy Vissar, Rockford Register Star

and entangled in a seemingly
endless sequence of court
rulings and remedies, the
lawsuit took on a life of its own
in which the sustaining force
appeared to be the lawyers'
appetite for fees rather than the
welfare of children in the
district. It was cold comfort to
learn that Rockford was one of
approximately 1,000 school
districts nationally whose
desegregation programs were
being monitored by the federal
courts; for the only lasting
reform of public education in
this country was going to come
from the voluntary efforts of
students, parents, and educators
working together in an open,
commercially-competitive
system. If the free market, in all
its dynamism, had changed
society in the years since the
Second World War, then similar
market forces would be needed
to restructure public education,
which reflected a social order
and system of enterprise that no
longer existed.

The dilemma that Rock-
ford faced at the end of the
twentieth century was a fundamental dilemma of the free
market system itself—an issue
that most of this country's
political leaders were unwilling
to discuss: how to restore a
process of upward mobility for
all sectors of our society, or how
otherwise to govern a society
that would be increasingly
polarized according to income
and education in the future.

*The two oldest marchers in the 1979
Memorial Day Parade, Art Rudelius and
Elzie Ulrey, pass the Alexander Lieberman
sculpture at the intersection of State and
Wyman Streets downtown. Photo by Jim
Quinn, Rockford* Register Star

9

Chronicles of Leadership

R ockford's industry began with water and wood. The wood came from the heavy forests that lay along the route between Chicago and Galena, and it was the raw materials of wagons, boats, and buildings. The water was the Rock River, a highway and the source of power to turn waterwheels that ran mills to grind grain and saw timber.

Then came metal. In 1837 in Grand Detour, a day's journey from Rockford, John Deere made the first steel-bladed plow in his smithy, revolutionizing midwestern agriculture, and the uses of metal grew apace.

And then came the railroad. Completed to the west side of the river in 1853, it gave Rockford a link with the outside world, a link along which raw materials and goods came in and goods made in Rockford flowed out. A dam was constructed across the Rock River. The following year Rockford's first foundry company, still operating today, began the manufacture of

everything a midwestern farm family would need, from stoves to trailer hitches.

Rockford was an established industrial center. Its population more than tripled in a decade, from 2,093 in 1850 to 6,979 in 1860.

The next great milestone for Rockford industry, ironically, was a disaster: the great Chicago fire of 1871. Among the victims of that conflagration were many furniture manufacturers. The craftsmen, many of Swedish ancestry, went elsewhere for work, a number of them came to Rockford. It was the beginning of a furniture industry that served the nation by the first decade of the twentieth century, and those names became part of the cityscape of Rockford.

The first furniture maker, Forest City Furniture, was founded in 1874 at Seventh Street and Railroad Avenue. Its first president was Gilbert Woodruff; a street of that name runs along the railroad through what became the center of the city's furniture-making area. Union Furniture Co. was founded in 1876; its president, John Erlander, lived in what today is the Erlander Home Museum in Rockford's historic Haight Village One of the key figures in Rockford's furniture industry was Pehr August Peterson. When he died at the age of 80 in 1927, he was president of nine companies, owned part of or was on the board of more than 50 others, and left an estate of more than $4 million. His home at 1313 East State Street is a Rockford landmark.

The furniture industry established a large, stable work force in Rockford, and others were able to build on this foundation to broaden and diversify the city's industrial base. Key participants in this process were a small group of creative people whose inventions and enterprises launched some of the city's largest companies: Amos W. Woodward, Howard Colman, Robert L. and Ralph S. Greenlee, Winthrop Ingersoll, and Seth B. Atwood.

With the establishment of the Rockford Tool Co. in 1905 by Levin Faust, Elmer Lutzhoff, and Swan Anderson, the Rockford machine tool industry was launched. And the fastener industry, a natural extension of the metalworking that was already going on there, followed in subsequent decades.

The organizations whose histories are detailed on the following pages have chosen to support this important literary and civic project. They illustrate the variety of ways in which individuals and their businesses have contributed to Rockford's growth and development.

This early twentieth century view of the old Shumway Market, taken from the present site of the Midway Theatre, shows the Hess Brothers Store and State Street Baptist Church in the background. The church was razed in 1949, the Hess Brothers Store in 1973. Since the Second World War, the Market has declined in size and importance. Today it survives as a kind of summer novelty, opening on Saturday mornings as a farmers' market and serving the rest of the year as a municipal parking lot. Courtesy, Rockford Public Library

ROCKFORD ACROMATIC PRODUCTS CO.

The only things that have not changed about Rockford Acromatic Products Co. are its address—611 Beacon Street, Loves Park—and its ownership by the same family since 1948.

But the offices of chairman Dean A. Olson II are quite literally on the roof of the original building. The company has grown from seven employees to 700, from 2,000 square feet to 55,000. And its product has evolved from general machining work to some very specific products for the automotive industry, products in which Rockford Acromatic is far and away the dominant supplier.

Dean Olson and his brothers, James N. Olson, president, and Nobel D. Olson, vice-president and secretary, continue in the tradition and pattern of success established by their grandfather and father.

Both these antecedents worked their way to success. Otto Olson, the grandfather, was the first apprentice toolmaker at Barber-Colman and worked for many years as plant superintendent at Roper Corp. Dean A. Olson, the father, had received an education, worked for Barber-Colman, been an ord-

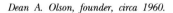

Dean A. Olson, founder, circa 1960.

Rockford Acromatic Products Co. is still at the original 611 Beacon Street location, which has grown from a 2,000- to a 55,000-square-foot facility since 1948.

nance officer in the South Pacific in World War II, and directed a tractor-manufacturing operation in a Korean auto factory during the U.S. occupation. After returning to Rockford, the younger Olson resumed his position at Barber-Colman.

Then came 1948. Rockford Acromatic, a general machining shop founded in the early 1930s, was in receivership. The two Olsons took it over. Their first big customers were John Deere and Caterpillar. For these and others, Rockford Acromatic did custom machining.

In the early 1950s the firm began the manufacture of automotive bearings, first in standard designs, then with designs and processes the company itself developed. It was the beginning of a 20-year period in which the organization became the dominant supplier of specialty automotive bearings, mostly universal joints.

By 1974 Rockford Acromatic was manufacturing 36 million units per year. "We were doing it all," Dean Olson says.

Since that time the company has followed the U.S. auto industry into front-wheel-drive technology. By the late 1980s the universal-joint manufacture had largely been supplanted by constant-speed automotive drive-line components.

In addition to its automotive

parts manufacture at the Loves Park plant, Rockford Acromatic is a dominant manufacturer of aviation-quality gearing, such as auxiliary gearboxes for flaps and power takeoffs.

This part of the company's business began with the 1968 purchase of the gear division of the Hupp Corp., once the maker of the Hupmobile car. Now a wholly owned subsidiary of Rockford Acromatic, this operation employs 400 people at a plant near Midway Airport in Chicago, and another 100 in Phoenix, Arizona.

Rockford Acromatic remains rooted in Rockford. Both Otto and the elder Dean Olson were active in civic affairs. Otto was a Mason for more than 50 years; by the time of his death in 1961 he had attained the 33rd degree. Dean was active in Boy Scouts all his life, eventually becoming a member of the national council. He was a founder of Junior Achievement in Rockford and was the founding president of Rock Valley College.

Dean Olson died in 1987. By then the company he and his father had established was doing $50 million per year in sales. And his sons are carrying on.

CARLSON ROOFING COMPANY

Carlson Roofing Company, which observed its centennial in 1988, began because its founder asked for five cents an hour more than the $1.25 per day he was already making.

Instead, the owner of the company offered to sell David Carlson the business. The 31-year-old roofing mechanic, who had come to the United States from Sweden eight years before, bought the firm and changed its name to the David Carlson Roofing Company.

The Carlson Roofing Company of 1988 has indeed come a long way. The largest commercial roofing company in the Rockford area, the operation has put roofs on such buildings as the Rockford Metro-Centre and the Winnebago County Public Safety Building and numerous other commercial and industrial buildings. The organization uses computers, synthetic materials, and other high-technology processes at every step in its roofing jobs, from the preliminary estimate to the regular follow-up inspec-

David Carlson, founder of the David Carlson Roofing Company, emigrated from Sweden in 1880.

tions.

But for all its growth and evolution, it is still Carlson Roofing. Larry Carlson, the company's president since 1982, is the great-grandson of the founder and part of an unbroken line of family leadership.

In the beginning David Carlson and four employees worked from Carlson's home at 622 South Fifth Street. The railroad ran nearby, hauling gravel, pitch, and other supplies of the time up to a barn near the house. From there the supplies were hauled by horse-drawn wagon to the work sites, which included the Palace Theatre, the city's vaudeville stage, and the Jarvis Inn Hotel in the 100 block of South Main Street. The latter job, completed in 1906, was done for 4.5 cents per square foot and, the original invoice solemnly proclaims, was guaranteed for five years.

David Carlson died at the age of 58 on March 14, 1915. His son, Edwin W., known as Bing, was 26 years old and working as a railroad clerk; at first he tried to sell the company, but took it over when he was only offered $500. His uncle, Alfred, who had been with the firm for 20 years, was his mentor, and they were joined by Bing's brother, Inar, in 1921.

The company built a warehouse at 2501 Charles Street in 1925 and the following year entered the residential roofing market. Though the warehouse was destroyed by the tornado that swept Rockford in 1928, the company prospered, putting roofs on more than 4,000 houses by 1941, as well as on both of Rockford's new high schools, East and West, and Washington Junior High

School in 1940.

By 1941 the firm had eight trucks and 56 workers. With the coming of World War II, it was chosen to put roofs on more than 500 new buildings at Camp Lewis in Macomb, as well as on buildings at Camp Grant near Rockford.

Edwin W. Carlson, Sr., died at age 66 on February 1, 1955, and

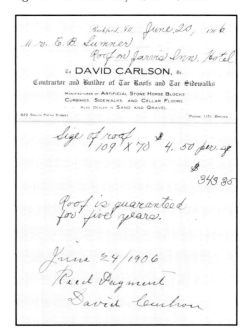

The original invoice for a roof installed on the Jarvis Inn Hotel, 110 South Main Street.

Inar succeeded him, running the business for 10 years. He was succeeded as head of the company by Bing's sons, David A. (1965-1978) and Edwin W. Jr. (1978-1982).

The year after Bing Carlson's death, the name of the operation was officially changed to Carlson Roofing Company. In 1961 it devoted itself exclusively to commercial and industrial roofing. Corporate offices were moved to their present location—828-21st Street—in 1971.

Edwin W. Carlson, Sr., was for many years active in the Rockford Park District Board, as was his son and namesake.

IDEAL UNIFORM SERVICE

The Great Depression was a time of ends and beginnings. For Raymond Maitzen (1890-1958), it was the end of a job as a dispatcher for a Chicago trucking company. And it was the beginning of what became Ideal Uniform Service.

The year was 1931. Maitzen, now among the legions of the unemployed, needed income to support his wife and two children. He bought a small industrial dry-cleaning route that covered Rockford and surrounding smaller towns. Each day he called at gas stations and garages to deliver and pick up dry cleaning. Each evening he would deliver overalls and coveralls he had picked up to Des Plaines—today an hour and a half away by tollway, but more than twice that in the days before U.S. 20 was built—and return to Rockford with the cleaning he'd left before.

Two events changed this pattern. Some smaller companies on Maitzen's route decided they wanted to rent clothes instead of buy them. And Maitzen decided it would be easier to wash clothes in the family basement instead of carting them all the way to Des Plaines.

Thus began Maitzen's first company, Ideal Overall. Raymond Mait-

Still a family business, Ideal Uniform Service, now at 5100-26th Avenue, employs 130 people that serve customers in four states.

zen handled pick-up and delivery, while his wife, Katharine, did the washing.

Ideal Overall grew steadily until World War II. With the war, however, came gasoline rationing and other shortages—including labor, with men who might have cleaned uniforms for Maitzen wearing them for Uncle Sam instead.

As during the Depression, Maitzen had to be resourceful. Gasoline rationing and the need to make do with old trucks sharply limited pick-up and delivery. Maitzen reduced his delivery area, served some accounts with steamer trunks carried by Railway Express, and imposed upon friends who happened to be going in the right direction.

Steady growth resumed after the war ended. With the building of new, better highways—culminating in the interstate highway system—Ideal Uniform expanded further, into adjoining states. The

firm added new buildings at its original plant, an old, 1,500-square-foot woodworking plant at 1608-13th Street. Around 1950 a new building was erected at 1404-21st Street, with additions being made over the years until both operations were merged at the present 65,000-square-foot location, 5100-26th Avenue.

Now, in the late 1980s, Ideal Uniform is still a family business, but it serves customers in four states, employs 130 people, and contributes more than $2 million in salaries to the Rockford economy.

Where once the Maitzens washed overalls in the basement, Ideal Uniform Service workers today use electronic sorting machinery. And they handle products ranging from industrial work uniforms, including clean-room garments, air-filter bags, and dust-control products, to dress slacks, shirts, and blazers.

The machinery has improved from 50-pound washers to 1,000-pound washers, and the productivity of pressing equipment has gone from 30 garments per hour per person to more than 900 per hour per person.

The original plant at 1608-13th Street. Mrs. Maitzen is on the right.

ESTWING MANUFACTURING CO.

Estwing Manufacturing Co. is a rare manufacturer, in Rockford or anywhere else: Its original product is still its mainstay.

That product is the finest hammer in the world. The Estwing one-piece solid steel hammer contains patented design elements that cannot be copied. Its design

Ernest O. Estwing obtained a patent in 1922 for a one-piece, all-steel hammer and founded Estwing Manufacturing Co. The hammer still is the firm's major product.

preempts dangerous loosening of the head, and its solid steel shank overcomes the weakness of wood handles and of the head-handle connection.

The one-piece, all-steel hammer design was patented in 1922 by a 38-year-old immigrant from Sweden who had learned to operate milling machines—and to speak English—in the plants of Rockford industrialist Levin Faust. A

year after getting the patent, Ernest O. Estwing founded the company that bears his name.

Estwing made his first hammers in his basement. Their two-dollar price, twice that of a top-quality wood-handled hammer, made sales growth slow at first, but an advertisement in a 1925 issue of *Carpenter Magazine* brought an excellent response. To meet the demand Estwing bought a plant on 18th Avenue and equipped it.

That plant was destroyed in the 1928 tornado that ravaged the city. Estwing acquired a plant on Eighth Street off Harrison Avenue. The firm has been at that location ever since.

Then came the Great Depression, but in the hard times that followed no married Estwing employee was laid off.

With the onset of World War II came other difficulties: The company had only one forge hammer, steel was hard to get, and many of the workers went to serve. But the firm carried on.

After the war the company added two forge hammers and continued to expand. The year 1946 also saw Norman Estwing, Ernest's son, come to work at the plant on a full-time basis; he had worked summers at the plant since age 14.

A few years later, he recalls, Norman got a taste of work in the plant. A forge worker had quit and another worker talked Norman into trying his hand. "The temperature was 95 degrees," Norman says. "That was the nitty-gritty."

Norman went on to do "every job in the plant" as the company continued its "steady growth, with some ups and downs." Ernest Estwing served on the Rockford school board and the City-County Planning Commission. Later in life he became a "rockhound," using a prospecting pick made by his com-

pany.

Ernest Estwing died in 1982, at the age of 97. Norman Estwing succeeded his father as head of the company, and growth has continued. The firm that had one forge hammer in World War II and three in the late 1940s now has 14. **The operation that began with**

Norman E. Estwing succeeded his father as president and still serves in that capacity. Under his leadership, the company has become one of five leading hammer manufacturers in the world.

one man making hammers in his basement now has 385 employees making 150 different tools in a 100,000-square-foot plant.

"Estwing Manufacturing Co. is today one of the five leading hammer manufacturers in the world," a company publication tells employees. "The pride and quality you put into your work here can just as easily be sold in Sydney, Australia, as in Chicago, Illinois."

UDL LABORATORIES, INC.

UDL Laboratories, Inc., headquartered at 1718 Northrock Court, is known by thousands of health care providers throughout the nation as a leading manufacturer, packager, marketer and supplier of multi-source and single-source generic pharmaceutical products predominately in unit-dose form.

Founded in December of 1980 with only three employees and thirteen products, the company has grown steadily over the past sixteen years. "Generics were just starting, so we decided to take a gamble," says Michael Reicher, President and co-founder of the Company. The gamble has paid off. "Anything not patented, we either make or distribute," Reicher says. Presently, there are 203 people working at the Rockford facility and an additional 127 employees at the Largo, Florida location.

UDL has developed its dominant role by being able to offer a wide range of products to the institutional market. At this time, approximately 450 line items are packaged at the Rockford facility including unit-dose oral solids and liquids, special-use packaging such as Emergi-Script, the most commonly dispensed generic pharmaceuticals, uniquely prepackaged in convenient 24 hour supplies for hospital use and

Sherri MacDonald, Sr. V.P. of Administration

Bingo Card, which is compliance packaging for nursing homes, as well as special-market products.

The Florida facility develops and manufacturers more than 80 liquid products for the institutional market. UDL is dedicated to the development of generic liquid products and currently has more than twenty in various stages of progression.

In virtually every health care delivery setting, providers are doing their best to maintain a delicate balance between quality of care and cost of delivery. UDL believes that helping to deliver value to both providers and patients is their first responsibility.

Reliable supply, reasonable costs and dependable service, along with convenience and personal attention, have become synonymous with the name UDL. It is this type of corporate philosophy that sets UDL apart from its competitors.

The success of any company is dependent upon many components, the most important being its people. UDL enjoys the benefits of a team of hard working, loyal employees who take great pride in their work, their company and their community.

Sally Claassen, V.P. of Manufacturing

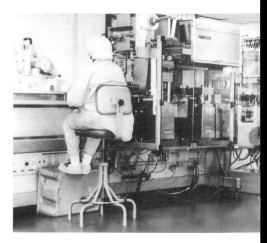

Sherri MacDonald joined UDL as an administrative assistant and is now Senior Vice President of Administration. Sally Claassen, Vice President of Manufacturing, started her career at UDL as a receptionist and studied for her degree at night. These Rockford success stories are prime examples of the employee work ethic and the company's policy of promoting from within.

In February of 1996, the country's leading independent drug manufacturer, Mylan Laboratories Inc. acquired UDL. Mylan and UDL are recognized in the industry for their integrity, quality products and personal service. The merger of these two companies provides UDL with the unique opportunity to continue its growth in the managed care marketplace as a subsidiary of a large, diversified pharmaceutical company.

ROCKFORD PARK DISTRICT

The mission of the Rockford Park District is to *"help people enjoy life"* by providing a quality park and recreation system, implemented in a responsive, efficient, creative, collaborative and flexible manner.

The Rockford Park District consistently strives to maintain a high

Aldeen Golf Club and Golf Practice Centre is the premiere golf experience in the Midwest. Industrialist Norris A. Aldeen generously donated his family farm to create this unique and challenging masterpiece.

level of citizen confidence and support, and has been awarded the National Recreation and Park Association's highest honor, The National Gold Medal for Excellence in Parks and Recreation Management, on two occasions (1989, 1995).

As determined by Illinois case law, the State's purpose in establishing park districts was to provide a

structure for local communities to establish and maintain public park and recreation systems that provide for the *health, welfare,* and *entertainment* of their citizens.

Founded in 1909, the Park District was essentially a land-only park system and performed this

stewardship role admirably. Land acquisition and facility development (golf courses, swimming pools, neighborhood parks, and picnic areas) were the focus.

Early in the 1950's, there were community leaders and citizens who felt it was not enough to have just outstanding parks, but had a shared vision to offer year round recreation programs and activities for all ages throughout the community. In April of 1956, the citizens of the Rockford Park District favorably supported a

referendum that would allow the District to begin providing tax-supported recreation programs and activities year round.

During the past forty years, there has been tremendous growth in recreation facilities, and with those facilities came new programs. Most all of the projects were created and developed through cooperative partnerships.

Today, the District offers about 750 different recreational programs, activities, and spectacular special events throughout the year, and operates 30 different recreational facilities. Over nine million visits to parks and recreation facilities by local residents, visitors and tourists occur each year.

Recreational opportunities are endless with 176 neighborhood parks, some of the finest, most affordable golf courses in the United States, and league play in every sport, for every ability and age level.

Families enjoy year-round ice skating and fair-weather water sports, miles and miles of bike and jogging paths, and some of the most imaginative playgrounds around.

The Rockford Park District has vital partnerships with approximately 350 community organizations and agencies (YMCA, YWCA, Boys & Girls Clubs, neighborhood community centers, both Harlem and Rockford School Districts, Ski Broncs, BMX Club, Pine Tree Pistol Club, Rockford Amateur Astronomers, festivals, etc.) to provide recreation services to the community in a comprehensive, holistic manner.

The Rockford Park District is governed by an elected five-member Board of Commissioners who serve six-year terms without compensation. It is the second largest municipal park system in Illinois, serving the communities of Rockford, Loves Park, Cherry Valley, and New Milford and adjacent unincorporated areas.

ADVANCED MACHINE & ENGINEERING COMPANY

Advanced Machine & Engineering Company represents the latest technology in design, engineering, and manufacturing of components for industry. The company also represents Willy Goellner's desire to successfully integrate his technical knowledge into a thriving company. Mr. Goellner holds several U.S. Patents and is the author of several technical articles. He was also instrumental in bringing the following companies to Rockford: Centro Inc., Fibro Inc., Hennig Inc., Krause GmbH, and A. Ott.

Goellner, born in Poland to German-speaking parents in 1931, was educated in Germany and received a mechanical engineering degree from the five-year Federal Technical College in Steyr, Austria, in 1954. After working in the machine tool industry in Germany, he came to the United States in 1958, landing his first job as a contract engineer in Chicago. He soon after came to Rockford to work for Ingersoll Milling Machine Co. His work there involved new special machine tools and associated research and development. In 1966 he formed his own company, which he began with $5000 in savings. Its first location was 1,000 square feet of space at 515 Loves Park Drive, Loves Park, Illinois. The firm moved to 2500 North Main Street two years later.

In 1980, Willy Goellner and partner Martha Roper, founded Advanced Boring Inc. (ABI) to do large boring and milling as a specialized contractor. ABI purchased machinery and equipment and rented space from another Rockford company, Martin Automatic Inc. ABI was merged with Advanced Machine & Engineering Company in 1984.

The company purchased its own 50,000 ft facility at 2500 Latham Street in 1985.

In 1993, a new air-conditioned manufacturing building was built to house the CNC Coordinate Measuring

AME Building 1 purchased in 1985 to house offices and manufacturing facilities

Machines (CMM's) and the large Boring Machines. Together, the new and existing facilities represent over 62,820 square feet. Each year, more state of the art equipment is added to keep the company competitive and profitable.

From the beginning, management has pursued the goal of providing total turnkey service for customers which means both custom manufacturing and distributing products manufactured by others. To the latter end, the company began acquiring manufacturing rights to product lines they had already been marketing. At the same time, the company concentrated on research and development of its own products, acquiring over 30 by 1995. New products are perpetually developed and introduced to ensure continued growth.

Through the efforts of Mr. Goellner and the rest of the team, AME has accomplished a great deal in

the 30 years since beginning as a one-man engineering firm. They have branched into contract manufacturing as well as developing a number of unique product lines of their own. Growth has been cultivated by maintaining AME as an innovative and flexible organization which has been able to survive even the most severe economic conditions.

Advanced Machine & Engineering Co. now employs 136 people in the Rockford area. The growth of the company is expected to continue. AME was given an award for being one of the top "Job Creators" in 1995 by the Rockford Area Chamber of Commerce, and Willy Goellner was nominated for Entrepreneur of the Year the same year.

AME Building 2 built in 1993 to house boring division and quality inspection services.

THE ROCKFORD REGISTER STAR

The Rockford Register Star, the city's only daily newspaper, continues a tradition that by the late 1980s dated back almost 150 years and had included 26 newspapers.

Rockford's first paper was the *Express,* founded by B.J. Gray on May 5, 1840, and lasting a year. The *Rockford Star,* founded in the autumn of 1840 and edited by Philander Knappen, lasted only slightly longer. Other newspapers came and went in the 1840s and 1850s, briefly riding the crest of political waves: Whig, Democrat, Free Soil, even spiritualism.

In February 1855 Elias C. Daugherty, a native of New York and not yet 30 years old, founded the *Rockford Register,* the first forerunner of the *Register Star.* The paper was not published in the years 1859 to 1873 and 1874 to 1877, but after its revival by Charles L. Miller and N.D. Wright, it grew and merged with other publications.

Another of the *Register Star's* precursors was the *Rockford Gazette,* founded in November 1866 by I.S. Hyatt as an advertiser and expanded into a semi-weekly by 1878 and a daily in August 1879.

The longest-lived Rockford newspaper name began with the appearance of the *Rockford Morning Star* on March 20, 1888. Its precursor, the *Winnebago Chief,* founded in 1866, was the first Rockford paper to propose a trolley car system and to publish statistics. The *Morning Star* embraced the Democratic party from its beginning, controversial in solidly Republican Rockford.

The *Register* and the *Gazette* merged to form the *Register-Gazette,* first published January 1, 1891. The owners of the new publication were Kalamazoo, Michigan, men: Edgar E. Bartlett, W.L. Eaton, and Eugene McSweeney.

Another Rockford daily arose in

The News Tower, an art deco building, is home to the Register Star.

April 1890, named for the political party whose tenets it put forth: *Republican.* Miller and two partners, Harry M. Johnson and John E. Warfield, purchased controlling interest in the paper and changed its name to the *Rockford Daily Republic.*

The three papers—*Daily Republic, Morning Star,* and *RegisterGazette*—carried on through the eventful first two decades of the twentieth century. In 1928 the *Daily Republic* and *Register-Gazette* merged, and two years later this company merged with the *Morning Star.* Rockford Consolidated Newspapers, Inc., published the *Morning Star* and the afternoon *Register-Republic.*

In 1932 the operation moved into an attractive art-deco building designed by Rockford architect Jesse Barlogga. The structure, the News Tower, stood at the east end of the State Street bridge over the Rock River, on land formerly occupied by the *Daily Republic's* production plant.

E. Kenneth Todd, a Rockford

newspaperman since 1923, became business manager of Rockford Consolidated Newspapers in 1933. In 1952 a company headed by him, Winnebago Newspapers, Inc., acquired both publications. Todd and his son, William K, ran them until they were purchased in 1967 by a nationwide newspaper chain that owned 30 daily newspapers: The Gannett Co., Inc.

The two newspapers became the morning and afternoon *Register Star* in January 1979; that October the *Register Star* became only a morning newspaper.

In the late 1990s *The Rockford Register Star* was one of 92 daily newspapers published by the Gannett Co. Inc., one of the largest news and information companies in the U.S. Gannett also publishes the internationally known newspaper, *USA TODAY.*

Production workers check the press before publication of the Register Star.

OSF SAINT ANTHONY MEDICAL CENTER

When The Sisters of the Third Order of St. Francis moved OSF Saint Anthony Medical Center to the East State Street corridor in the early 1960s, the only neighbors were farmers. Some businessmen questioned the wisdom of moving the hospital to such an isolated area.

Today, the 120-acre campus is surrounded by the hottest property in Rockford. OSF Saint Anthony is a Level I Trauma Center and a 254-bed tertiary care facility. Patients are drawn from a 10-county area for services including trauma, as well as the Regional Burn Unit, Regional Heart Institute, Illinois Neurosciences Institute, and strong service lines in orthopedics, neurosurgery and cardiac surgery.

The Sisters' healthcare network, The Sisters of the Third Order of Saint Francis, through its subsidiary, OSF HealthCare System, owns and operates healthcare facilities in three states. The corporation, based in Peoria, includes OSF St. Francis, Inc., OSF HealthPlans, and OSF Medical Group.

This large healthcare network had very humble beginnings. The Sisters' entire ministry, was founded on nothing more than faith, prayer and very hard work.

The Sisters came to the United States in 1875 to escape religious persecution in their native Germany. They initially took refuge in Iowa City, Iowa, and pledged themselves to

ABOVE: OSF Saint Anthony Medical Center is located in the heart of the bustling East State Street corridor.

RIGHT: The former Schmauss home was the site of the original hospital, located at East State and Summit streets, the site of the current Camelot Towers.

the care of the sick and poor.

Word of their good works spread, and soon the Sisters were opening hospitals in central Illinois. In 1899, five Sisters arrived in Rockford with little more than their deep faith and a desire to serve. They enlisted the aid of real estate agent William Crotty, who raised a public subscription of $12,000 to purchase the Schmauss home at the corner of East State and Summit streets. Crotty persuaded local merchants and civic leaders to donate furniture for the new hospital.

The German-speaking Sisters quickly learned Swedish to care for their new community. Their hospital grew, and in 1915 the Sisters opened a School of Nursing to supply a ready workforce. Today that school is an accredited College, which offers a bachelor of science in nursing degree.

In 1958, the Sisters saw the need to expand again. But instead of building on the old site, the corporate board voted to move to the current location. The new building opened in January 1963, and a $10 million expansion was completed in 1973. Construction has continued ever since.

The latest addition to the

complex, the Center for Cancer Care, was opened in 1995. The Center offers radiation therapy, including brachytherapy, a first for this region, chemotherapy, physician offices and support services to the patient in a unique, one-stop approach.

Innovative firsts for the Rockford area performed by the physicians affiliated with OSF Saint Anthony Medical Center include open-heart and

total hip replacement surgeries, innovative valve-replacement cardiac surgery, implantable cardiac defibrillators, pain-relief devices, and the use of Integra artificial skin for burn patients. The hospital has participated in numerous national and international research trials.

A teaching hospital, OSF Saint Anthony is affiliated with the UIC College of Medicine at Rockford, and is the site of a School of Medical Technology, as well as the Northern Illinois Mobile Intensive Care Program for paramedic training. CT scanning services, MRI, nuclear medicine, home care, lithotripsy, occupational health services, and the Center for Sports Medicine and Health Fitness are featured. A Cardiomyopathy Clinic is operated in conjunction with Rush University, Chicago.

OSF Saint Anthony Medical Center and The Sisters of the Third Order of St. Francis have come a long way from those humble beginnings 100 years ago. Despite the growth in size and technology, one constant remains. Tender, compassionate, quality care is offered to all in need, regardless of their ability to pay.

BARKER ROCKFORD COMPANY

"Pierce Barker Jr. represents the true entrepreneurial spirit on which Rockford was built," says Pierce Barker III of the man who founded Barker Rockford Company in 1956. Graduating in 1941 with a BS in Mechanical engineering from the University of Michigan gave him the knowledge and skills to work for Hudson Motor Car in Detroit during WW II. While in Detroit, he saw the value in the emerging new technology of *Fluid Power.*

A sales opportunity with a fluid power manufacturer brought him to Rockford in 1946. Designing and selling systems during the day and building his first house in the evenings consumed all of 1950 for Barker. Then, in the spring of 1956, he saw the opportunity to serve the Rockford marketplace and Barker Rockford Co. was born.

For the first several years the company specialized in the design and construction of hydraulic systems for local machine tool builders. The first hydraulic power unit was designed in the attic of his northeast Rockford home at night, built in the garage and sold to a local machine tool builder in the spring of 1957.

Four times business outgrew space and the company moved; finally to it's 52,000 sq. ft. present location at 29 Airport Drive in 1968.

Growth and success continue for Pierce Barker Jr. In 1977 he was named "*Illinois Small Businessman of the Year.*"

The *Systems Division* manufactures hydraulic power units for many different industries, including paper making, machine tools, automotive and snack foods. Outstanding accomplishments include power supplies for the Trans-Alaskan Pipeline, the B-1 bomber program and the Space Shuttle.

The Chicago based *HECO Division* designs and builds fluid power

test stands and ground support equipment for international markets, with customers as far away as China. They also participate in the Air Force F-16 and F-18 fighter test programs.

Forming a relationship in 1971 with Parker Fluid Power that continues to this day, the *Fluid Power Distribution Division* was born. This group specializes in the application of air and hydraulic fluid power and motion control systems. Several sales/application engineers on staff and many years of experience make the technical support unsurpassed in the area.

In 1980, with foresight and the ability to take an educated risk always his strong suit, Barker purchased a small company in Peoria Illinois, *Dove Equipment.* Nurturing and growing this business took many years. Today they are one of the largest finishing equipment distributors in the Midwest, with locations in Peoria, Chicago, Rockford, Quad Cities, Cedar Rapids and Des Moines Iowa; and the latest expansions in Monterey and Guadalajara, Mexico.

In 1984, Barker established the *Electronic Systems Division.* A completely separate sales and marketing staff brings computers, electronic systems and controls to the marketplace in this division. In 1989 ESD formed a distribution relationship with Siemens, an international leader in the electrical/electronic industry. This move brought the company into the electrical construction and control

Barker Rockford Company's office and factory building is located at the northwest corner of the Rockford Airport at 29 Airport Drive.

market.

In 1995 Barker again stepped out on his entrepreneurial spirit, forming a partnership with several other local "Best of The Best" distributors in Rockford. Further reducing cost, the new company "*iPower Distribution Group, LLC of Illinois/Wisconsin*" brings full EDI (Electronic Data Interchange) to their customers. With the ability to blend this group of distributors into a solid, cohesive team the growth continues.

"*We have a long and <u>undistinguished</u> list of failures... and a few great successes!*" he quips about his entrepreneurial history.

When asked about his accomplishments, Barker only nods with a gentle smile. "*A company is nothing more than it's people,*" he says, taking pride in being able to make family relationships work in business. Many parents and their children have formed strong alliances working at Barker Rockford Company.

The energetic Barker still headed the company into the late 1990's with his son serving as vice-president/sales; Ian Proudfoot, who joined Barker in 1957 as vice-president/administration; his son, Doug Proudfoot as ESD manager; son-in-law Steven C. Stutsman as vice-president/engineering.

HYDRO-LINE, INC.

HYDRO-LINE, Inc. was founded in 1946 by G.A. Markuson, G. J. Peterson, H. W. Johnson, and Ray O. Harding, four entrepreneurs who possessed little more than a dream and desire to succeed. During this same year, "ENIAC", the first computer or "electronic brain" as it was referred to at the time, was dedicated in Philadelphia; airplanes had not yet broken the sound barrier; the duplicating process of "Xerography"

HYDRO-LINE, INC. Headquarters, 4950 Marlin Drive, Rockford, Illinois

was invented; the Chicago Bears defeated New York in the NFL Championship and the 48 United States were rebuilding a war torn economy.

HYDRO-LINE continued to grow and eventually occupied a 6,000 square foot plant located at 711 - 19th Street in Rockford. By 1953, additional capacity was needed to accommodate anticipated future growth. As a result, a larger facility at 5600 Pike Road was acquired, which after five additions totaled 80,000 square feet.

A solid reputation for high quality products and services brought more growth and additional space was needed once again. Between 1965 and 1981 strategically located branch facilities in Michigan, New Jersey, California, and Alabama were established to service focused geographic areas. These plants increased HYDRO-LINE's marketshare and when Winnebago County issued $3.5 million of Industrial Building Revenue Bonds, a 143,000 square foot corporate headquarters was built on a 26-acre

site at 4950 Marlin Drive. Construction was completed on May 18, 1979, and the total transition completed in only three (3) days with minimal customer inconvenience.

The U.S. economy was strong and HYDRO-LINE's growth continued until the recession of 1981-82. Rockford was seriously affected by the recession as unemployment soared to over 20%. The machine tool, foundry and automotive industries, key industries to HYDRO-LINE's success, hit all-time lows. To assure continued customer service and to maintain a strong workforce, HYDRO-LINE responded with a decision to consolidate all branch facilities into the Marlin Drive location and use a three shift workforce when marketplace demand increased.

As the recession turned into an unprecedented economic recovery, HYDRO-LINE began to position itself for competition in a global economy. In 1984, HYDRO-LINE resumed its aggressive posture and acquired Sierra Engineering Company, a $2.1 million, welded cylinder manufacturing plant, in Reno, Nevada. This acquisition allowed HYDRO-LINE to serve customers in the western United States and western Canada.

Even though HYDRO-LINE was expanding its international presence, making the Rockford workforce the most highly skilled in the industry was a major goal. Due to this focus, Prairie State 2000 Authority (of Illinois) awarded HYDRO-LINE funds to train 173 people in high-tech manufacturing techniques, such as computer-controlled machinery, quality circles and materials-planning systems.

These investments attracted the attention of other firms within and outside of the fluid power industry and in 1989, HYDRO-LINE was

acquired by M-C Industries of Ann Arbor, Michigan. Along with the acquisition came additional resources for investment and expansion and in 1992, a manufacturing facility was established in Charlotte, North Carolina to serve the expanding needs of the southeastern United States. This same year, a joint venture with ENIDINE, Inc. was established to sell HYDRO-LINE products in Europe through Midland Pneumatic, Ltd., an ENIDINE subsidiary and leading manufacturer of stainless steel cylinders, valves, filters, regulators and lubricators, located in Wolverhampton, England.

The successful joint venture resulted in HYDRO-LINE being acquired by ENIDINE, Inc. of Orchard Park, New York in December 1993. Additional acquisitions to strengthen competitive positioning facilitated the formation of International Motion Control Incorporated (IMC) in 1994 as the parent company to four operating groups offering a complete range of motion control products. HYDRO-LINE and International Motion Control Ltd. (Midland Pneumatic) form the *Fluid Power Group*; Enidine, Inc. comprises the *Energy Absorption Vibration Isolation Group*; Dynact, the leader in electromechanical actuators forms the *Controls Group*; and the *Distribution Group* handles distribution of all motion control devices throughout the world.

By selling to end-use markets and utilizing sales agents and distributors, HYDRO-LINE continues to build on one of the most successful fluid power distribution networks in the world. Today, HYDRO-LINE, Inc. has about 300 employees worldwide, and is considered an expert in hydraulic and pneumatic applications for a broad spectrum of industrial applications. Always innovative and continually

responsive to changing market requirements, HYDRO-LINE is able to produce "engineered" as well as "standard" products with manufacturing flexibility that is unparalleled in the industry and keeps them in the forefront of fluid power actuation technology. HYDRO-LINE has achieved a significant worldwide penetration in the plastics machinery, machine tool, agriculture, amusement, rock crushing, and material handling industries.

Through the years, HYDRO-LINE accomplishments have been formally acknowledged by such companies as Boeing and Cross Sales Company. Boeing entered HYDRO-LINE into the APOLLO/SATURN V of Honor for the design, fabrication, and testing of a pneumatic cylinder used in the Saturn SIC ground support equipment for the 1969 APOLLO/SATURN trip that took three men to the moon and back; and Cross Sales awarded HYDRO-LINE its "Supplier of Excellence Award" in 1992 for outstanding delivery and service performance. Similarly, as we celebrate our 50th year of business and dedication to the Rockford area, the Mayor of the Village of Machesney Park proclaimed August 2, 1996 "HYDRO-LINE, Inc. Day" in recognition of providing employment for many Village residents and achieving many successes that include ISO-9001 certification and 50 years of growth in the Rockford community.

HYDRO-LINE's 50 year milestone bears testament to the dedication and perseverance of the entire HYDRO-LINE team. HYDRO-LINE is very appreciative of the support from the Rockford area and residents and looks forward to expanding the presence of Rockford, Illinois on the international map of success.

GREENLEE TEXTRON

"Enduring tools, enduring company."

The motto sums up the products and the history of Greenlee Textron, which began during the Civil War, making tools for the woodworking industry, and, 126 years later, was eminent for its tool manufacturing for the electrical industry, as well as for its distribution and training programs.

As a wholly owned subsidiary of Textron, Inc., Greenlee markets more than 5,000 tools and accessories for professional electricians, electrical contractors, electrical utility crews and electrical maintenance workers, including extensive lines of knockout punches, cable pullers, cable connectors and crimpers, fish tapes, conduit benders, hand tools, test instruments, and hydraulic operated tools.

Greenlee Textron has endured by changing with the times. Indeed, the company's beginnings were in change. Before the Civil War, Robert Lemuel and Ralph Stebbins Greenlee, identical twins with identical beards, had worked with their father to develop a barrel making machine for the Pennsylvania oil fields. But the demand there dwindled, so in 1862 the twins came to Chicago, where there was need not only for barrels, but also for buildings and sidewalks. The firm prospered. The 1871 Chicago fire was so ruinous for so many, but the rebuilding added to the brothers' prosperity.

The year 1874 was the company's first great milestone. That year the brothers developed the hollow chisel mortiser, which combined the cutting edge of a chisel with a boring bit. It literally used a round bit to cut square holes.

From this invention, and the

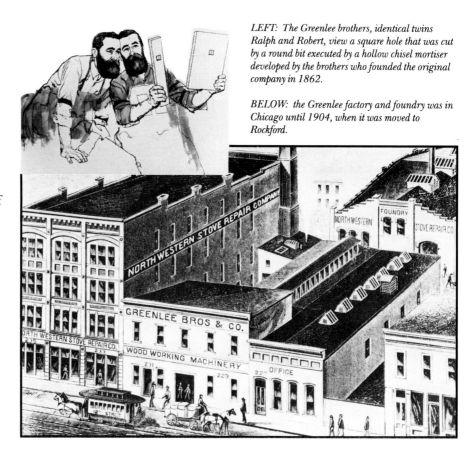

LEFT: The Greenlee brothers, identical twins Ralph and Robert, view a square hole that was cut by a round bit executed by a hollow chisel mortiser developed by the brothers who founded the original company in 1862.

BELOW: the Greenlee factory and foundry was in Chicago until 1904, when it was moved to Rockford.

capital it generated, came a long line of woodworking machines, ranging from a self-feeding rip saw to an entire self-contained railroad tie factory carried to the site in a freight car. Transfer machines the brothers developed were among the earliest of their kind, the antecedents of the huge automated transfer lines of today's heavy industry. The brothers' automated processes preceded even Henry Ford's mass production innovations.

The prosperity of Greenlee Bros. & Co. continued into the last decade of the nineteenth century. Then, in January 1897, a fire destroyed the company's Chicago plant. The factory and its foundry were rebuilt, but the decision had already been made to relocate the business. After many sites were considered, the firm moved in 1904 to Rockford, which had ample room for growth and railroad service

from the Illinois Central.

The opening of the Rockford plant began an expansion of the company's manufacture of auger bits, hollow chisels, and other quality small tools. With growing demand for both the machine tools made in Chicago and the smaller tools made in Rockford, the managers of Greenlee Bros. & Co. decided to create a separate operation, Greenlee Tool Company, solely for the small-tool portion of the business. This firm was established in 1927, with Robert's only son, William B. Greenlee, and George Carr Purdy in charge.

Purdy had seen that the future of the machine tool industry was in metal, not wood, and Greenlee Bros. had begun moving in this direction before World War I. After the war the company had developed new products for woodworking,

One of the company's early products was the hydraulic conduit and pipe bender (inset) shown here (left) being used by an employee.

such as the electric double-end tenoner, introduced in 1926. But then in 1928 came a line of metal hole punches for use by plumbers, construction workers, and electricians. They were the firm's first milestone in metalworking tools.

Early in 1930 the company began manufacture of a pipe and conduit bender, a self-contained hydraulic unit that bends up to three inch diameter pipe with up to 25 tons of ram pressure. In 1936 came a cable puller for electrical contractors.

Since then Greenlee Textron has continued to refine the products that established its eminence. The original metal hole punches are still in the firm's catalog, with two unique developments which split the slug in half for easy removal. The first pipe and conduit bender has evolved into the electric motor driven bender which combines updated bender technology with an on-board computer for figuring layouts for complex bends and assuring accurate repeat bends. The company's early success with wood boring bits gave rise to the line of wood bits which can bore through nails that would dull or break ordinary bits.

In 1969 Ex-Cell-O Corporation

acquired Greenlee Tool. Since then the innovations have continued: The company's central distribution center, opened in 1982, uses state-of-the-art computer technology for the storage and distribution of more than 5,000 stock items. And the technical and education center, opened in 1986, is the center for the most modern training the firm can give its distributors and contractors, as well as the home of the company's engineering and administrative sections.

As part of Ex-Cell-O Corporation, Greenlee Tool was acquired by

Greenlee Textron's technical and education center where the most modern training is provided for distributors and contractors. The building, opened in 1986, also houses the engineering and administrative sections.

Textron, Inc., in 1986. A year later the firm observed its 125th anniversary. Then in 1992, to expand its product offerings to the electrical utilities market, Greenlee Textron purchased Fairmont Hydraulics, a manufacturer of hydraulic powered tools, located in Fairmont, Minnesota. Manufacturing continues at that location today.

In mid-1996, Greenlee Textron expanded their global marketing reach and their growing product base with the acquisition of Klauke, a well established and respected German manufacturer of cable connectors and cable crimpers.

Under the leadership of president and chief executive officer Barclay Olson, Greenlee Textron takes pride in both its past and its future.

CENTURY 21 COUNTRY NORTH, INC. REALTORS

Jan Mansfield became a Realtor in 1973, and immediately enjoyed the challenges that this exciting career presented. Very young to be handling the most expensive purchase that most people will ever make— their home, and a woman in a man's world, she definitely had her work cut out for her. But work she did, achieving her GRI (Graduate of Realtors Institute) designation in her first year, and entering the coveted Million Dollar Circle in her first full year of sales(one of only 19,

Century 21 Country North, Inc. Realtors office at 7210 East State Street.

Jan Mansfield, President and CEO of Century 21 Country North Realtors in Rockford.

three of whom were women), in spite of an average sale price at that time in the $20s.

She started her company in 1977 and through three company name changes and histrionic industry changes, she hung on tight as the roller coaster of business and personal life, including divorce, merger, de-merger, recession, and dramatic company growth, on occasion left her a bit frayed around the edges. She fundamentally credits her success to a basic sense of fairness, a "Golden Rule" philosophy, and a true and unshakable

belief that the customer is always right.

Jan, a native of the Missouri "boot heel" and mother of two, had both of her children before she was 20 and remembers that they always felt as if the three of them grew up together. She relocated to Rockford in 1965 and has always been more than pleased about the choice of their new home. "Rockford has been very good to me," she reflects.

Though the original name, Country North Realtors, was chosen because of its "north of Rockford" location of the first office at 11607 Main Street, Roscoe, it no longer reflects the organization's present existence. The economic slump that hung like a pall over the Rockford area in the early 1980s brought an end to the literal truth of "Country North" when, amid the slump in the housing market, the Roscoe office was closed in August of 1982. In 1996, with five locations in four counties, they are, ironically, located south, east, and west of Rockford, with no office to the north.

The Rockford office, which opened originally in 1978 and has changed locations four times, moved in January, 1996, into the stately Century Plaza Building, 7210 East State Street, which Jan designed and built. It was built with customer

convenience and employee comfort in mind with a large comfortable reception area, spacious conference rooms, and a "kiddie" conference room complete with TV, VCR, and toys. The agents and staff enjoy the "fifties diner" break room, the communication center which they call "mission control", and the large meeting rooms and fully equipped health club in the lower level.

In 1991 the Byron office was opened and in 1995 an excavating accident caused the collapse of the historic limestone and stucco building it occupied. In 1996 the old building was demolished and replaced with a gorgeous new brick building, following the same format as Century Plaza.

In 1994, Century 21 Country North purchased Northwind Realty in Oregon, the county seat of Ogle County, and proceeded to purchase the prime corner in town, just across the street from the court house. To the delight of Oregon residents, they quickly converted the unsightly abandoned gas station into another office showplace, which boasts the same traditional flavor as the other office locations. Also, in

1994, Century 21 Country North expanded to Belvidere, and currently has plans for the construction of another new building for the Belvidere location.

In 1996, Century 21 Country North purchased one of the top real estate agencies in Freeport, Hersh Realtors, and has dramatic plans for expansion and growth in Stephenson County. "I really see an untapped market in Freeport," says Jan, "and we are thoroughly enjoying getting to know the local people. Everyone is really great, which is what we've found in every market into which we've ventured." They plan to build a new and similar home for the Freeport office in 1997.

If you're starting to see a pattern here, you're absolutely correct. Since serious Realtors spend more of their awake hours at work than they do at home, Jan believes that it's her responsibility to provide a very nice working environment for her agents and staff, as well as for their customers. Her personal

The "kiddie" conference room delights the young visitors to Century 21 Country North's office.

vision of the future of real estate, her bold flair in presentation, and her willingness to tread in unknown territories shows in every area of the organization.

As the real estate industry is changing dramatically and rapidly, Century 21 Country North is adjusting to what they believe the consumers want, value for their money and

the ultimate in convenience. They have created a "one stop shopping" environment that brings together in one location everything the customer needs to buy a new home or an investment property. The real estate agency, the lender, the attorney, the insurance agency, and the title company are in one convenient location, so the customers' needs can be handled from start to finish. In addition, there's a Commercial Department, an International Division (with 12 languages spoken and a dedicated Spanish telephone line), a Property Management Division, an Auction Division, a Land Development Department, and a New Construction Division. They also have a telex machine to receive calls from the hearing impaired, and a registered signer on staff.

Century 21 Country North is very "high energy" and they believe in the concept that the company that plays together stays together. They provide their own entertainment at award dinners with massive participation. Lovingly named the Mighty Mansfield Maniacs by their audiences, the word quickly spread and they have performed by invitation at national real estate conferences from Chicago to San

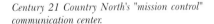

Century 21 Country North's "mission control" communication center.

Jan at work in her office.

Francisco. All audiences have enjoyed their impersonations, which have included Elvis, the Blues Brothers, Tina Turner, Willie Nelson, Julio Iglesias, Marilyn Monroe, Elton John, and Madonna, just to name a few.

Century 21 Country North is innovative and creative, with unusual marketing promotions and eye catching ads, including the use of their highly recognized zebra icon. They have been promoting their listings on television for years and were the first company in the Rockford area to put all their listings on the Internet.

"I believe that my job as the leader of the Company," says Jan, "is to anticipate change and to keep us ahead of our competition. In today's changing world," she continues, "technology is opening doors that only the brave of the real estate profession are walking

through, and contrary to our initial concerns, this evolutionary process is bringing us closer to our customers instead of moving us further from them. We are still caring and compassionate, yet far more professional and business oriented than ever before, building long term relationships and creating

customers for life."

The original five person Country North office in Roscoe has evolved through the years to become the largest and highest producing real estate company in

The receptionist is always available to greet customers.

the Greater Rockford Area, with over 20 staff members and over 150 sales associates. Century 21 Country North Realtors is consistently named in the top 250 real estate companies in the country by *National Relocation and Real Estate Magazine's* "Top Power Broker" report and ranks in the top five companies within the Century 21 system.

Jan was the 1993 President of the Rockford Area Association of Realtors, has served multiple terms on Century 21's National Brokers Communication Congress and National Advisory Board, and is a speaker at the national level on the topics of real estate management, agent recruitment, and fun in the work place. She was named "Today's Realtor" in the Large Broker category for 1996 by *Today's Realtor Magazine* which is published by the National Association of Realtors.

The plant filled foyer of Century Plaza has a homey feel.

At the local level, she was presented the Connie Tremulis Award for Business Owners at the YWCA Leader Luncheon in 1991, and in 1996 she was the inaugural winner of the Chamber of Commerce's "Top Woman Business

One of Century 21 Country North's unique "zebra" ads that contributes to their leadership in the field.

Owner Award". She has, also, been active on local civic committees and boards of directors, such as the Fourth of July Civic Committee, March of Dimes, Muscular Dystrophy Association, and New American Theater.

ECLIPSE, INC.

Eclipse, Inc., has evolved from a manufacturer of a single product—a rigid meter bar for mounting gas meters—made in one plant, to a widely diverse product line manufactured and marketed worldwide. Eclipse today is both different from and similar to the company that Garnet W. McKee founded in Chicago in 1908 and moved to Rockford two years later.

One link between yesterday and today is the company's commitment to heat processing of industrial products—a commitment that began when McKee, shortly after founding his company, published a book on the heat treatment of steel. Today Eclipse, through its many business units, continues to be a key manufacturer and supplier of high-quality industrial heat-processing equipment, heat exchangers, valves, controls, gas vaporizing and mixing equipment and related services for its many customers.

Garnet W. McKee, founder of Central Appliance Co. (now Eclipse, Inc.), obtained a patent for this rigid meter bar—his first commercial invention.

When the firm moved to Rockford in 1910 as part of the Eclipse Gas Stove Co., it occupied 2,000 square feet of space in Eclipse Gas Stove's facility at 711 South Main Street.

But the Eclipse of today is much more. The products and expertise that are offered in Rockford alone embrace much of the energy industry—natural gas, oil, and propane/air. Eclipse Combustion, a subsidiary of Eclipse, Inc., manufactures burners and burner systems used in incinerators, kilns, ovens, dryers, and furnaces.

Eclipse, however, has grown far beyond Rockford. They have added two domestic, wholly owned subsidiaries: Exothermics, Inc., Toledo,

The Eclipse RatioMatic burner for process air heating.

Ohio—a manufacturer of aluminum and stainless steel heat exchangers; and, Sam Dick Industries, Inc., Seattle, Washington—a manufacturer of propane gas standby systems.

Internationally, there are six Eclipse wholly owned subsidiaries — three in Canada, one in England, one in Spain, and another in Holland, with branch companies in France and Germany. In addition, Eclipse is also involved in joint ventures in Mexico, Australia, India, Taiwan, Korea and Hong Kong. The firm directly employs about 550 people worldwide (250 in Rockford) and has annual sales of approximately $85 million. Despite its worldwide presence and influence, Eclipse, Inc., remains a Rockford company. Its corporate headquarters and main plant are at 1665 Elmwood Road.

SUNDSTRAND CORPORATION

Left:
In 1926 the Rockford Milling Machine and Rockford Tool companies merged to form the Sundstrand Machine Tool Company, located at 11th Street and Harrison Avenue.

Right:
The Sundstrand Corporation world headquarters was constructed in 1987 and is located at 4949 Harrison Avenue.

Sundstrand Corporation, one of the eminent design and manufacturing concerns in the international aerospace and industrial markets, is Rockford's largest industrial employer.

Sundstrand's corporate headquarters and Aerospace Division are based in Rockford, with eight office and manufacturing facilities and 3,000 of the company's 10,000 employees worldwide.

The Aerospace Division product lines include electrical power generating systems, engine accessories, actuation and control systems, missile and space products, aircraft fans and blowers, auxiliary power units, turbo machinery, and torpedo propulsion systems. Virtually every commercial jet aircraft in the free world has Sundstrand-manufactured components.

The company that has become Rockford's most prominent aerospace and industrial business began in 1905 as the manufacturer of a small cutter chuck for the city's thriving furniture industry. Rockford Tool Company was founded by Levin Faust, Elmer Lutzboff, and Swan Anderson. That year the firm brought out two new products, which put it on solid footing.

Hugo Olson, a mutual friend of the three partners, joined the company about that time as financial adviser. He would become the first president of what became Sundstrand Corporation.

In 1909 the Rockford Milling Machine Co., owned by Oscar Sundstrand and his brother-in-law, Edwin Cedarleaf, opened in the same building as the Rockford Tool Company. Rockford Milling Machine moved to the corner of Harrison Avenue and 11th Street in 1911; the tool company moved across the street the following year.

Oscar Sundstrand's business launched a subsidiary, Sundstrand Adding Machine Co., to market a 10-key adding machine his brother David had invented in 1914. At Hugo Olson's suggestion, the Rockford Milling Machine and Rockford Tool companies merged to form the Sundstrand Machine Tool Company in 1926. Several months later Sundstrand sold the rights to its adding machine to Underwood-Elliot-Fisher, but continued manufacturing the machines until 1933 under the agreement.

In the early 1930s Sundstrand developed hydraulic machine tools that worked with greater precision. This led to the development of a fuel pump for oil burners on home furnaces, leading the way to automatic heat in the home and the company's recovery from the Great Depression.

In 1936 Sundstrand acquired the American Broach and Machine Company of Ann Arbor, Michigan.

Throughout the next three years the firm developed a hydraulically driven milling machine called a Rigidmill, an automatic stub lathe, and other new tools.

During World War II the company grew rapidly. From 1945 to 1946 it expanded its product lines, building on the hydraulic technologies applied in its machine tools. As a result of several years of research and development, the firm developed a new variable displacement hydraulic transmission for aircraft. The aviation division was formed to further develop these hydraulic systems. In 1946 this system, called a constant speed drive, was installed on the Air Force's B-36 bomber, to convert the variable speed of the aircraft's engine to a constant speed to drive an AC generator. In later years this product would launch Sundstrand into the markets and industries that made it the worldwide corporation it is today.

Hugh Olson died in 1949. His son, Bruce F. Olson, succeeded him and served as president of the company until 1968, when he was elected chairman of the board and chief executive officer, the position he held until his death in 1979.

By 1957 Sundstrand employed about 5,000 people at four plants and had annual sales of $77.5 million. Two years later the company became Sundstrand Corporation.

BERGSTROM INC.

Bergstrom Inc., an ISO-9001 registered designer and manufacturer of climate systems, finds itself today developing new technology for thermal management, and practicing integrated supply base management. While this sounds like pretty heavy stuff, and it is, Bergstrom's growth and success for nearly five decades is due to a very simple rule: Always Deliver to Your Customer State-of-the-Art "Quality Products and Services."

The company still makes HVAC units for trucks, buses, and off-highway vehicles, as it did in 1949 when the company was founded in Rockford, Illinois, by Adolph G. Bergstrom. These devices combine items as ordinary as a fan and as state of the art as complex integrated electronic circuits. Bergstrom's 325 employees produce products for customers that include, Caterpillar, heavy truck makers Kenworth, Peterbilt, Navistar, and Volvo, and school bus maker Thomas Bus.

Adolph G. Bergstrom's father, a Rockford fireman, had marked a

Bergstrom Inc. takes pride in its beautifully landscaped grounds at it s Rockford, Illinois facility.

path for his son by inventing a new design spark plug, the Fyrac, which resisted fouling. The younger Bergstrom acquired experience selling automobile heaters for the Burd Piston Ring Company in Rockford. The Burd car heater was

Bergstrom (Europe) Ltd. is located in a very nice business park in Sutton coldfield, United Kingdom

sold under the brand name Ha Dees. "The company motto was, 'Hotter 'n HaDees,'" recalls Elvin "Al" Rydell, who joined Bergstrom in March, 1951, and is now the company chairman.

Burd moved, and some of its former employees came to work for Bergstrom. Another who came aboard the first year was Victor Mandell, nephew of a Rockford-born world-champion lightweight boxer of the mid-1920's, a Navy veteran and former worker at a Rockford furniture factory. "There were three other people there," says Mandell, who was still with the company in the early 1990s. "We drilled and tapped the heaters, assembled 'em, packed 'em, and shipped 'em."

That first product was a cast aluminum hot water heater for trucks and school buses. From the beginning the product line began to expand to accommodate the widening customer base. But the original cast heater, with some modern touches, is still made by the company, Mandell observes.

Bergstrom's first home was in an alley behind the 300 block of East State Street, in one of Rockford's oldest retail areas. It quickly expanded into another building, and that building's address became the firm's -115 North Madison Street. The assembly room had formerly been used for horseshoeing, Al Rydell recalls.

Mandell recalls how Bergstrom was part of Rockford's teeming downtown life in its early days, with employees going to State and Madison for coffee, patronizing barbers and other businesses. "We'd be spraying, looking out the back window, and watch the bustle of the streets." The view then was of a downtown much different than today. Mandell also remembers the early closeness of the company, and of Adolph Bergstrom's shirtsleeves management style: "He always helped out. He wore a suit, but he got dirty." Adolph Bergstrom died in 1964. The following year the company branched into vehicle air conditioning, developing a combination heater-air conditioner unit for Kenworth, a truck maker, and

---

Bergstrom's state-of-the-art environmental chamber can simulate a wide variety of conditions including temperature, humidity, wind and solar load.

Victor Mandell (center) hired by A.G. Bergstrom (photo) in 1949, with Elvin Rydell (left), Chairman, and David Rydell (right), President. Victor retired in 1992 after forty three years of service to Bergstrom.

Caterpillar. The firm kept expanding and growing. It took over the former location of Rockford Illustrating, but by 1970 it needed still more space. The decision was made to build the Blackhawk Road plant and leave the downtown.

"I hated to leave downtown; there was a closeness there," Victor Mandell says. "The new plant was out in the sticks. But I was glad for the growth. And there was quite a change in downtown."

The new plant had 58,000 square feet of floor space at first. By 1978 another 40,000 square feet were added for fabrication and punch press areas. Formerly the company had had to "job out" some of its sheet metal fabricating, Mandell recalls. Thereafter it did all its own. Such was typical of the firm's growth and expansion. There have been other additions to the Blackhawk Road plant since, and currently it encompasses nearly 200,000 square feet. The factory is now segregated into five separate Business Units. Each with its own people, equipment, and processes necessary to serve their own specific customer.

Bergstrom has found that being a global supplier is absolutely necessary. Therefore, Bergstrom

(Europe) Ltd. was founded in 1990 in Birmingham, England. Today the company has 40,000 square feet, 45 employees, and serves many off-road customers such as Caterpillar, Massey Ferguson, New Holland, and JCB. By the mid-1990's Bergstrom was also actively pursuing a presence in Asia.

Dave Rydell, who joined the company in 1963 and has been its president since 1985, says Bergstrom's products remain "whatever the customer needs," the definition of those needs is in large part left to Bergstrom as their customers look to them as the "Climate System Experts"

Bergstrom Inc. remains privately owned. Both Al and Dave Rydell have been active in civic and charitable activities - Al in the Red Cross, Rotary, Protestant Community Services, and Swedish American Hospital, and Dave in the YMCA, Rotary, United Way, the Rockford Museum Center, the Center for Sight and Hearing Impaired, and Swedish American Hospital.

"I never thought it would grow that big," Victor Mandell says of Bergstrom. "It just keeps on growing." And he offers clues to the reason why: "There were good men there doing it. They knew the stuff, and they got the ol' power goin'."

As for him, "I was always just thrilled to work there."

THE INGERSOLL MILLING MACHINE COMPANY

In an age of miniaturization and microelectronics, in a city known for the manufacture of tiny screws and fasteners, The Ingersoll Milling Machine Company is distinguished, among other things, for the big scale of its products.

In the 1970s, for example, Ingersoll supplied the most extensive complete machining system ever for a customer in Europe to automate the production of diesel engines used in heavy trucks. At about the same time, a huge numerically controlled machining center was supplied for use in the construction of nuclear power plants. This was the biggest machine tool in the world, standing 60 feet high and weighing 600 tons.

The largest CNC machining center ever built, a gantry-type adjustable rail, was shipped in the early 1990s to Argentina. It housed a 33-foot diameter rotary table and could accommodate work pieces as large as 500 tons.

This bigness is not an end in itself; however, it is a by-product of Ingersoll's approach to a job, an attitude of taking a customer's problem and finding a complete, comprehensive solution to it.

Ingersoll is also distinguished for having uninterrupted work since 1887: It has carried on through depressions and recessions, without labor unrest, changing and broadening its products to adapt to the needs of the world marketplace.

Ingersoll in Rockford has over 2,000 employees and is comprised of The Ingersoll Milling Machine Company, at 707 Fulton Avenue and The Ingersoll Cutting Tool Company at 505 Fulton Street. There are affiliate organizations in Midland, Michigan (Ingersoll CM Systems) and in Germany (Ingersoll Maschinen und Werkzeuge GmbH, with four subsidiaries and over 2,000 employees).

Ingersoll's history, so bound up

The Ingersoll buildings in 1892.

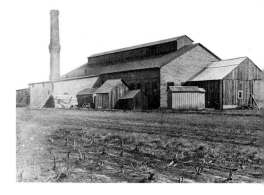

with Rockford, nonetheless did not begin here. Young Winthrop Ingersoll of Cleveland, Ohio wanted to play professional baseball, but his father, Judge Jonathan Ingersoll, did not agree. The father's solution was to purchase an interest in W.R. Eynon & Co., a local machine tool company. The year was 1887.

Winthrop eventually took over Eynon, and in 1891, with a loan of $29,000 from Rockford businessmen, moved the company there. "One of the prettiest places I have ever seen," Ingersoll explains. And they have the very best class of mechanics."

The first shop was 50 by 150 feet; the first payroll was for 19 employees. But Winthrop Ingersoll established his company's approach to a job—and to bigness—early. In 1903 he doubled the size of the company in a bid to win a large contract from General Electric Co. Ingersoll obtained the order, and by 1906 the firm had completed the largest milling machine of its time—157.5 tons—for GE.

The company grew on the crest of the boom in the automobile industry in the first 15 years of the twentieth century, and then on that of World War I production. By 1916 the firm had recorded its first million-dollar sales year, was adding an assembly shop, and was more than doubling the payroll, to 451.

In 1917 the company built $750,000 worth of machinery to build 50-caliber machine guns. By the end of the year there were almost 600 employees. One of those who joined that year was Robert M. Gaylord, who had married Ingersoll's daughter, Mildred.

Profits passed the million-dollar mark in 1918. The following year Winthrop Ingersoll, responding to the

urging of his employees, put in writing the policy that Ingersoll would conduct its operations in ways that labor unions would not be needed. It has remained so to this day.

The company weathered the post war slump and grew steadily through the 1920s, developing continuous milling machines for engine blocks in the automobile industry and other equipment used in the manufacture of locomotives. In 1924 Ingersoll built the first transfer line for the automatic machining of engine blocks in the U.S. In 1928 Winthrop Ingersoll died, and Robert Gaylord succeeded him. Despite

Ingersoll Rockford headquarters today.

the death of its head, the company stood on the threshold of more growth in 1929.

But then came the Great Depression. The firm struggled from 1931 to 1936, and the financial situation was grave. As prosperity began to return in the late 1930s, the company purchased the Schuman Piano plant, built a new assembly shop, and added office and garage space.

The Ingersoll Milling Machine Company joined the massive gearing up of war production that was the United States' response to World War II. The company built a 175-ton, swivel head boring machine to cut and machine armor plate for naval vessels. It was so effective that the Navy honored Ingersoll with the prestigious "E" Award. The firm also built large-scale machinery used in the manufacture of reduction gear drive cases for battleships, hulls and turrets for battle tanks, torpedo tubes and

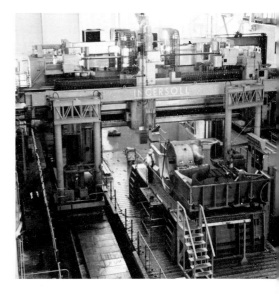

In 1969 Ingersoll completed two of the world's largest machine tools for General Electric Company to help produce turbine generator sets for electric power utilities. Two freight trains could pass each other between the vertical columns of each machine.

antiaircraft gun mounts. It also pioneered the development of carbide cutting tools. By 1942 sales had risen to $11.5 million, and the work force to 1,200.

Sales and production slumped briefly after World War II ended, but had picked up by the 1950s. That decade the company added many new buildings for assembly, office and engineering space, storage, the manufacture of cutting tools, and fabrication.

And the tasks Ingersoll undertook grew. In 1953 the company built the largest milling machine in the world for installation in its own plant. The machine measured 133 feet long and weighed 500 tons. By the late 1950s several more of these "giants" were added to the plant, making Ingersoll's Rockford facility one of the most modern and productive big machining shops in the world.

Ingersoll's customer base expanded into the growing aluminum industry, and into the manufacture of diesel engines for locomotives in the 1950s. The company sold to customers in India, Australia, the Soviet Union, and France, among others.

The 1960s began with projects to build two large transfer lines for an Opel automobile plant in West Germany. The order heralded the massive growth of the foreign customer base in the 1960s. Ingersoll joined with the West German company Waldrich Siegen to build a cutting tool plant in West Germany, and in 1966 a similar venture led to construction of a plant in England.

That decade Ingersoll also led the way in new technology, developing and

building electrical discharge machining (EDM) and numerical control (N/C) equipment.

By 1970 annual sales totaled $37 million, and Ingersoll was ranked 15th in size among 250 U.S. metal cutting tool manufacturers. The firm's acquisition of H.A. Waldrich of Siegen, West Germany, and later Waldrich Coburg in Germany marked even further growth and firmly established the company as a dominant international builder of machine tools and complete manufacturing systems.

In the 1980s Ingersoll joined in partnership arrangements with Boeing, General Motors and others to provide large manufacturing systems for major aircraft components and powertrains for the automobile industry.

In 1996 Ingersoll introduced High Velocity machines which are rapidly transforming the manufacturing process to provide agility and flexibility for many manufactured parts throughout the world. These machines are being shipped to Europe and Asia, as well as Ingersoll's customers in the Americas.

Today, with worldwide employment of more than 4,000 workers and annual shipments of over $500 million, Ingersoll ranks among the top handful of special machine builders in the world.

HOMEBANC

Swedish Building & Loan Association was formed in 1889 with assets at the end of the first year of $21,665. After years of community service as Home Federal Savings and Loan Association, headquarters of the institution now known as HomeBanc is just a few blocks away from the original location on East State Street and assets have grown to $338 million.

One of the first homes financed by the Association with a $1,100 loan in 1889 still stands at 518 Union Street as a tangible link in the unbroken chain of community service to generations of HomeBanc customers. "You saved our home," was a testimonial expressed many times over the years as the Swedish Building & Loan successfully weathered the Depressions of 1893, 1897, 1907, 1914, and the Great Depression of the 1930's. The operation suspended all payments of principal and "encouraged people to stay in place and pay what they could." Loan customers kept paying interest to indicate their intention. By its 50th anniversary in 1939 the Association has financed over 3,000 homes and had assets of $1,792,188.

Within three years the United States was in World War II and association members were among the mass of men joining the military. The Association responded as it had during the Depression, holding the soldier's loans in abeyance. By January 1945, the Association also had purchased $735,000 in war bonds. The Association had stood sturdily and assets totaled $2,345,114.

Growth into the Eisenhower era was modest reaching $7 million by 1959. That year the transition from a state to federal-chartered institution began under

HomeBanc at its current location, 1107 East State Street

Raymond E. Reimer's guidance. The 1960's laid the groundwork for the 1970's expansions with mergers and branch office openings. By his retirement in 1981, accounts were insured, today's headquarters at 1107 E. State Street was constructed, a federal charter was granted, and assets reached nearly $200 million.

Steve Sjogren, who joined Home Federal as a loan officer in 1972, assumed leadership and the bank continued to grow despite Rockford's economic difficulties in the early 1980s. Subsequent mergers expanded the bank's service area from Rockford to Freeport, Dixon, Loves Park and Cherry Valley.

On June 22, 1990, Home Federal Savings converted from mutual to stock charter becoming HomeBanc, a federal savings bank providing a wide variety of consumer financial services at its headquarters and nine other offices and a network of automated teller machines. HomeBanc's diverse services include savings, checking and money market accounts; traditional, first mortgage and home equity loans; consumer, commercial and construction lending; real estate development, and financial brokerage services. As President, Sjogren states, "In the tradition of meeting our customers needs, we try to do 1,000 things just one per cent better."

A&B FREIGHT LINE, INC.

"There was no big breakthrough that made us jump right up," Fredrick "Fritts" Blume says of his company, A&B Freight Lines, Inc. "It took quite a few breaks to get us where we are today."

Where the firm is today is at 4805 Sandy Hollow Road, a sprawling truck yard and building complex with 38 freight doors, garage space for all 60 truck tractors in the company's fleet, and room for most if not all of its 250 trailers.

It is a long jump indeed from the one tractor and two straight-unit trucks with which Fritts' brother, Alvin Blume, began in 1955, operating in a building in Loves Park, across North Second Street from the garage the brothers' father, Homer, had founded in the 1930s.

"Al" Blume and Fritts, who joined him as a partner, improvised. Their first loading dock was a 50-foot flatbed. "We had a little problem with snow and rain," Fritts Blume recalls, laughing.

They were at that location for roughly a year. Then the brothers and their company of four moved to a location on Falund Street,

A&B Freight Line has grown steadily over the years since its founding in 1955.

A&B Freight Line is at 4805 Sandy Hollow Road, with 38 truck doors and room for most of its 250 tractors at the sprawling terminal yard.

which today is at the foot of the Manley Melin Bridge across the Rock River. That building had housed a rendering plant, Fritts Blume recalls, and the "massive" remodeling job the brothers had to do included blasting down a 50-foot chimney.

But A&B contracted to haul for a Chicago company, K&R Delivery, and thereby did all the hauling for three big retailers: Montgomery Ward, Spiegel, and Alden's. And the firm's clientele grew from there.

A&B moved to Sandy Hollow

Road in 1979. Three years later Al Blume passed away, and the company passed to Fritts. He is pleased to note that his children will one day assume control of the business.

By the late 1980s the company offered direct service to over 419 points in Illinois, plus many more throughout Iowa and Southern Wisconsin. Through its brokerage operation and other partnership, the company serves all the Midwest.

Fritts Blume credits much of the venture's success to his parents, Homer and Marie, both for the brothers' upbringing and their company's start: "They really got things going," he says.

But what of the name? According to Fritts Blume, his brother did not start the company, but took it over from two Belvidere men whose names, Atkinson and Brown, are enshrined in the initials.

PIERCE CHEMICAL COMPANY

When Dr. Alan Pierce founded Pierce Chemical Company in 1948 as the first commercial producer of Ninhydrin—a chemical used in amino acid (protein) analysis—it consisted of a collection of small wooden buildings and a staff of two.

Did he imagine that within 40 years it would expand to become a large, modern, 85,000-square-foot complex with 150 employees and worldwide distribution? The successes he experienced almost from the beginning were a good clue.

In 1951, three years after the

Pierce Chemical Company, at 3747 North Meridian Road, is a leading supplier of high-purity, research-grade chemicals to the biotechnology industry.

establishment of Pierce Chemical Company, annual sales totaled $7,740.35, with a good portion of the revenue still generated from the sale of Ninhydrin. By 1960, with annual sales of more than $100,000, Dr. Pierce made the decision to incorporate. Pierce Chemical Company then had a staff of seven, including Dr. Pierce, president and treasurer; his wife, Barbara, vice-president; Roy Oliver, vice-president; and Darlene Anderson, secretary.

In 1960 Roy Oliver became the company president. In an effort to search out international sales opportunities and markets, he traveled to

Europe in 1961. Contacts he made there resulted in a joint venture four years later with Koch-Light Laboratories, an English company that manufactured biochemicals.

That same year Pierce Chemical Company became Pierce Organics, although the original name was retained for the joint-venture relationship with Koch-Light. (By 1970, however, Pierce had gained total ownership of the joint venture.)

Pierce Organics had gained a foothold in a new market in the mid 1960s—aromatic fluorine compounds and organic silicon compounds used for electronics, chromatography, and specialty chemicals. Then, again in 1965, Pierce Organics added another product, Tri-Sil, a chemical used in gas chromatography (a process that separates and identifies chemical and biochemical compounds). This was the firm's entry into the area of formulated reagents—a field in which it would later become widely known.

During this growth period the Pierce facilities had also expanded. A building that housed offices and shipping facilities was erected in 1963. Within three years an upper floor was added to this building, along with a two-story production laboratory.

The year 1969 marked the first

million-dollar year for Pierce Organics, and it was also a landmark year for Pierce in terms of international sales growth. For that was the year Pierce became involved in another joint venture with Hicol, b.v. The sales company formed with this Rotterdam, Holland, chemical supplier was named Pierce Eurochemie, b.v.

International expansion continued when four years later, Pierce Organics was instrumental in the formation of Pierce and Warriner (U.K) Ltd. This Chester, England, company joined with Pierce to promote and distribute Pierce products in the United Kingdom.

As the 1960s came to a close, Pierce Organics had established itself in both the British and European markets. Still, the 1970s were to see a number of significant changes for Pierce Organics.

The first occurred in 1971, as the last of the many original small wooden buildings was demolished. Then, in 1975, Pierce reverted to its former name, Pierce Chemical Company. At the same time both Hicol, b.v., and Pierce Eurochemie, b.v., were brought under a single corporate umbrella. Pierce Eurochemie, b.v., later became Pierce Europe, b.v., which acted as Pierce's European distribution and stocking center until replaced by a network of European distributors in 1995. Hicol, b.v., until the end of its corporate existence, about 1990, served as the European sales and service center for Perstorp Analytical, the Perstorp business group to which Pierce belonged at that time.

As the mid-1970s approached, Pierce Chemical Company saw increasing opportunities in supplying products to researchers involved in the high-tech area of biotechnology. It was during this time that Pierce began its move away from manufacturing bulk chemical products —and

Founded in 1948 with a staff of two, Pierce Chemical Company has grown to 150 employees providing worldwide distribution of products used for immunology and biochemical research.

toward the production of high-purity reagents for biotechnology research.

In 1980 Roy Oliver, the driving force behind Pierce's overseas and domestic expansions, retired as president of Pierce Chemical. By this time sales of Pierce products to overseas markets accounted for approximately 40 percent of total shipments. Pierce had become a profitable company with a reputation for supplying innovative products of the highest purity to the scientific research community.

In 1983 Pierce, which had been owned largely by its employees, was acquired by Perstorp, AB, a Swedish holding company with annual sales of two billion dollars. Perstorp's Swedish management style, emphasizing continuity and a "family" work environment, meshed well with the similar management style Pierce had known for years.

With the full support of Perstorp, Pierce Chemical now had the resources necessary to more vigorously pursue opportunities in the competitive biotechnology industry. Robb Anderson, president of Pierce since December 1980, worked hard to guide the firm toward these goals. And many significant events have occurred since the mid-1980s, all designed to enhance Pierce's abilities to meet the needs of researchers in

this high-tech industry.

The first was in 1986, when an 8,000-square-foot wing was added to the main Pierce building to house the growing marketing, customer service, and international sales departments. Then, in 1988, a 10,000-square-foot research and development center was completed. Both expansions increased Pierce's abilities to hire people and purchase the necessary technologies to gain a strong position in the biotechnology markets.

In 1988 alone 30 employees were hired. Most came to Pierce with vast experience and expertise in research technologies. This allowed Pierce to further develop new products on target with the biotechnology strategy. It has been these additions, along with the experience and dedication of veteran Pierce employees that allowed Pierce to introduce almost 300 new products in January 1989. Most of these introductions were in the area of high-purity antibody products for immunochemical research techniques.

And it has been the continued support of its parent company, Perstorp, that has allowed Pierce to become a leading supplier of high-purity, research-grade chemicals to the immunology and biotechnology markets.

Although Pierce has become an international force, it has managed to maintain its small-town ties through community involvement. The firm is

a member of the chamber of commerce and the Council of 100, which guides Rockford's economic development. In addition, Pierce works closely with the University of Illinois School of Medicine, Rockford, in the field of immunology. And the company endows five research grants and awards each year, including the E. Melvin Gindler Award, given at

Robb Anderson, president (left), and Dr. Alan Pierce, founder (right).

Rockford College.

One of the largest contributions Pierce makes to Rockford is the creation of jobs and the flow of revenue into the area. Virtually no Pierce revenues are taken directly from the community—all sales are generated outside of Rockford. Still Pierce pumps money back into the city by way of the taxes it pays and the dollars spent in the Rockford area by the company and its employees.

Pierce attained ISO9001 certification of its Quality Systems in August, 1994. Pierce plans for the future are very aggressive, and include major technology transfer acquisitions, the introduction of unique new products for the biotechnology research industry, and custom production of biochemicals.

There looks to be a very bright future for Pierce Chemical Company—and for Rockford.

CAMCAR DIVISION OF TEXTRON INC.

Camcar Division of Textron Inc. is both a part of and apart from Rockford's fastener industry. Its three founders came up through that industry. But the company began with the goal of performing a job the industry said could not be done.

The year was 1943. The job was to manufacture, by the cold heading process, a particular type of threaded electrical terminal needed for military airplanes in World War II. The three people were Robert H. Campbell, a fastener salesman based in Chicago; Ray H. Carlson, who had started in the industry as a header machine operator 10 years previously; and Eugene H. Aspling, who had worked in the tool room of the same Rockford company that employed Carlson.

The three pooled their knowledge of cold heading—shaping fasteners with impact instead of forming them by heating—and decided to go against the conventional wisdom of the industry. They acquired a 40-year-old header machine and set up shop in one corner of a building on Broadway Court. The founding date was August 1, 1943; Campbell was president, Carlson vice-president and general manager, and Aspling secretary and general superintendent.

The three successfully manufactured the terminal, and Camcar has built upon this success ever since. Over a half-century later Camcar—the name combines the first syllables of Campbell and Carlson—is a leading producer of custom-engineered components and fasteners for the automotive, business equipment, electronics, railroad, appliance, and truck-trailer industries. It employs over 3,200 people in 13 plants in six states, Canada and Malaysia. Camcar's customers range from Harley Davidson to IBM to General Electric to General Motors.

Camcar's founders, Ray H. Carlson, Eugene H. Aspling, and Robert H. Campbell, in front of the company's original building.

James R. MacGilvray, current President of Camcar Textron.

Products and processes developed by the firm have revolutionized the fastener industry, and are licensed for use worldwide.

Growth was occasionally precarious, but always steady. Campbell once recalled how the company had to ask for early payment from customers and how the three founders used personal belongings as collateral to raise operating cash. But the firm prospered in the manufacturing boom of the World War II years, and, because Campbell, Carlson, and Aspling planned for the transition to a civilian economy—automotive and appliance products—Camcar's growth continued after the war ended. By the end of 1946 the company had outgrown its original plant. That December it moved to the facility that is still its main plant and corporate headquarters, 600-18th Avenue.

That plant was doubled in size in 1948, and additions were built in 1950 and 1951. A second plant, now the firm's Taptite Products plant, was begun in 1950, and the company's SEMS Products plant at 1818 Christina Street was established in 1953. Plants number 3 and number 4 were added on 18th Avenue in 1957.

The firm became a division of

Textron Corp. in 1955. Textron originally began as a manufacturer of products for the textile industry, but its founder, Royal Little, was one of the early builders of the diverse conglomerates that today dominate the corporate economy of the United States and the world.

With larger capital resources thus available, Camcar was poised for new growth. By that year the company employed approximately 300 people. Camcar's products were innovative, but with two introductions the firm and Carlson went beyond innovation to transform the industry with the Raycarl Process.

The first introduction was the Raycarl Process. This new process of extruding and heading cold-formed products was, one industry magazine said, the first significant breakthrough in cold forming in 50 years. As a direct result of this innovation, the entire industry was able to overcome previous limitations on the size and configuration of cold formed fasteners, and to operate more efficiently. Camcar began licensing the use of the Raycarl

High-tech manufacturing equipment improves productivity and reduces costs.

Process industrywide in 1963, and thus established itself as one of the industry's leaders. Today the Raycarl Process is used worldwide.

The second introduction was the TORX Drive System in 1972. This drive uses a hex-lobular recess for driving fasteners. The design puts less concentrated strain on both tool and fastener, resulting in longer life and lower cost. Developed by Bernard Reiland and patented by Camcar, TORX Drive fasteners are used throughout the world's automobile industry, as well as in consumer products.

The company also developed a new process for heading titanium, and was the first to manufacture a

fastener that withstood pressures of 245,000 pounds per square inch, and manufactured more than 600 different parts for the engines that launched mankind's first trip to the moon.

Campbell retired in 1967 and Carlson succeeded him as president. The growth continued. By the mid-1980s, 125 domestic and foreign companies were manufacturing TORX Drive products under license. General Motors was using 341 separate part numbers based on the TORX system, and in one year more than one billion TORX fasteners were used in the auto industry. Today 50 percent of Camcar's production incorporates the TORX drive system. The firm currently holds more than 75 foreign and 37 United States patents.

Carlson retired in 1979. Only 16 days later, he died. The company and the industry mourned and paid tribute.

Carlson's successor as president was Robert C. Sellin, who had been one of two vice-presidents during Carlson's presidency. Sellin led the firm until November 1986, followed by Bob Rothkopf.

Rothkopf resigned in 1989 and was replaced by James R. MacGilvray, who continues to lead Camcar as they approach the 21st century. Under the leadership of MacGilvray, Camcar has grown significantly in the global marketplace, with a new manufacturing facility in Malaysia and the development of the TORX PLUS Drive System. Since 1990, sales have increased approximately 70%. Camcar's success can be attributed to a company-wide commitment to developing innovative processes, materials and products. As part of the Textron Fastening Systems group, Camcar will continue to be a world leader in the fastener industry.

Innovative products and processes have allowed Camcar to solve assembly line problems for customers in a variety of industries.

SWEDISHAMERICAN HOSPITAL

Nothing better summarizes the history of SwedishAmerican Hospital than its name.

By the early part of the twentieth century, Rockford had become heavily populated with immigrants from Sweden, most of whom came here to work in the furniture industry. Most settled along Seventh Street between State Street and Broadway, and in the businesses and churches of that area, Swedish was spoken at least as much as English.

One Swedish immigrant, O.F. Nilsson, wrote a letter to the editor of *Swenska Posten*, a popular periodical, challenging the Rockford Swedish community to establish a Swedish hospital. He enclosed one dollar to start a fund. Responses flooded in, and by 1911 enough money was deposited in the Swedish American National Bank (now Amcore Bank) to buy land in the 1400 block of Charles Street. A 55-bed hospital opened on the site in 1918.

From the beginning the hospital has grown in size and broadened in its range of services to respond to the needs of the Swedish community of both Rockford and the surrounding area as a whole. The hospital's first board of medical staff included a

The surgical area of SwedishAmerican Hospital in the 1950s.

A dollar and a challenge from a Swedish immigrant in 1911 started the fund that created the first SwedishAmerican Hospital.

chief of surgical service, consulting surgeons, associate surgeons, and an eye, nose, and throat specialist. A School of Nursing was established in 1919, with a class of five.

But the Swedish identity was preserved, chiefly through the formation in the early 1920s of the Jenny Lind Ladies Auxiliary. In the early 1920s, with the hospital's entire annual electric bill totaling about $1,300 and its entire annual income about $55,000, the hospital suffered one annual loss of $17,000. But the Jenny Lind Ladies Auxiliary, working with

the board of trustees and the Swedish churches, raised enough money to begin work on expansion of the hospital in the early 1930s.

The first of the institution's major expansions, an addition with 75 beds on the east side of the original building, was completed in 1953. Ten years later an imposing 10-story tower was added, and the hospital's capacity was increased to 330.

By the late 1980s the hospital's capacity had increased to 427; the hospital complex had grown to fill almost the entire area bordered by State, Ninth, Charles, and 11th streets; and SwedishAmerican's comprehensive health care program embraced all the types of care the public had come to expect, including cardiology, maternity, pediatrics, and cancer treatment. Many of the programs were pioneered at SwedishAmerican.

The hospital is particularly proud of its Center for Cardiovascular Medicine. The very latest in advanced technologies are in a constant process of evolution and successful state-of-the-art methods of treatment are being employed on an on-going basis. SwedishAmerican was among the first to offer coronary angioplasty. Today, treatment methods run the full gamut—from new clot-dissolving

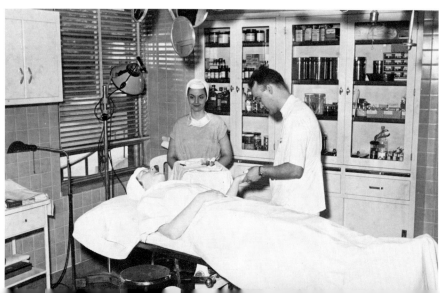

The hospital's addition after completion in 1953

drug therapies to by-pass surgery to laser surgery.

By the late 1980's Swedish-American's Family BirthPlace offered expecting families a full range of options that make the birth of their child a special experience. To help families prepare, SwedishAmerican sponsors educational classes on early pregnancy, prenatal care, Lamaze-type training, pre and postnatal exercise, parenting, infant and child CPR, and first aid. SwedishAmerican is the University of Illinois College of Medicine at Rockford's site for obstetrical teaching services.

Pediatric care began with a separate ward for children whose illnesses required a hospital stay. By the late 1980's SwedishAmerican's pediatric program included an intensive care unit for critically ill children, the first in Illinois. There is also CuddleCare, day care for sick children who do not require hospital care but whose working parents cannot miss work time to stay home with them. In 1988 the pediatrics unit underwent a major renovation. Through regional outreach programs affiliated with the University Child Health Services the pediatric team of physicians is able to respond to patients with complicated and often

uncommon illnesses.

Cancer care began with surgery to remove tumors. Medical understanding of the disease has widened the response to include radiation, chemotherapy, and other therapies. The Regional Cancer Center at SwedishAmerican offers services for cancer prevention, early detection, treatment and supportive follow-up of patients and care-givers. Follow-up services include supervised home healthcare, as well as I CAN COPE, CAN SURMOUNT, LIVING WITH CANCER, US TOO and COPING WITH LOSS support groups.

SwedishAmerican's commitment to medical education and involvement with other community agencies is reflected in its expanded partnership with the University of Illinois College of Medicine at Rockford by

relocating the Residency Program and Office of Family Practice on the SwedishAmerican campus in 1996.

The hospital has also been a pioneer in hospital administration and management. In 1980 it established the SwedishAmerican Medical Foundation, and two years later reorganized under the Swedish-American Corporation. With this organizational structure the hospital has expanded its range of services through the establishment of subsidiaries to include physician offices, an insurance company and Swedish-American Home HealthCare.

In the early 1990's, Swedish-American Hospital was a two-time national award winner in the Rochester Institute of Technology/USA Today Quality Cup competition. In 1995, the Joint Commission on Accreditation of Health Care Organizations awarded accreditation with commendation to SwedishAmerican Hospital, making it the only provider of its type in Rockford to earn this select achievement. These initiatives mark the ways that SwedishAmerican has evolved from a small community hospital to a major regional medical center.

The cardiology team performing surgery at SwedishAmerican Hospital.

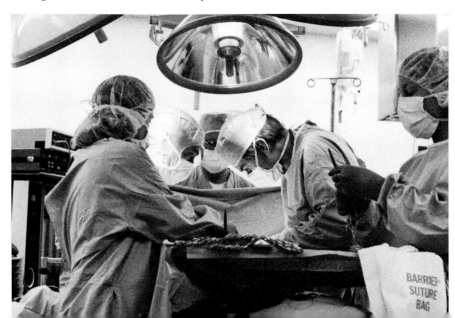

SPECIALTY SCREW CORPORATION

Of the history of the company he helped found, Arvid "Bill" Johnson says, "There's not any one thing that stands out as more exciting than another; however, it has been very exciting for me to see the company grow."

The name of Specialty Screw Corporation best summarizes what the firm does: The 95 employees, working in a 77,000-square-foot plant, produce specialized fasteners—mostly screws, bolts, and pins—by the coldforming process for about 400 customers nationwide. About half the fasteners are used in the automotive industry, with the remainder divided among lawn-and-garden, appliance, household product, and caster manufacturers. Specialty Screw is also in a joint venture with a Swedish company that manufactures hose clamps used in the automotive industry. The company, ABA, Inc., at 4004 Auburn Street in Rockford, employs 15.

The story of Specialty Screw Corporation began in 1953, when Harold Dahlberg, Willard Wise, Arthur Novak, and Wallace Carpenter mortgaged their homes, raised $30,000, and formed a fastener company. The four were all former employees of one of Rockford's large fastener businesses. They rented a truck, purchased used equipment, which they overhauled themselves, and set up shop at 711-19th Street. Their sales totaled $50,000 the first year.

Bill Johnson and Frank Brady, both manufacturers' representatives in the Detroit area, had acquired interests in the company shortly after its formation. The firm grew, and Johnson and Brady increased their interests. By 1972 Willard Wise, the only remaining partner of the original four founders, had died; the following year Johnson and Brady acquired all outstanding stock.

By 1979 Specialty Screw Corporation had grown to 25 employees, and Johnson and Brady needed more room. That year the plant and equipment of Time Screw and Manufacturing Corporation, at 2801 Huffman Boulevard, became available. With the help of economic development bonds from the City of Rockford, Specialty Screw acquired the Time Screw assets, which otherwise were to be auctioned. Most of Time Screw's employees were also taken on.

Specialty Screw has been on Huffman Boulevard since then.

Arvid "Bill" Johnson (right) has been head of Specially Screw Corporation since 1983, and his son, Russell (left) is president.

Johnson became president and chief executive officer in 1973. Brady retired the following year, and Johnson acquired his interests. The firm established a Scanlon participative management program, whereby production teams in various departments elect their own representatives and meet monthly to formulate suggestions to improve the company and the product.

Specialty Screw Corporation prides itself on its meticulous quality control, largely through the use of statistical process control and the use of state-of-the-art equipment, and on its streamlined information systems that allow the most rapid processing of customer quotations, specifications, and shipments.

Bill Johnson continues as head of Specialty Screw Corporation. His son, Russell, has been with the company since 1980 and is its president. Russell has changed the spelling of his surname to Johansson, to restore the original Swedish heritage.

LANDSTAR INWAY, INC. (INWAY)

Landstar Inway, Inc., also known as "Inway", has been in existence since 1982, and has grown into one of Rockford's most dynamic companies and one of the most significant success stories of the U.S. trucking industry.

Landstar Inway, headquartered at 2330 - 23rd Avenue, was born as the result of an immediate need: In July 1982 a Chicago-area trucking company ceased operations, leaving 72 commercial trucking agents and 276 tractor-trailer owner/operators out of business. Landstar Inway was then less than a month old and based in Jacksonville, FL, where it shared a computer system with a sister company. It picked up the closed firm's customers, key agents, employees and owner operators - and established itself on Pyramid Drive in Rockford.

From its inception, the firm's core business has consisted of three types of equipment; flatbed, van, and specialized equipment. Each of Landstar Inway's local business owners (agents) and business capacity owners (owner/operators) is a small business; together they make up one large business and are essential to its growth. Landstar Inway has grown, one of its officials said, by being in the "small-business" business.

Landstar Inway has grown from 72 local business owners and 276 business capacity owners in 1982 to more than 360 local business owners, 2,175 plus business capacity owners, and 295 employees, whose jobs contribute to the Rockford area economy. Its revenue grew from $8.25 million for the six months of operation in 1982 to in excess of $289 million for 1995. Landstar Inway's network of regional offices and terminals is located throughout the continental United States and Canada. And other than UPS,

Architect's drawing of Landstar Inway's new building located at 1000 Simpson Road, anticipated completion date is Spring 1997.

Landstar Inway is the largest Illinois-based carrier.

The company takes pride in its relationships with its business capacity owners as well as its customers. More than 95 percent of the business capacity operators participating in 1994 were retained in 1995.

The foundation of Landstar Inway's success can be traced to it's 1996 mission statement: *"Continue on a more profitable basis to expand our core businesses of flatbeds, van and specialized equipment through a business capacity owner, local business owner and employee-based company. Deepen the understanding between these partners to offer a high quality, safe service to our customers. Continuing an adherence of accurate, timely and consistent service to our customers, business capacity owners and local business owner family. Remembering the fact that as much as we are in the transportation business, we are in the business of profiting a conducive atmosphere for small businesses to succeed."*

Landstar Inway's commitment to high quality, safe service can best be demonstrated by the safety and quality awards bestowed upon them. Among some of these awards are: American Trucking Association's Fleet Safety Award, First Place (1993, 1994, 1995...no other trucking company has received this award three times in a row); American Trucking Association's Presidential Award, Finalist; Landstar's Presidential Award for Achievement in Safety, First Place; Specialized Carriers & Rigging Association (SC&RA) Fleet Safety Award, First Place; Trailmobile Fleet Safety Improvement Award; United Parcel Service (UPS), Exceptional Performance.

Landstar Inway's commitment to the Rockford area can also be demonstrated by its new $7 million, 60,000 square foot facility, located at the Southrock Industrial Park, which will be completed in late winter or early spring, 1997.

Landstar Inway's present location at 2330 - 23rd. Avenue is the hub of an expanding nationwide network.

DAN-CAR SPRINKLER CO.

Barney Danis came to Rockford in 1968 as a fire sprinkler engineer to start the fire sprinkler division of Simon Carlson and Son, a large plumbing company. In 1977 he purchased that division from Simon's son, Roland, and the new firm was named Dan-Car Fire Sprinkler Company after the new and old owners.

The first office was located at the corner of 20th and 23rd Streets in Rockford. Approximately ten employees averaged about $500 per week for a $5,000 weekly payroll.

As the business grew, the need for expanded facilities mandated the move to the company's present location at 11028 Raleigh Court in Machesney Park in 1986. That same year John Danis purchased the company from his father.

In the very consistent fire sprinkler industry, Dan-Car Fire Sprinkler Company's team approach has enabled it to use such technological advances as computer design to provide its customers with excellent service at a competitive price. In the words of owner John Danis, "Even though quality products with excellent service at a competitive price sounds like a cliché, our team firmly believes that if you maintain a proper mix of these ingredients, customers will come back and be your best advertisement."

Over the years this philosophy has built a substantial customer base for Dan-Car Fire Sprinkler Company including the State of Illinois and major contractors in the Rockford area. Dan-Car has been fortunate to participate in various Rockford area landmark projects including Metrocenter, Rockford City Hall retrofit and expansion, the downtown Luther High Rise, and the New American Theatre.

Satisfied customers have spread the word so that Dan-Car's work force of twenty in 1986 has grown to approximately 150 today to serve a market extending into Northern Illinois and Southern Wisconsin, with clients such as Chrysler in Belvidere. Future commercial, industrial, and institutional growth is targeted to extend beyond those boundaries.

Another future growth area is residential fire sprinkler protection, which is still in its infancy. "I have the utmost confidence," states John Danis, "That once the public is educated about the affordability and the protection provided by a residential fire sprinkler system, we will see an increasingly rapid growth in that market. Dan-Car

Bernard "Barney" J. Danis, founder of Dan-Car sprinkler company.

Fire Sprinkler Company intends to be in the vanguard."

A special historic area of interest for Danis is the unique Rockford-made pottery of the Norse Pottery Company.

Dan-Car Sprinkler Company is located at 11028 Raleigh Court.

NORSE POTTERY COMPANY OF ROCKFORD

Although there are examples of sixty-two different Norse patterns in his collection, "I've rarely found a piece in Rockford," states collector John Danis of the Norse Pottery Company—an historic Rockford company. For sixteen years the owner of Dan-Car Fire Sprinkler Co. has searched for pieces of this unique pottery that originally cost from $ .25 to $15.00 and now commands $100 to $1,000.

It all started in 1903 when Danish immigrants Thorwald P.A. Samson and Louis Ipson began producing pottery based on the designs of newly excavated ancient Scandinavian and Viking objects they saw on exhibit in Copenhagen. Arthur W. Wheelock, one of their customers who had established a large Rockford retail/wholesale crockery business in 1888, was so impressed with the decorative pieces that he bought the Edgerton, Wisconsin firm and moved it to Rockford in 1904.

Ipson and Samson came along as mold designers. When Wheelock became comfortable with their work, he encouraged them to use their talents to add imaginative designs with art nouveau and American Indian motifs to their Scandinavian designs. The production plant was at 111 South Water Street where the *Register Star* now stands. The retail outlet and business office were at 107-109 South Main Street.

Wheelock's Rockford store sold the black matte finished pieces whose glaze imparted a green or blue-green verdigris effect on brass, bronze or copper. The ashtrays, bowls, candlesticks, cigar jars, vases and other pieces also were sold in his Milwaukee and Des Moines stores and in Midwest stores owned by Wheelock relatives. Wheelock traveled as far as New York wholesaling his pottery, each identified by its distinctive model number.

By 1913, ads indicated that there were 128 different designs and each had a number. Every piece bore the Norse logo and was boxed with a design information card.

Tall vase applied with a lizard and gold wash. Norse pottery model number 25.

But 1913 also signaled the eventual demise of Norse pottery. Even though three pieces of Norse pottery had been accepted for the Smithsonian collection in 1906, by 1913 the Rockford City Directory had no listing for Norse Pottery.

In 1917 Wheelock ended his pottery business by selling the store and purchasing the controlling share of Forest City Wholesale Grocery Co. Extensive publicity about the sale/purchase made no mention of Norse Pottery. According to grandson Robert Porter of Barrington who owns no Norse pottery, Norse molds were sold to Hager Pottery. But fourth-generation Hager president Lexy Estes has no knowledge about the Norse molds and is researching the mystery of their disappearance.

John Danis hopes that more information can be found in the future about this important part of Rockford history. He has sought employee records, production records, molds, production catalogs, sales brochures, history cards and even original boxes and packing materials. His desire would be to see the publication of a book about this unusual pottery that was made from Rock River bank clay and made its way to our nation's foremost museum.

A three legged covered jar on a pedestal, with an impressed seahorse design. Norse Pottery model number 84.

ROCKFORD MEMORIAL HOSPITAL

There was no hospital for Freddie Griffen to go to after he was run over by a train. Had there been, the six-year-old might have survived. Because he didn't survive, Rockford Memorial Hospital began.

Freddie was struck by a switch engine where the tracks cross South Main Street on October 2, 1883. Five doctors worked frantically, amputating three limbs. But the boy died five hours after the accident.

There was no hospital in Rockford, in part, because Rockford was not large enough to sustain the almshouses that passed for public hospitals in the nineteenth century. In small cities and large, such medical care as there was in the nineteenth century was centered in the home. But the concept of a "cottage hospital" had begun to evolve, and there was a tradition of benevolence brought to Rockford by its New England settlers. And there was a need: Rockford, ideally situated for industrial growth, was experiencing it.

The *Rockford Daily Gazette* raised a hue and cry about preventing "urchins" from playing on the

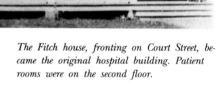

The Fitch house, fronting on Court Street, became the original hospital building. Patient rooms were on the second floor.

tracks—and about the need for a hospital. By December 1883 a committee of the Winnebago County Medical Society had incorporated the Rockford Hospital Association, and a group of lay trustees had set about raising money.

Two members of this group came to the fore: William Talcott, the secretary/treasurer, and Adeline Talcott Emerson, his sister and the wife of his business partner. The committee solicited the help of physicians, each of whom received a quota of 3,500 shares they could sell or buy for them-

selves for $10 each. One Rockford physician, Dr. William Fitch, offered his home at the corner of Court and Chestnut streets as a site, and he and the trustees agreed to terms in mid-1884.

Despite slow sales of shares and some fear that a hospital would spread disease, the effort gained momentum. Shares sales picked up in 1885, and companies made donations in kind to improve the Fitch house. By that autumn an eight-member medical board had come together. This board appointed the first hospital matron, Martha Jane Smith.

Rockford City Hospital opened on October 1, 1885, two years almost to the day of Freddie Griffen's death. Support, in money and in kind, came slowly, but it came. Financial support by late 1887 was sufficient for design of a new wing, and it opened in March 1888. It included an operating room, nursing superintendent's quarters, and patient rooms with a homelike decor.

The year 1887 also marked the beginning of a training school for

Rockford Hospital's Ward 8 in the early 1900s.

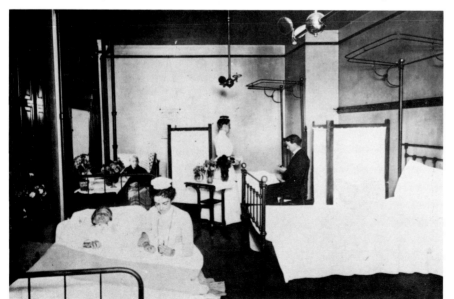

Rockford Memorial Hospital as it appears today, with the newly constructed Professional Office Building standing on the far left.

nurses. Elizabeth Glenn, a Chicago nurse with excellent credentials, was hired to head it. Under Glenn's guidance the curriculum expanded to two years. Glenn became superintendent of the hospital and the training school in 1900, but resigned a year later.

The hospital grew apace with improvements in medical care, particularly surgery. Plans for a new operating room were begun in 1890. By July 1901 there were plans for a new building. With the help of large donations from the Walter Forbes family, five current or former trustees, two railroads, and the Daughters of the American Revolution, the board had the cost of the new building paid within two years of its opening in 1904. But the new facility was outgrown within five years. The Ralph Emerson family paid for a new building and created a $60,000 fund for an adjacent hall that bore the Emerson name. It was completed in 1913.

From the beginning the hospital had struggled with matching income and expenses. The early problem was care for patients who could not pay. As the concept of hospitals changed and medical care grew more complex, sophisticated, and expensive, the problem of paying for innovations such as X-ray, laboratory services, and more advanced drugs was added.

Rockford City Hospital came into the modern era of hospital administration in 1919, when C.K. Muir became its first business manager. Two years later the hospital's governing board was reorganized,

turning control over to physicians, and Stanley L. Davidson was hired as business manager that April.

Davidson was at the hospital only two years, but his influence far outlasted his tenure because of the standard of professionalism and management skill he established. When the post-World War I economic slump and 50 percent unemployment increased the number of undernourished children in the city, he established the hospital's outpatient department to care for them. Before his administration no

An early surgical procedure performed at Rockford Hospital.

Rockford hospital had a laboratory; under Davidson, Rockford Hospital opened one.

The sense of community service widened with the establishment of the Rockford Hospital Auxiliary by Alma Fringer in 1922. From the start its job was fund raising, but it gradually assumed other roles, including volunteer help in the hospital itself.

With the onset of the Great Depression in 1931, admissions fell off, but expenses did not. The

steady growth of five decades abruptly ended. The nursing staff was cut. But the hospital carried on, and by 1938 there was already concern with the need for a new facility.

Not only was the hospital outgrowing its buildings at Court and Chestnut streets, but downtown traffic and development were overwhelming it. With the coming of World War II, wartime prosperity brought the city back from the depression.

It took until 1954 for the institution to achieve a new location and a new name, however. The war effort stalled fund raising and further development during the war years. But local industrialists, led by Robert Gaylord of Ingersoll Milling Machine Co., rallied to the need for a new hospital.

Operation Big Switch, the move to the new facility at 2500 North Rockton Avenue, took place just after Independence Day, 1954, and involved hundreds of volunteers, as well as 40 trucks. By July 10 the old hospital stood empty.

By 1972 Rockford Memorial Hospital was a 410-bed facility with a 90-percent occupancy rate, 7 specialty care clinics, a charity clinic, 14 health profession education programs, a medical-dental staff of 279, and 1,100 employees. In the early 1970s it became a teaching hospital for the University of Illinois College of Medicine.

In 1994, as part of its continued growth, the hospital merged with the Rockford Clinic network and established its own managed care company, Rockford Health Plans, to become Rockford Health System, the region's first vertically integrated health care system.

BEST WESTERN CLOCK TOWER RESORT AND CONFERENCE CENTER

In an age when identity disappears into an acronym or a trademark, the Clock Tower of its namesake still presides over a Rockford-area oasis of travel and convention services that has become a destination in itself.

Gerald Ford and Bob Hope slept there. So did a couple of Georges—Bush and Burns. Red Skelton chatted with staffers as he sat in the lobby and drew clown faces. The Beach Boys danced in Quark, the discotheque, and Kenny Rogers played tennis on its courts. The guest list also includes Dr. Kenneth Cooper, the founder of aerobics; the Harlem Globetrotters; tennis stars Billie Jean King and Bjorn Borg; and even the three Rin Tin Tins.

For four years the resort has been the home of a jazz festival that has featured talents such as Anita O'Day and Wild Bill Davison, and has attracted performers and devotees nationwide. There have even been two annual Murder Weekends, in which guests play detectives—or suspects—in a staged murder mystery.

One industry publication described the Clock Tower Resort and Conference Center as "a hotel with a variety show of restaurants, a resort with emphasis on fitness, a conference center with a penchant for small groups, an affiliate of a referrals chain with more and more leading-hotel-in-the-community properties in its membership."

It is an apt summary. In the late 1980s the facility included 253 guest rooms, 26,000 feet of meeting space (including a theater that seats 170), three restaurants (ranging from a cozy coffee shop to a gourmet dining room), indoor and outdoor swimming pools, and a shop complex. There is something else: a world-class museum. And its theme, fittingly enough, is clocks.

The Time Museum contains more than 3,000 items, collected during the past four decades by Seth G. Atwood, whose family has owned the Clock Tower complex from the time it opened in 1967. The complex has housed the collection since 1970.

The scope of the Time Museum's collection spans the entire history of timekeeping, from about 3000 B.C. to the present. There are detailed models of Stonehenge and the first atomic clocks; there are tiny wristwatches less than one inch across; there is a nineteenth-century German astronomical and automaton clock that stands 10 feet high and eight feet wide. Sundials with no moving parts point the passage of a day, and the most complicated astronomical clock in the world charts the movement of all the planets in the solar system, as well as the procession of the earth's axis.

The museum is an aesthetic experience, with some items standing out because of their austere, utilitarian beauty—others for their rococo adornment. It is also a comprehensive overview of human ingenuity harnessed to the precise measure of time. The presence of the Time Museum—as well as each item in it—makes the Clock Tower Resort and Conference Center unique.

In dining, the Clock Tower experience includes the elegance of Bellamy's, the exciting modernity of Figgs, the atrium restaurant, and the everyday goodness of the coffee shop. There is also finger food to be had amid the lights, colors, and big beat of Quark.

The Racquet Club's seven indoor tennis courts, two racquetball courts, and fitness center attract both guests and area residents, as does the indoor pool. So does the dinner theater, with productions mounted by veteran dancer-director

Chuck Hoenes, whose troupe also performs throughout Florida.

Rockford's pioneer Atwood family had prospered in industry and banking, and did not intend to enter the motel-restaurant-convention business. But when Max Liebling, who conceived the inn, died shortly after building it, a loan the Atwoods had made to him was defaulted, and patriarch Seth B. Atwood and his family found themselves the owners of the motel, which then had 120 rooms, a coffee shop, two meeting rooms, and an outdoor pool.

With the move of the Time Museum to the facility, it became the Clock Tower Inn. Two years later, in 1972, an indoor pool, 30 guest rooms, and a 10,000-square-foot convention area were added.

The following year United Realty, the Atwood family's company, took over operation of the motel from Henrici's, a management company. A total of 53 more rooms were then added, and the motel took over the adjacent Racquet Club. That same year Rex Parker was hired as general manager, a post he still holds. In 1974 arcade shops and the theater were added, and the Racquet Club doubled in size.

An important milestone was passed in 1980: The food and beverage operations, previously run by Henrici's, were taken over by the Clock Tower. Now it was all one facility owned and operated by one company.

Bellamy's opened in 1982, elevating the standard of gourmet dining for the entire Rockford area. Quark, with its lights and videos, and Figgs opened a year later.

The room expansion has continued. Fifty-four new rooms were added in 1982.

So the Clock Tower Resort and Conference Center maintains the steady route of expansion and improvement established at the beginning by Seth B. Atwood. There is also the continuing tradition of Atwood family involvement: The founder's grandson, Bruce Atwood, is president of the company, and other grandchildren—Diane Atwood, a Chicago architect, and Seth Lang, of Genoa, Nevada—also have taken active roles.

Then there is the most important ingredient of all: the highest level of attention to the needs and wishes of guests. Madge Gulley, manager of the Rooms Division, says she doesn't remember the famous guests during her 19 years under the Clock Tower, but thinks of "taking it day to day, listening to guests, responding, serving each individual guest as a special, warm human being with special needs.

"You need to be a showman in this business," says Madge. "And a servant. You are a servant, and we are in show business, creating an atmosphere. The guests are enveloped in a feeling of warmth and caring. They're in the hands of the experts.

"It's the Seth B. Atwood philosophy: 'Always give the customer what you promised, and more.'"

Bruce T. Atwood (right), president of Best Western Clock Tower Resort and Conference Center, with Rex A. Parker, C.H.A., vice-president and general manager.

RENO, ZAHM, FOLGATE, LINDBERG & POWELL

The law firm of Reno, Zahm, Folgate, Lindberg & Powell had its beginnings in 1923 when two young State's Attorneys, Shelby L. Large and Guy B. Reno, struck out on their own and formed Large & Reno, with offices on the fifth floor of the old Swedish-American National Bank Building on Seventh Street. Their clientele consisted almost exclusively of SwedishAmerican factory workers (many of whom later became factory owners and community leaders.) This was before the 8-hour day, 40-hour week; evening and Saturday office hours were therefore the order of the day to accommodate the clients who waited their turn with the "Advokat" while sitting on the steps between the fourth and fifth floors. Associates during this pre-depression period included Wilbur Johnson, James Berry and Oscar Dahlquist.

In 1932 two important changes occurred: Ralph S. Zahm joined the firm which shortly thereafter became Large, Reno & Zahm, and Large and Reno were each elected to the Board of Directors of Swedish-American Bank. As a result, the primary focus of the firm shifted from trial practice to include corporate and business law and such associated fields as labor law and estate planning.

John B. Anderson, later State's Attorney, U.S. Congressman and candidate for President, and H. Eugene Hallstrom were associates during the late 1940s and 1950s. Roger Reno and H. Emmett Folgate came in the early

Camelot Tower, home of Reno, Zahm, Folgate, Lindberg & Powell

1950s, followed by Wesley E. Lindberg and Robert K. Skolrood. Large died in 1960, Guy Reno in 1972 and Zahm in 1978.

Lindberg and Skolrood were instrumental in the construction of Camelot Tower at the site of the old St. Anthony Hospital on East State Street, which has been firm headquarters since 1970.

Also joining the firm during this period were William B. Powell, R. Jerome Pfister, Angus S. More and J. Todd Kennedy (both of whom are now Associate Circuit Judges.)

In the 1980s Skolrood resigned from the firm to become Dean of the Oral Roberts Law School, Reno opened an of-counsel branch office at the site of the original Seventh Street office, and Edward J. Fahy, veteran labor lawyer, joined the firm as of-counsel. More recent partners and associates include Robert A. Fredrickson, Jack D. Ward, Jan H. Ohlander, James D. Zeglis, John H. Young, Jamie Swenson Cassel, Craig P. Thomas, Arthur G. Kielty and Suzanne Kiwaiko Robinson.

While the purpose of serving its clients over the 73 year period of its existence has remained constant, the firm has participated in a technological revolution in its delivery of services. Gone are the days of open windows for lack of air-conditioning, thirteen sheets in the manual typewriter separated by twelve carbons, with typewriter erasers to use on each sheet in the rare event of error, and evening and Saturday hours. The firm looks forward to serving clients into the next Century, even under more rapidly changing conditions, recognizing that the tools of the lawyer's trade remain his time and skill.

Bibliography

I have made extensive use of the manuscript and photographic collections of the Rockford Museum Center and the Rockford Public Library (Local History and Genealogy). Of particular value in the latter were the Rockford City Directories (1857-present), the "Nuggets of History" newsletters circulated by the Rockford Historical Society, and the library's "Rockfordiana" file of old newspaper clippings. I also took advantage of the microfilm files of old Rockford newspapers in the library. Among the most helpful manuscripts were Robert Borden's dissertation on "John H. Manny's Contribution to the Development of Harvesting Machinery 1848-1856" ; the Brown's Hills-Knightsville history; John R. Conley's paper on "The Socialist Party of Rockford, Illinois" ; W.A. Dickerman's "Memorandum Relative to My Trip To Rockford, 1844, and My Impressions of It" ; Ralph Emerson's "Short Auto-Biography 1831-1914" ; Levin Faust's "History of the Swedes in Rockford" (Rockfordiana file); Daniel Shaw Haight's "Scrapbook Commenced in 1842 and Made by Himself" ; David Williams McCormick's dissertation on "Partisan Politics in a Middle-Sized Midwestern City: A Case Study of Rockford, Illinois" ; John Molyneaux's short history of "Rockford's Limestone Buildings 1853-1860" ; Dean Olson's paper on "Rockford Watches" ; R.P. Porter's "Sketch of the First Settlement of Rockford and Winnebago County. Written June 20 1876."

Addams, Jane. *My Friend, Julia Lathrop.* New York: The Macmillan Company, 1935.

Alexander, John W. *Geography of Manufacturing in the Rock River Valley.* Madison, Wisconsin: University of Wisconsin School of Commerce, 1949.

Baie, Lyle. *Rockford's Harlem Park: The People and the Times.* Rockford: John Gile Communications, 1987.

Barrows, Harlan H., and Rollin D. Salisbury. *The Environment of Camp Grant.* Urbana, Illinois: Illinois State Geological Survey, Bulletin 39, 1918.

Bishop, David, and Craig G. Campbell. *The History of Winnebago County Forest Preserves.* Rockton, Illinois: Balsey Printing, 1979.

Breasted, Charles. *Pioneer to the Past.* New York: Charles Scribner's Sons, 1943.

Brown, Eugene, and F. Ford Rowe. *Industrial and Picturesque Rockford.* Rockford: Forest City Publishing Company, 1891.

Chapman, Barbara. *That Men Know So Little of Men.* Rockford: Rockford Public Library Special Project III, 1975.

Church, Charles A. *History of Rockford and Winnebago County, Illinois.* Rockford: W.P. Lamb, 1900.

——————. *History of Winnebago County* [Volume II of *Historical Encyclopedia of Illinois,* Bateman, Newton, and Paul Selby, editors]. Chicago: Munsell Publishing Company, 1916.

——————. *Past and Present of the City of Rockford and Winnebago County, Illinois.* Chicago: S.J. Clarke Publishing Company, 1905.

Clausius, Gerhard P. "The Little Soldier of the 95th: Albert D.J. Cashier." *Journal of the Illinois State Historical Society,* 51 (Winter 1958), 380-387.

Clemens, Walter. "Where Jack Benny Bombed." *Newsweek,* December 24, 1973, 93-98.

Cole, Harry Ellsworth. *Stagecoach and Tavern Tales of the Old Northwest.* Cleveland: The Arthur H. Clark Company, 1930.

Costello, David F. *The Prairie World.* New York: Thomas Y. Crowell Company, 1969.

Croy, Homer. *Corn Country.* New York: Duell, Sloan and Pearce, 1947.

Daly, Charles L. *The City of Rockford and Her Men of Affairs.* Rockford: C.L. Daly, 1920.

Decker, Taylor, and Clement Burns. *Germanicus A. Kent.* Rockford: Rockford Historical Society, n.d.

Eads, A.B. *Illustrated History of Rockford.* Chicago: A.B. Eads, 1884.

Eby, Cecil. *"That Disgraceful Affair," The Black Hawk War.* New York: W.W. Norton and Company, 1973.

Estwing, Ernest. *Exciting Life and Success.* Rockford: E. Estwing, n.d.

Faust, Levin. "The Rockford Swedes." *Swedish-American Historical Bulletin,* III (June 1930), 61-72.

Hassell Burt R.J. *A Viking with Wings.* Edited by Mary Hassell Lyons and Dean Todd. Bend, Oregon: Maverick Publications, 1987.

Havighurst, Walter. *The Heartland: Ohio, Indiana, Illinois.* New York: Harper and Row, 1974.

History of Winnebago County, Illinois. Chicago: H.F. Kett and Company, 1877.

Hulbert, Archer Butler. *Pioneer Roads and Experiences of Travelers.* 2 volumes. Cleveland: The Arthur H. Clark Company, 1904.

Johnson, Paul Cornelius. *Farm Inventions in the Making of America.* Des Moines, Iowa: Wallace-Homestead Book Company, 1976.

Keister, Philip L. *The Rockford and Interurban Railway.* Chicago: Electric Railway Historical Society Bulletin, 22, 1956.

Lundin, Jon. "A Sign of Other Times." [*Rockford Register-Star*], April 5, 1981, 4-7.

——————. "The Last Victorian House." [*Rockford Register-Star*], May 31, 1981, 4-6.

McCleneghan, ALex C. *Six Years in Heaven.* Chicago: Laird and Lee Publishers, 1894.

Madden, Betty L. *Art, Crafts, and Architecture in Early Illinois.* Chicago: University of Illinois Press, 1974.

Manufacturing and Wholesale Industries of Illinois. Volume III of 3 volumes. Chicago: Thomas B. Poole Company, 1919, 1-45.

Manufacturing Rockford, Illinois. Smith Publishing Company, 1892.

Nelson, C. Hal, editor. *Sinnissippi Saga. A History of Rockford and Winnebago County, Illinois.* Mendota, Illinois: Wayside Press, 1968.

————. *We, the People . . . of Winnebago County.* Mendota, Illinois: Wayside Press, 1975.

————. *Rockford College: A Retrospective Look.* Rockford: Rockford College, 1980.

Parsons, Alice Beal. *The Trial of Helen McLeod.* New York: Funk and Wagnalls Company, 1938.

Peterson, Rudolph E. *A Swedish-American Family.* Mendota, Illinois: Wayside Press, 1979.

Picturesque Rockford. West End Pharmacy, n.d.

Pierce, Frederick C. *Picturesque and Descriptive History of the City of Rockford.* Rockford: n.p., 1887

Portrait and Biographical Record of Winnebago and Boone Counties. Chicago: Biographical Publishing Company, 1892.

Quick, Graeme R., and Wesley F. Buchele. *The Grain Harvesters.* St. Joseph, Michigan: American Society of Agricultural Engineers, 1978.

Randall, Ruth Painter. *Colonel Elmer Ellsworth.* Boston: Little, Brown and Company, 1960.

Rockford and Its Points of Interest. Rockford: Commercial Publishing Company, 1899.

Rockford. Compiled by Workers of the Writer's Program of W.P.A. [American Guide Series.] Rockford: Graphic Arts Corporation, 1941.

Rockford Industries, Enterprises, Etc. Rockford: *Rockford Gazette* Extra, 1884.

Rockford Morning Star Centennial Edition. 1952.

Rockford Morning Star Civil War Edition. 1965.

[Rockford] *Register-Gazette Historical Edition.* 1904.

Rockford Streamlined 1834-1941. Rockford: Graphic Arts Corporation, 1941.

Rockford To-Day: Historical, Descriptive, Biographical. Rockford: *Rockford Morning Star,* 1903.

Rockford 1912. Rockford: *Rockford Morning Star,* 1912.

Rockford 50,000, 1909-10. Rockford: *Rockford Morning Star,* 1910.

Rockford - 50,000 People - No Saloons. Chicago: n.p., 1910

Seventy Years of Progress 1834-1904. Rockford: *Register-Gazette,* 1904.

"A Sociologist Looks at an American Community." *Life Magazine,* September 12, 1949, 108-119.

Spalding, Albert G. *America's National Game.* New York: American Sports Publishing Company, 1911.

Stevens, Frank E. *The Black Hawk War.* Chicago: F.E. Stevens, 1903.

Thurston, John H. *Reminiscences, Sporting and Otherwise of Early Days in Rockford, Illinois.* Rockford: Daily Republican Press, 1891.

Trillin, Calvin. "U.S. Journal: Rockford, Illinois." *New Yorker Magazine,* November 8, 1976, 146-154.

Warner, W. Lloyd. *Social Class in America.* New York: Harper and Row, 1949.

Index